Are You Happy?

It depends on how many of these questions you answer "yes" to:

- **Do you feel safe in your everyday life?** If you feel unsafe, that's all you can focus on — you don't have time or space to be happy.

- **Do you feel you have enough of what you need to be happy?** Having enough of what you *need* isn't the same as having everything you *want*. Sure, you may be dying for a new car, but do you have a car that gets you from point A to point B? If so, you have what you need.

- **Do you have moments when you look at the totality of your life instead of the events of the day?** This is called *taking stock,* and it helps you appreciate the whole of your life rather than just the part you're living today. You could just be having a bad day in an otherwise good week.

- **Do you often find a quiet place to enjoy a moment of self-reflection?** Sanctuary is a good thing. Unfortunately, in today's hectic, fast-paced world, most people have too little of it. A quiet moment here and there can make all the difference in how you feel throughout the day.

- **Are you satisfied with your finances, relationships, and career?** Being satisfied doesn't necessarily mean that you have all the money in the world, a perfect marriage, or an outstanding career. It just means that things are all right for the moment.

- **Are you optimistic about your life?** From where you're standing, does the future look bright? Do you envision more good times than bad in the months ahead? Are you hopeful about the future? If so, you can move forward with joyful anticipation.

- **Are you grateful for the way your life is unfolding?** Being grateful can be as simple as waking up every morning and saying "thank you" for the challenges, promises, and opportunities this day offers you.

- **Do you often experience peace of mind?** Can you actually hear yourself think without the noisy outside world intruding? Can you feel the power of silence? ***Remember:*** A quiet mind and a quiet body go hand in hand.

- **Would you rate your health and well-being as above average?** You don't have to be a perfect 10 — anything from 6 on up means you're ahead of the game. If you're comparing yourself to others, make sure it's a fair comparison. A 60-year-old can't rate his health as above average if his standard is the way he felt when he was 20.

- **Do you often find yourself feeling content?** Being content means you're comfortable with where you are at this moment in life and you have no burning desire to make a change. Life is good and you want to savor it.

For Dummies: Bestselling Book Series for Beginners

Happiness For Dummies®

Cheat Sheet

What Happiness Isn't

If you're like most people, you're not entirely sure what happiness is. I can tell you what it *isn't*:

- **Happiness is not about being wealthy.** Money buys you comfort, support, and freedom of action, but it doesn't make you happy.

- **Happiness is not about being powerful.** Power is about exerting your will on others; happiness comes from working together in mutually satisfying ways.

- **Happiness is not about achieving success.** Some of the most successful people I know are very unhappy — and vice versa. The only exception: people who decide to *succeed* at being happy.

- **Happiness is not just about being excited.** If I fall down a flight of stairs, believe me I'm excited — but I'm surely not happy! Sadly, excitement often creates an *illusion* of happiness — and that illusion doesn't last.

- **Happiness is not a life-transforming experience.** Happiness is momentary — it comes and goes — but it doesn't change your life in any significant way. Enjoy happiness while you have it!

- **Happiness is not always an easy thing to achieve.** Most people have to work at being happy, which is what this book is all about.

Work 101: How to Be a Happy Employee

If you're tired of being unhappy at work, here are some things you can do to remedy the problem:

- **Always say "please" and "thank you" to your fellow employees.** The better you treat others, the more willing they'll be to help you get the job done.

- **Establish healthy boundaries.** Don't confuse personal and professional relationships — look for intimacy in other areas of your life.

- **Avoid toxic co-workers.** These people are the naysayers, complainers, and spoilers who want to rain on everyone else's parade. The more you're exposed to them, the unhappier you'll feel.

- **Look for win-win solutions.** It's a fact: Employees who engage in win-lose battles with each other waste a lot of productive energy and end up exhibiting counterproductive work behavior. Why not try compromising, accommodating, or collaborating once in a while? Believe me, things will go more smoothly.

- **Handle your anger constructively.** If anger leads to an improvement in how you and your co-worker relate and work together, then it's constructive. If it simply ends up hurting the other person, it's not.

For Dummies: Bestselling Book Series for Beginners

Happiness FOR DUMMIES®

by W. Doyle Gentry, PhD

Wiley Publishing, Inc.

Happiness For Dummies®

Published by
Wiley Publishing, Inc.
111 River St.
Hoboken, NJ 07030-5774
www.wiley.com

WILEY

About the Author

W. Doyle Gentry, PhD, is a clinical psychologist living in Lynchburg, Virginia. He is a Fellow in the American Psychological Association and was the founding editor of the *Journal of Behavioral Medicine.* In Dr. Gentry's 40-year career as a scientist-practitioner, he has authored over 100 publications in the fields of health psychology and behavioral medicine, which he helped pioneer. He has previously served on the faculty of Duke University Medical Center and the University of Texas Medical Branch, Galveston. Gentry has conducted training seminars for lay and professional audiences throughout the United States, Canada, and Europe. He has also served as a consultant to major industry, where he specializes in conflict management, team building, and health promotion. Articles referring to Dr. Gentry's work regularly appear in a variety of contemporary magazines, and he is frequently interviewed on radio and television. He is the author of three earlier self-help books: *Anger-Free: Ten Basic Steps to Managing Your Anger* (William Morrow), *When Someone You Love Is Angry* (Berkley), and *Anger Management For Dummies* (Wiley).

Dr. Gentry is available for speaking engagements and workshops. Interested readers may contact him via e-mail at HappyUBE@aol.com.

Dedication

I dedicate this book to the countless numbers of people who, in one way or another, have brought happiness into my life.

Author's Acknowledgments

I want to thank a number of fellow collaborators without whose efforts writing this book would not have been possible or nearly as enjoyable. As always, I want to express my appreciation to my agent, Maura Kye, of the Denise Marcil Literary Agency. Once again, she has served my interests well!

The team at John Wiley & Sons, Inc. — in particular, Mike Baker, Elizabeth Kuball, Lindsey Lefevere, and Diane Steele — was a pleasure to work with at all phases of the project. I greatly appreciate their encouragement and professionalism, as well as their thoughtfulness and patience throughout. Their collective enthusiasm for the *For Dummies* brand is definitely contagious.

Lastly, I want to thank my loving family — Catherine, Chris, and Rebecca — for their unending support for my life's work and, more important, for bringing so much happiness into my life each and every day.

I believe that happiness is the only really important goal, and yet we are all dummies when it comes to pursuing it in our everyday lives. If this book brings even one additional moment of happiness to the life of a single reader, then my time spent on this project will have been well worth it.

Publisher's Acknowledgments

We're proud of this book; please send us your comments through our Dummies online registration form located at www.dummies.com/register/.

Some of the people who helped bring this book to market include the following:

Acquisitions, Editorial, and Media Development

Project Editor: Elizabeth Kuball

Acquisitions Editor: Mike Baker

Copy Editor: Elizabeth Kuball

Editorial Program Coordinator: Erin Calligan Mooney

Technical Editor: Donna Allen, PhD, MS Ed, CHES, FAWHP

Senior Editorial Manager: Jennifer Ehrlich

Editorial Supervisor and Reprint Editor: Carmen Krikorian

Editorial Assistants: Joe Niesen, David Lutton, Jennette ElNaggar

Cover Photos: © Stock Connection Distribution / Alamy

Cartoons: Rich Tennant (www.the5thwave.com)

Composition Services

Project Coordinator: Katie Key

Layout and Graphics: Melissa K. Jester, Ron Terry, Julie Trippetti, Abby Westcott, Tobin Wilkerson, Christine Williams

Proofreaders: Joni Heredia, Jessica Kramer

Indexer: Valerie Haynes Perry

Publishing and Editorial for Consumer Dummies

Diane Graves Steele, Vice President and Publisher, Consumer Dummies

Joyce Pepple, Acquisitions Director, Consumer Dummies

Kristin A. Cocks, Product Development Director, Consumer Dummies

Michael Spring, Vice President and Publisher, Travel

Kelly Regan, Editorial Director, Travel

Publishing for Technology Dummies

Andy Cummings, Vice President and Publisher, Dummies Technology/General User

Composition Services

Gerry Fahey, Vice President of Production Services

Debbie Stailey, Director of Composition Services

Contents at a Glance

Table of Contents

Introduction

Happiness is an important part of life — no less than anger, sadness, and fear. It begins with life itself: What mother doesn't recognize the look of happiness on the face of her newborn? Human beings are wired with an innate, neurological potential for happiness, but whether this potential eventually becomes a reality depends on how we choose to live our lives. In other words, happiness isn't an accident, and it isn't a gift from the gods — it's the gift you give yourself!

Unlike Shangri-La, a mythical paradise on Earth, happiness is not confined to a particular place, nor is it the result of any one specific activity or life circumstance. Happiness is a personal state of physical, spiritual, and emotional well-being that you can experience anywhere at any time. This morning, for example, before I began to work on this book, I spent a few happy moments sitting in my driveway quietly watching my two basset hounds, Max and Dixie, experiencing another day through the many divergent smells on a crisp fall morning in Virginia.

If you're like me, you're far too passive when it comes to experiencing happiness. You wait for it to find you instead of exercising your right to pursue it. It's *because* most people are passive when it comes to happiness that happiness seems so elusive! Face it: We live in proactive times. People around the world don't *wait* for freedom — they fight for it. Wealth is no longer something you have to inherit (despite what Paris Hilton may think) — you can *create* it. People are living longer these days. Why? Because we're learning that we can improve quality of life through the everyday choices we make. *Happiness For Dummies* tells you how to fight for, create, and live a long and happy life. It makes you the master of your own happy destiny!

About This Book

How do you know when you're happy? Are you as happy as most people? If you have lots of money or a fancy title at work, shouldn't that be enough to make you happy? What does happiness have to do with health? Is there such a thing as eternal happiness? Can you really make yourself happy by putting a smile on your face? Type B personalities tend to enjoy less material success than Type A's, so why are Type B's so much happier? These are just a few of the important questions that *Happiness For Dummies* answers.

In writing *Happiness For Dummies*, I had five basic goals in mind:

- ✔ **I wanted to show you that happiness is not a simple emotion — it's an extremely complex experience that results from feeling safe, satisfied, and grateful.** By understanding all the key ingredients that are involved, you can make up your *own* recipe for happiness.

- ✔ **I wanted to tell you what happiness *isn't* — it isn't power, money, success, or excitement.** Happiness is something much more than that!

- ✔ **I wanted to show you how to develop those personality attributes that maximize your potential for happiness — optimism, hardiness, and conscientiousness.** These are not qualities that you inherit at birth through some genetic "good fortune" — they're learned traits, and if you haven't learned them yet, this book can help.

- ✔ **I wanted to offer you actionable strategies for pursuing happiness.** In other words, I wanted to show you how to get into the flow of everyday life, how to find the silver lining in what you otherwise might view as an all-bad situation, how to develop an abiding sense of self-confidence, and how to smile for the right reasons. Think of this book as your happiness toolbox!

- ✔ **I wanted to emphasize the importance of striking the right balance between the essential opposing forces that constitute human life, like that between work and play or between selfishness and generosity.** Happiness is never found at the extremes of life — it's in the middle. That's why they call it the "happy medium"!

Happiness For Dummies is not one of those 12-step books where you have to read and follow the advice of Step 1 before you can proceed to Step 2, and so on. It's a resource book that contains everything I know about how to achieve happiness after four decades of professional experience, both as a scientist and as a clinician — and after more than 60 years of personal experience living my own life!

I did not want *Happiness For Dummies* to be another one of those pie-in-the-sky books containing more fluff than substance. This book is intended to show ordinary people how to pursue and achieve happiness. Simply put, it's a road map that guides you to the most sought-after destination in life — happiness. Buying this book means you want to get there — *Happiness For Dummies* shows you how.

Conventions Used in This Book

Happiness For Dummies is not a book about the science of happiness. Even though the principles contained in the book are based in part on science, I've eliminated all the professional jargon and instead used terms and concepts that the average person without a degree in psychology can understand. Instead of looking at tables and charts, you read about happy people — composites of real people like yourself who represent friends, relatives, and clients I've had the good fortune to learn from over the years. The quotations and two-person dialogs that I include in these stories are based solely on my recollections of conversations I had. And, yes, you find a few reflections on my own most memorable moments of happiness sprinkled throughout —one of the perks of being an author is sharing my experiences!

You don't have to know psychology to understand *Happiness For Dummies*. But I do use a couple of conventions that you should be aware of:

- ✔ When I introduce a new term, I put the word in *italics* and define it shortly thereafter (usually in parentheses).
- ✔ When I give you a list of steps to perform, I put the action part of the step in **bold,** so you can easily follow along.
- ✔ When I list an e-mail address or Web address, I use a special font called `monofont` so you know exactly what to type.

When this book was printed, some Web addresses may have needed to break across two lines of text. If that happened, rest assured that we haven't put in any extra characters (such as hyphens) to indicate the break. So, when using one of these Web addresses, just type in exactly what you see in this book, pretending as though the line break doesn't exist.

What You're Not to Read

Look on the bright side: I won't be giving you a test after you've had a chance to read *Happiness For Dummies*. So, you don't have to read every single word, sentence, chapter, and/or part of the book to get your money's worth. And don't feel compelled to remember everything. If it strikes a nerve, believe me, you'll remember it!

Throughout the book, I include lots of sidebars — text in gray boxes. Sidebars make me happy! Although they aren't an essential part of the overall message conveyed in this book, they are things I thought you might find interesting. You can think of them as side dishes to the main course. If you're hungry for every morsel of information there is on how to pursue happiness, then by all means gobble them up; otherwise, you can skip them altogether and still satisfy your appetite.

You can also safely skip any paragraphs marked with Technical Stuff icons (see "Icons Used in This Book," later in this Introduction, for more information).

Foolish Assumptions

I made a few assumptions about you when I was writing *Happiness For Dummies*:

- ✔ **You want to be happy — but so far happiness has been elusive.** You bought this book, not because you want or need someone to convince you that happiness is a good thing, but because you haven't been able to achieve it on your own. You know it's out there; you just don't know how to find it.

- ✔ **You're open-minded about discovering more-efficient ways to achieve happiness.** People don't typically buy books simply to reinforce their own fixed ideas about life or to have someone else tell them about experiences they've already had. They're looking for something new, something different, something that will both guide and inspire them — something that will help them not only survive but, more important, thrive on life.

- ✔ **You see yourself as part of the "let's do it" generation and you want to be a player, not a spectator, when it comes to achieving true happiness.** This attitude portends one of the key personality traits underlying happiness — hardiness — which I cover in this book. You may be farther along in your pursuit of happiness than you realized!

How This Book Is Organized

I organized *Happiness For Dummies* into 6 parts and 23 chapters. Here's what you can find in each part.

Part 1: Defining Happiness

In these first four chapters, I acquaint you with some basic ideas about happiness as a universal emotion, the benefits that positive emotions have for health, the key ingredients that make up happiness, and what happiness isn't. (Knowing what happiness *isn't* is important because many people spend most of their lives searching for happiness in all the wrong places.) I show you how to calculate your HQ — happiness quotient — and help you compare yourself to others so that you know whether you're ahead of or behind the curve. I also explain how happiness is simply your nervous system's feedback about whether you're living the right kind of life — and fill you in on what *right* means in the context of achieving happiness.

Part II: Personality Attributes That Lead to Happiness

In this part, I introduce concepts — in this case, personality attributes — from the emerging field of positive psychology that greatly influence the extent to which you experience happiness. Not everyone learns early in life (if at all) to be optimistic, hardy, and conscientious, so in these three chapters I show you how to be that type of person and get a leg up in your quest for happiness. It's not hard — trust me.

Part III: Behaving Your Way toward Happiness

Chapters 8 through 12 show you specific ways to behave — always look for the silver lining, have a heart-to-heart with a higher power, make a daily confession of the positives in your life — that increase your potential for achieving happiness. Chapter 12 talks in depth about the power of a smile and gives you a heads-up about which smiles will *not* bring you happiness. The idea here is that happiness is no mere accident — it's something that you have to work for!

Part IV: Striking the Right Balance

If you're like me, your everyday life is mostly out of balance. Sad to say, you approach life from one extreme or another — you work too much and play too little, you have too many hassles and not enough of life's little pleasures, and you're either too selfish or too selfless. Am I right? This part of the book helps you find a happy medium along some of the more important dimensions of life.

Part V: Achieving Happiness in Key Relationships

People tend to compartmentalize their day-to-day lives into three main areas of interaction — at work, at home, and in intimate relationships. The three chapters in this part offer situation-specific strategies designed to increase happiness. Interpersonal happiness is all about reciprocity — or, as the saying goes, "What goes around comes around." Here I show you how to calculate your workplace positivity ratio, which determines whether employees flounder or flourish at work; tell you which parenting style leads to a happy home life; and illustrate how marital happiness is really a three-legged stool.

Part VI: The Part of Tens

If you're looking for quick ideas about how to raise a happy child or the ten most common roadblocks to becoming a happy person, or you just want an easy-to-remember checklist of personal habits or thoughts that foster happiness, this is the part for you.

Icons Used in This Book

Icons are those little pictures in the margins throughout this book that are there to draw your attention to certain types of information.

This icon suggests practical how-to strategies for achieving happiness.

This icon alerts you to important ideas and concepts that you'll want to remember and that you can use when you don't have *Happiness For Dummies* in hand.

Every once in a while, the scientist in me gets a little chatty, and when I do, I mark the paragraph with this icon. You can read these paragraphs if you want, but the information they contain isn't essential to your understanding of the topic at hand.

This icon appears when I think a cautionary note is in order or when you need to seek professional help.

Where to Go from Here

You don't have to begin by reading Chapter 1 and continue straight through to the end of the book. Each part and chapter of this book is meant to stand alone in its discussion of how to achieve true happiness. When I was writing, I skipped around, writing chapters in no particular order — when I finished one chapter, I looked at the table of contents to see what interested me next and went with that. It made the writing more fun. Feel free to do the same — choose a topic that interests you and dive in!

A word of caution

If after reading *Happiness For Dummies* and trying the behavioral strategies set forth in this book, you still find yourself struggling to find happiness, talk to a professional — a licensed clinical psychologist or mental-health counselor, for example. Tell your counselor that you've already read *Happiness For Dummies* and, if she hasn't already, suggest that she do so as well — that way, you can ensure that you're both on the same page and she'll know that you've already done your homework in trying to become a happier person.

I don't recommend looking for a medical remedy for unhappiness — one that focuses on pre-scribed medication. There is no known pill that will create a sense of enduring happiness, only ones that treat some of the obstacles to happiness, such as depression.

Finally, if you've been diagnosed with clinical depression, you owe it to yourself to get help. For more information on depression, check out *Depression For Dummies,* by Laura L. Smith, PhD, and Charles H. Elliott, PhD (Wiley).

You may want to head straight for those chapters that focus on how to achieve happiness in your key relationships — at work, at home, and with your loved ones (Part V). Or you may want to take a quick look at the ten most common obstacles to happiness (Chapter 22). The choice is yours. In the end, it really doesn't matter where you start — what matters most is where you end up, I hope a much happier person!

Part I
Defining Happiness

The 5th Wave   By Rich Tennant

"Mom and Dad get like this everytime they watch back—to—back episodes of 'The Love Boat.'"

In this part . . .

I talk about why happiness is a universal emotion and help you begin to appreciate just how complex an experience true happiness is. I explain why there is no such thing as eternal, everlasting happiness and why it's important to enjoy those precious moments. I show you how to quantify happiness and break down happiness into its various components — pleasure, gratitude, contentment — so that you know how close you are to achieving your goal of being a happy person. I also tell you where *not* to look for happiness — power, status, wealth, and success. If that's all you pursue in life, you can only end up being *un*happy! Finally, I explain what your nervous system is telling you when you find happiness — the answers to four crucial questions that determine your overall quality of life.

Chapter 1

Anyone Can Be Happy

In This Chapter

▶ Experiencing happiness anywhere

▶ Meeting some happy people

▶ Calculating you happiness quotient

▶ Benefiting from positive emotions

*W*hat do children in an Israeli kibbutz, students at the College of William and Mary, and preliterate tribesmen in the wilds of Borneo share in common? Not their language or customs. It's their innate ability to experience happiness. Nowhere on this planet is there a group of human beings who lack the capacity for joy, satisfaction, peace of mind, and well-being.

Unlike its counterparts — anger, sadness, and fear — happiness is a *positive* emotion. Happiness is the glue that binds us all together and underlies all forms of civilized behavior. Happy employees are more productive. Happy couples have more enjoyable sex. Happy children make good students. Just as anger repulses people, happiness attracts. Happy people enjoy more support from those around them and are more sought after in social situations. Happiness offsets the burdens of everyday life and can be a healing force for the injured and infirm.

In this chapter, I fill you in on the many benefits that come from positive emotions and show you how to assess how happy you are at any point in life. I show you that it's possible to be happy no matter what your social and economic circumstances. And I introduce you to four people whose stories illustrate some key ingredients to how you can go about achieving happiness.

Happiness: The Universal Emotion

Happiness is everywhere — in every country, culture, big city, jungle, canyon, and apartment building in the world, anywhere that human beings reside. Thus, happiness — along with anger, curiosity, fear, disgust, and sadness — is considered a universal emotion.

Psychologist Paul Ekman, professor emeritus at the University of California Medical School in San Francisco, spent his entire 40-year career circumnavigating the globe, and everywhere he went he found the same smiling faces. His research pointed the way to our understanding that emotions are not learned behaviors — we're born with them. What you *can* learn, however, are ways of accessing happiness.

Find a quiet spot somewhere — your favorite coffee shop, the YMCA, your local shopping mall, a park bench — and, like Dr. Ekman, observe the faces of people around you. Count how many smiling faces you see in a period of 30 minutes. You'll probably find that there's a lot more happiness in the world than you imagined.

Happiness from the Individual Perspective

Other people are the best teachers, no matter what you're trying to learn. So, if you want to know how to be happy, what better way to start than by asking people who show happiness more than most people?

I interviewed four people whose stories are not only interesting but instructive. Here's what they had to say:

✔ **Diane** is a 64-year old grandmother of eight. She's what's known as a "mover-shaker" in the real-estate business, a very successful woman, who has an infectious laugh and looks much younger than her age. Diane has had, in her words, "a blessed life," and her only major current stress is caring for an aging parent. She attends church regularly and has for most of her life. On a happiness scale from 1 to 10, Diane rates herself "at least 9" and she believes that people who know her would give her that same score. I asked Diane what the secret to her happiness is, and she said:

> That's easy. I had happy parents. We didn't have a lot of money, but they managed to make me feel special and a very important part of their lives. They were very positive about whatever I wanted to do when I was growing up. And, most important, they showed me I had a choice about how to see life — if you look for the positive, you'll find it. And the same goes if you're always looking for the negative.

That positive outlook Diane learned from her parents has served her well in her business. As she put it, "In real estate, looking for the positive helps when you have to deal with difficult people and I think it makes it easier for me to find solutions to problems."

✔ **Lanny** is 74 and widowed. He has one grown daughter and two grand-kids, who are the joy of his life. Lanny retired after a long and very successful career as a stock broker, and now he spends a lot of his time doing volunteer work for various community agencies. He believes it's important to give back some of the good fortune he's accumulated throughout his life. Lanny also attends church regularly.

At the time I interviewed Lanny, there were no significant stresses in his life, but there had been in the past — the deaths of four siblings, his parents, and his wife, all as a result of severe and lingering illness. Still, on that 1-to-10 happiness scale, Lanny rates himself a 10. He believes it's important to look for opportunities to be happy and to work hard to achieve that end. His motto: "Only *you* can make it happen!"

Like Diane, Lanny doesn't look his age — he says, "I don't frown and have wrinkles, so most people think I'm younger than I am!" He also believes that happiness has had a lot to do with the fact that he's rarely been ill throughout his life. Lanny says he owes much of his ability to be happy to his mother, who from the outset taught him to "go to bed every night thinking about something positive you did today." He begins the day the same way, thinking about "someone I want to see today who means a lot to me" — this sets the emotional tone for his day. Lanny also makes a point of repeating to himself, both silently and aloud, "Life is good!", which keeps him focused on the positives in the world around him. Finally, he thanks people he encounters for "sharing their smile" with him, which they're glad to do.

✔ **Janine** is 56, has two grown sons, and is happily married. She spends much of her time lately doing volunteer work, which she describes as both a joy and a hassle, depending on which day you ask her. She attends religious services regularly. And you'd never guess it from her happy demeanor, but Janine has long suffered from chronic depression. Interestingly, part of her success in managing her depression comes as a result of her attempts to "keep others happy" — their happiness then bounces back on her and "helps me get through difficult times."

What's her recipe for happiness? She says, "My mother taught me that 'pretty is as pretty does' — in other words, a smile is more becoming than a snarl." Her mother also taught her to "not say anything about someone if you can't be nice," which remains a guiding principle in Janine's life. Her mother was a strong role model, a self-made woman with a generous spirit. Janine feels that happiness is a gift from her mother — a talent — that she, in turn, must share with the world. On the happiness scale, she rates herself a definite 9!

✔ **Cecil** is 60 and still actively employed in the insurance business, a profession he has succeeded at since high school when he began shadowing his father, who was also an insurance agent. He's married to the same sweet woman he met decades ago, whom he credits with being a major influence in his ability to be perpetually happy — "She pulls me up in life and always has." She's also taught Cecil to "loosen up" and enjoy life — and, be the type of person who always sees the glass half-full.

Cecil had a childhood illness that left him disabled, and he learned early on that humor defuses the awkwardness that often arises when you have a handicap. He attends church regularly and also looks much younger than his age. Cecil believes that happiness is crucial to good health — "At my age, I think it's remarkable that I don't take any prescription drugs." Laughter is Cecil's medication to be sure. He is legendary when it comes to telling jokes; as a close friend once said, "It's impossible to tell a joke that Cecil hasn't already told." He believes that happiness is contagious and he's apparently doing his best to infect the world around him.

Each of these people is unique in his or her own way, but there are some commonalities to their happy stories:

- ✔ They all attribute much of their happiness to the influences of significant others in their lives (parents, life partners).

- ✔ They all profess a belief that happiness is something you have to work for — you have to find it, it doesn't come looking for you.

- ✔ They all believe it's possible to be happy even when life doesn't always go the way you want it to (for example, when dealing with aging parents, coping with depression, or grieving the loss of loved ones to debilitating illnesses).

- ✔ They all believe in a higher power and practice their religion, and they think that helps them have a positive outlook on life.

- ✔ They all believe in beginning and ending the day with positive thoughts that lend themselves to happiness.

- ✔ They all believe that happiness insures good health and keeps you looking young.

- ✔ They all believe that happiness is something that increases with age (see the following section).

Talk to a happy person you know and see if you can find out what his secret to happiness is. If you're like me, you'll be surprised at how willing he is to talk about why he's happy, who in his life enabled him to feel this way, and what he sees as the benefits that come from always being positive.

The Demographics of Happiness

Happiness is a very democratic emotion — it isn't an emotion that's available to only a certain group of individuals and not others. But there *are* some demographic characteristics that increase your chances of being happy. I cover these in the following sections.

The happiest country in the world

Finland is purportedly the happiest country in the world. Their secret, so say the Finns, is that they're a culture of modest expectations. As a people, they want less out of life and are satisfied with what they have. Finland has a shortage of workaholics and there is little disparity as far as wealth goes. They don't suffer from all the social pressures and violence that typify most industrialized countries. They find a certain comfort in their collective humility — when it comes to materialism, they're content being the underdog.

Age

Age seems to increase a person's overall likelihood of being happy. If you think that young people have the advantage here, you're wrong. Most young people are happy to be sure, but research shows that you're much *more* likely to experience happiness the older you get. In one survey, 38 percent of respondents aged 68 to 77 reported feeling "very happy" as compared to only 28 percent of respondents between the ages of 18 and 27. This same survey showed a sharp increase in happiness scores beginning at age 45 and continuing into the mid-70s. (There was a similar decline in negative emotions with age.)

So, why do people tend to get happier as they get older?

- **Older people have reached a point of *satiation* in life.** They've had a sufficient amount of success and positive experiences to feel both grateful and content. Younger people are on the way, but they're not there yet.

- **Age alters a person's expectations.** Somewhere along the way, you realize that you don't get everything you want out of life and that life never was meant to be perfect. I tell people all the time, "If you want to be happy, you don't have to like the way life is — you just have to accept that it is that way."

- **With age comes *wisdom* — a perspective that results from a combination of accumulated worldly experience and knowledge — not often seen as people muddle through the first half of life.**

It's no coincidence that the people I interviewed (see the preceding section) were all between the ages 56 and 74.

Marital status

Marriage also seems to make a difference in people's happiness. Married people, generally speaking, are happier than those who are unmarried. This is true for both men and women. Marriage is one of the meaningful social ties I talk about in Chapter 16. Marriage brings coherence to people's lives (Chapter 10), gives them an opportunity to be less selfish (Chapter 17), and allows them to tend and befriend those they love (Chapter 20).

Although most of the research looks at happiness in married people, I think it's fair to say that these same benefits would accrue from other types of committed, long-term relationships as well.

Not all partnerships are happy. In Chapter 20, I point out the aspects of an intimate relationship that make for a happy couple. These include

- ✔ Understanding that being in an intimate relationship means being your partner's companion
- ✔ Creating a sense of equity and parity in the relationship
- ✔ Sharing interests, passion, and intimacy
- ✔ Avoiding contempt even when angry
- ✔ Practicing empathy
- ✔ Saying the magic words: "I am sorry."

Education level

The more education you have, the happier you're likely to be. This may be an indirect effect of the positive relationship that education has on a person's earning power, health, ability to cope with the stresses and strains of everyday life, and longevity. In short, education doesn't guarantee that you'll be happy, but it sure does increase your odds.

Sign up for a class or two at your local community college. Trust me, you'll be happy you did.

Happiness at Each Stage of Self-Actualization

According to psychologist Abraham Maslow, a forerunner of the positive psychology movement, if you're self-confident (as opposed to self-centered), enjoy solitude, have a need to serve the greater good, have a keen sense of humor, and aren't afraid to be creative and unique in how you approach life, you're a self-actualized person. Maslow said that happiness comes from satisfying a *hierarchy of needs* in an orderly manner. He argued that you experience happiness at each of five levels of self-actualization:

✔ **Level I:** The first level of self-actualization has to do with meeting your basic survival needs — air, water, food, and sleep. At this level, happiness is more about having something to eat than it is about tender, loving care.

✔ **Level II:** The second level of self-actualization has to do with safety and can include everything from a safe neighborhood to a financial safety net that comes from having a supportive family or by working hard to put aside money for your retirement years.

✔ **Level III:** The next level involves a sense of belonging — that is, feeling loved and needed by others.

✔ **Level IV:** The fourth level has to do with self-esteem. Do you feel like you're respected and appreciated by others? Do you like and respect yourself?

✔ **Level V:** The final level Maslow calls self-actualization. In essence, you're there, you've arrived, you've reached your full potential, and you are your happiest, most unique, most creative self. Classic examples of self-actualized people include Thomas Jefferson, Florence Nightingale, Albert Schweitzer, Albert Einstein, Eleanor Roosevelt, and Mother Teresa.

Having satisfied each level of need/motivation, you then move on to the next all the way to the "peak" of what life has to offer.

So, ask yourself: How satisfied am I as far as biological needs, safety, love, self-esteem, and creativity goes? You may be more self-actualized than you know.

Looking at the Benefit of Positive Emotions

Only in recent years have psychologists begun to appreciate the benefits of positive emotion — benefits that include everything from enhanced creativity to improved immune-system function. Dr. Barbara Fredrickson at the University of North Carolina, a leader in the field of positive psychology, posed the question, "What good are positive emotions?" and came up with the following possibilities.

Broadening your focus and expanding your thinking

Positive emotions — curiosity, love, joy, contentment, wonder, excitement — expand your focus of attention. When you're angry, your focus narrows to the source of your frustration and the object of your wrath. Your mind is like a heat-seeking missile, bent on destruction.

Contrast this with what happens when you get excited about something — your mind opens up and there's a free flow of ideas and intellectual possibility. Curiosity abounds. This is precisely why passion is so essential to artistic endeavors. This is also why you need a high positivity ratio in the workplace (see Chapter 18) if you want a high rate of productivity and a healthy bottom line. In short, your brain works best when it's high on happiness.

Dr. Fredrickson likens the cognitive changes that accompany positive emotion to a state of mania (great excitement), only in this case not the kind of mania that requires medical treatment.

All four of the happy people I introduce in "Happiness from the Individual Perspective," earlier in this chapter, also enjoyed success in their respective careers. When I talked to them, I could hear the excitement and passion in their voices, whether we were discussing the challenges of dealing with difficult clients in the real-estate business or how to thrive in the insurance industry. And that passion had obviously not diminished despite their age.

Psychologist Jon Kabat-Zinn at the University of Massachusetts Medical School teaches his patients the art of *mindfulness meditation* — a Buddhist meditation exercise — as a means of expanding their awareness of those things they fear most, for example, chronic pain and depression. He has patients relax their bodies while at the same time opening up their minds. The irony here is that the more clearly you think about your pain, the less it distresses you. (If you'd like to try meditation, but you're not sure where to start, check out *Meditation For Dummies,* 2nd Edition, by Stephan Bodian [Wiley]. It includes a CD of guided meditation exercises.)

When Kabat-Zinn and others studied the brain activity that accompanies this type of meditation, they found that it was the left frontal lobe of the brain that was literally turned on — the part that scientists refer to as the "happy brain."

Endorphins: The link between happiness and pain relief

The same chemicals that facilitate pain relief — often referred to as the body's own painkillers — also underlie feelings of pleasure, joy, and contentment. Those chemicals are called *endorphins,* and they have an opiate-like effect on a person's mental and emotional states. The so-called "runner's high" is an example of endorphins at work, suppressing the pain that would naturally come from long-distance running. In addition to exercise, activities that turn the brain on to endorphins include all forms of creative activity, competitive pursuits (as long as you don't get angry), fellowship with others, prayer, healthy sexual encounters, and being surrounded by things of beauty.

Improving your ability to problem-solve

Psychiatrist Avery Weisman, in his wonderful book *The Coping Capacity* (Human Sciences Press), lists 15 commonly used coping strategies, including "Laugh it off — change the emotional tone." That's right, when you're frustrated and you're having trouble solving some problem that confronts you, what you need is a good laugh. Laughter unfreezes a "stuck" brain. Think of humor as a lubricant that allows the wheels — your thought processes — to once again move toward a solution. The mechanism that underlies effective problem-solving is creativity, which is your brain's ability to come up with novel, unique answers to life's many challenges.

In the ten years that I ran an outpatient rehabilitation program for chronic-pain sufferers, one of the things that made our program more effective than most medically oriented programs was the fact that we went out of our way to create a positive environment for our clients. The four-hour-a-day, five-week experience we offered our clients was about much more than shots and pills. Getting people who experience pain 24/7 to lighten up and laugh is no easy task, I can assure you. But, in the end, I'm convinced that laughter is the best painkiller on the market. Typically, within only a couple of days, strangers whose only common link was their ongoing pain began to smile, giggle, tease one another, and, for the first time in years, exhibit a sense of hope and optimism. Suddenly, those who had steadfastly resisted engaging in any type of physical reconditioning were willing to tackle the treadmill, floor exercises, and exercise bike. In group discussions, patients were able to come up with creative solutions of how to live with pain — whereas before they could only envision a lifetime of misery and disability. They began to move about more freely — walking faster, limping less, and showing more signs of stamina. Pain management was now a possibility that they embraced rather than ran from.

Building physical, intellectual, and social resources

Positive emotions build the following resources:

- ✔ **Physical resources:** People are more playful when they're happy — they're interested in golf, tennis, marathon running, pick-up basketball games, adult softball leagues, scuba-diving, and water-skiing. Happy people are more likely to exercise on a regular basis. Part of this comes from the higher self-esteem seen in happy people. In short, happiness translates into physical fitness — stronger muscles, improved heart-lung function, and increased flexibility.

This relationship between happiness and physical resources explains, in large part, why the Baby Boomer generation is expected to live longer and healthier than preceding generations — as a group, they've been happier and more physically active throughout their lives and they have no intention of changing any of that even after retirement.

The next time you feel really happy, think about signing up at a local gym. That's where all the other happy people are!

✔ **Intellectual resources:** People learn better when they're in a positive frame of mind.

I once attended a workshop conducted by Patch Adams, the controversial physician who believes that positive emotions have the power to heal. What was unusual about this workshop was having my nose painted red by one of his assistants — who was dressed as a clown — at the beginning of the afternoon seminar. He didn't ask my permission — he just did it! And, you know what? The workshop was one of the best learning experiences of my entire professional life — I looked silly as hell, but I sure learned a lot. There's something about humility that opens the mind, relaxes the body, and makes the brain more receptive to incoming information.

The most effective schoolteachers are the ones who find ways to make education enjoyable — laughter makes kids pay attention and attention is the key to learning. The same is true when you go to a continuing education experience; you want a speaker who is not only knowledgeable about his subject matter, but who can be entertaining.

I tell my students at the community college to do something for fun before they sit down to study for a test and they'll get a better grade. If you engage in a fun activity first, your brain will be like a happy sponge and absorb all that material.

✔ **Social resources:** Human beings gravitate toward positive people and away from negative ones.

Think about the biblical prescription, "Do onto others as you would have them do unto you," and decide how you want to be treated. If you want to be treated badly, then by all means act badly toward others. However, if you want people to smile at you, you need to greet them with cheer and influence their lives in some positive way. More often than not, this is what you'll get in return.

Counteracting negative emotions

Happiness is one antidote to rage. Optimism can be an antidote to fear and cynicism. Joy is the opposite of misery. Humor defuses a desire for vengeance. Positive and negatives emotions can't exist at the same moment in time. Embracing one negates the other.

Once when I was being treated for depression, I was fussing about things I thought my family had done to agitate me, when my therapist interrupted to ask, "Do you love your wife?" Without hesitation, I said, "Of course, I do." He then told me to continue ranting and raving about my family, but I couldn't. My head wanted to, but my heart was no longer in it — it happened just that fast. Whenever I find myself getting angry at the people closest to me, I ask myself that same question, "Do I love this person?" and the anger disappears.

The next time you find yourself feeling negative — upset, angry, sad — try replacing that with a positive feeling and see what happens. Think about someone who makes you laugh, something that excites you, some activity that pleases you — it may provide just the escape you need from those negative emotions.

Protecting your health

You probably already know that getting upset or angry can raise your blood pressure and, in the worst-case scenario, precipitate a heart attack or stroke. But did you know that positive emotions can lower your blood pressure and risk for cardiovascular disease? Well, they can.

The pioneering work of Dr. Barbara Fredrickson illustrated that when stressed people watched a film that left them feeling amused and content, that led to quicker recovery of heart function. She also noted that stressed subjects who smiled while watching a sad movie had a more rapid heart rate recovery than those who didn't smile. Her thesis is that positive emotions *undo* the effects of stress and, therefore, protect a person's health over the long run.

The wrong time to be happy

There is one situation in which happiness doesn't pay — it's when you're trying to negotiate a resolution to some type of conflict or bargain with someone. If the opposing party sees that you're in a good mood, he's more likely to have a longer list of demands.

Research shows that parties concede more to an angry opponent than a happy one. So, if you want to strike a good deal, wipe that smile off your face and replace it with a frown — even if you don't feel all that negative. It's just good business!

Happiness detracts from the impression that you're a tough negotiator. It also implies that, no matter what you say, you'll be satisfied with whatever the last offer was. It encourages others to hold the line on what they're willing to give you. So, the next time you go to buy a car or a new house — where negotiation is expected — put on your serious face. You can smile after the deal is done.

Other studies have shown that something as simple as getting a light touch on your hand from a compassionate friend or the act of petting your favorite animal can also lower your blood pressure — and, neither requires a prescription, gets you into a hassle with your insurance carrier, or has negative side-effects.

Achieving Happiness Isn't Always Easy

You'd think it would be easy to be happy, but that's not always the case. You have to be aware. You can't be in a hurry. And you have to welcome the experience. In the following sections, I show you how.

Being mindful

Mindfulness is about paying attention. Being mindful requires that you stay in the present moment — the here and now — which isn't easy for folks whose minds are always dwelling on the past or skipping ahead to the future. If you're paying attention to the world around you, then you're said to be "mindful of your surroundings." In the case of emotions like happiness, mindfulness has to do with being acutely aware of your inner feelings — something most people don't do enough of.

Being mindful requires that you be able to focus your thoughts on one thing — how you feel — and nothing else. For some people, this is more difficult than it sounds. Often, for example, when I ask male clients how they feel about something, they answer by telling me what they *think* or what they *did*. They're simply not used to thinking in emotional terms. In the more extreme case, I end up saying, "Look, I don't care what you thought or what you did. I just want to know how you felt at the time — you know, like mad, sad, or glad. Which were you?"

Being mindful requires that you not critique, sensor, or judge whatever it is that you're focusing your attention on. There is no right or wrong to how you feel. If you feel happy, that's okay — if not, that's okay, too.

You may be happier than you realize because you're not paying attention. Your mind is always somewhere else — worrying about this or that, checking things off the never-ending to-do list, and so forth. If you stop for a minute to reflect — be mindful — you may be surprised at how good you feel.

Lingering in the moment

The dictionary defines *lingering* as "remaining in a place longer than usual or longer than expected." Lingering is, in effect, a measure of time — in this case, taking time to enjoy a moment of happiness. Hurrying is just the opposite. When you hurry, you quickly jump from one experience or task to another. You tell yourself you don't have time to stay with any one thing too long. Always moving forward, always too much left to accomplish.

In Chapter 15, I talk about some of the differences between Type A and Type B personalities and how this impacts the balance between work and play. Type A's hurry; Type B's tend to linger.

Kristin, a highly intelligent 30-year old, single woman, was very accomplished but also very unhappy. She was a workaholic, putting in at least 10 to 12 hours at the office each day. If there was a task to be done, Kristin was the one to do it — definitely a Type A! When I asked her to tell me about her feelings, she angrily replied,

> Dr. Gentry, I don't have time to have feelings — I'm too damned busy. The people who work under me, now *they* all have feelings. They're always mad about something or upset because of this or that, which, believe me, gets in the way of their work. So, when you ask me how I feel, the honest answer is, "I don't have a clue."

When I finally succeeded in helping Kristin explore her feelings, she became painfully aware of just how sad, depressed, anxious, and defeated she felt most days. (Sometimes, in counseling, people end up feeling worse before they feel better.) This then begged the question: "Is this how you want to feel at work for the next 30 years, or would you like instead to enjoy your job and be happy with what you've accomplished?" I'm happy to say that Kristin chose the latter.

Bottom line: Some people allow time in their busy day for a few moments of happiness, and others don't. Which kind of person are you?

Being happy about being happy

Some people just have a hard time letting themselves be happy. Take Rod, for example. He wants to be happy — he really does — but as soon as he finds himself enjoying life, he gets anxious. Deep down in his subconscious, Rod knows two things for certain:

✔ The minute he lets himself feel the least bit happy, something will come along and screw it up.

✔ For some reason, he doesn't deserve to be happy.

Where in the world did Rod get these screwy ideas? The answer is: He got them by being raised in an alcoholic home by parents who were emotionally unstable, unpredictable, and at times violent. Rod and his brothers could be playing happily one minute and the next minute all hell would break loose and somebody would end up hurt. "It was like you were afraid to let yourself relax and enjoy what you were doing because any second everything went from harmony to chaos," he said. Thirty-five years later, Rod is still afraid, always waiting for the other shoe to drop. Without realizing it, Rod is being self-protective. The logic is simple: You can't lose what you never had.

And why exactly does Rod feel like he doesn't deserve to be happy? Because the child in him — that part of his personality that never really grew up — thinks like all children that "if my parents are angry or unhappy, it must be because I did something wrong." Because the child did something wrong, he deserves to be punished. And what better punishment is there than a lifetime of unhappiness?

When you find yourself in a happy moment, does a little voice in the back of your head whisper, "Be careful, don't let your guard down — you don't deserve this"? If so, you may want to consider seeing a mental-health professional — part of a mental-health professional's job is to help people quiet those lingering childlike voices that often get in the way of people's adult lives.

Timing is everything

Maybe happiness is meant to be the *exception* rather than the *rule*. If you're happy too much of the time, you might get too comfortable — too complacent — with the way things are and not want to change anything. For example, if people had been happy having to light their homes with candles, we wouldn't have needed Thomas Edison to come along and invent the electric light bulb. If in the Old West, people had been happy with the Pony Express as the major communication link between east and west, we wouldn't have needed the telegraph, telephone, and eventual global telecommunication networks. If Americans had been happy using horses to plow their fields and take them into town, Henry Ford would never have brought us tractors and automobiles.

This could also explain why people tend to be happier as they grow older. Maybe it makes

sense that young people are more frustrated, angrier, and more restless about life — these feelings provide the energy necessary to make things happen in terms of productivity, entrepreneurship, creativity, and invention.

What I'm suggesting is that perhaps happiness is wasted on the young and is an emotion better suited to people in the second half of life. Why else would 38 percent of people between the ages of 68 and 77 report being "very happy" as compared to only 28 percent of those between 18 and 27?

Look on the bright side: If you're under age 40, you have something to look forward to — a happier time of life. If you're over 40, good news: You're already well on your way to compounding a life of happiness.

How Happy Are You?

Nearly everybody is happy at one time or another. Happiness, like all emotions — anger, pain, sadness — is a subjective experience, which means only *you* know how happy you are. On a scale from 1 to 10 (where 1 is not at all happy and 10 is the height of happiness), where are you right now? Divide that number by 10 (so if you said 6, divide 6 by 10, and you get 0.6, or 60 percent) to get your happiness quotient (HQ).

Happiness scores tend to be skewed toward the positive end, which means that the average person either is typically somewhere between 5 and 10 in terms of how positive he feels or he doesn't want anyone to think he's unhappy — probably a little of both.

If your rating HQ is 50 percent or below, you're less happy than most people. If you scored 10 percent, 20 percent, or 30 percent, you're basically saying you're *unhappy*. If your current HQ is 80 percent, 90 percent, or 100 percent, you're doing something right!

Happiness scores fluctuate — more in some people than in others. Some people are consistently on the high end of the curve; others are typically on the low end. To track your HQ scores over time, rate yourself at the same time every day for 30 days. Make a few notations each day alongside your score so that, when you're finished, you can go back and compare what was happening in your life on those days when you were the happiest versus those when you weren't. Think of it as a *happiness log*.

Chapter 2

The Recipe for Happiness

In This Chapter

▶ Understanding the complex nature of happiness

▶ Identifying the primary and secondary components to happiness

▶ Assessing how close you are to being happy and moving closer toward your goal

*E*very time my wife, Catherine, decides to make her legendary layered vegetable salad, it's a happy day for friends, family, even strangers. This salad is not some simple lettuce-and-tomatoes concoction — it's a carefully prepared mixture of 12 separate ingredients that, when combined, make for some very enjoyable eating.

Catherine's salad recipe

1. **Layer the following vegetables in a tall bowl in the following order:**

   1 small head of lettuce, shredded

   ½ cup to ¾ cup sliced celery

   ½ cup to ¾ cup chopped green pepper

   1 can sliced water chestnuts, drained

   1 small, red onion, sliced and broken into rings

   1 package frozen green peas, cooked until thawed and heated throughout

2. **Cover with 2 cups mayonnaise.**

3. **Sprinkle with 1 teaspoon sugar.**

4. **Top with a heavy layer of grated Romano cheese.**

5. **Refrigerate overnight or at least eight hours.**

6. **When you're ready to serve, garnish with the following:**

   2 hard-boiled eggs, chopped

   4 medium-size tomatoes, diced

   ½ pound crisp bacon, crumbled

And, so it is with happiness. In fact, a salad is the perfect metaphor for happiness, which is the end result of at *least* eight different components of psychological experience. As I explain in this chapter, some of these (like safety) are primary ingredients, while others (such as gratitude and a sense of satisfaction) are important add-ons that enrich the happiness.

This chapter shows you just how close you are to that perfect psychological salad called happiness.

The Four Basic Ingredients

The foundation for true happiness consists of four basic ingredients:

- ✔ A feeling of safety
- ✔ A sense of satiation
- ✔ A sense of perspective
- ✔ Quietude

These four ingredients are essential if your goal is happiness. You can't make chicken soup or chicken salad without chicken to start with. But your neighbor may put things in his chicken salad that you can't imagine putting in yours. Think of these four items as the chicken, and the ingredients later in this chapter as all the optional stuff that you can choose to add or leave out.

Safety

Not everyone lives in a safe world. There are unsafe neighborhoods, where crime is rampant and all the windows have bars. There are unsafe relationships, where a person's odds of being harmed — physically and/or emotionally — are exceedingly high. And, not everyone has a safety net when it comes to financial problems. Feeling unsafe carries with it fear, uncertainty, and bodily tension — hardly a context in which you can expect to be happy.

I once asked my friend Tony if he'd had a happy childhood. He said, "Well, yes and no." When he was at home with his biological family, Tony was never really happy. His father was an unpredictable alcoholic — sometimes violent — and his mother vacillated between episodes of loving behavior and sudden attacks of rage. All the time he was with his family, Tony was tense, cautious, anxious, always waiting for things to change from good to not-so-good.

On the other hand, when Tony spent time with his aunt and uncle, who had no children of their own, he was immensely happy. Why? Because his aunt and uncle were good-natured people, who always seemed happy to have him around. "I honestly don't ever remember either one of them getting angry, much less losing their temper," he said, adding, "If things were good, they stayed good." Ironically, Tony felt safer — and happier — with his aunt and uncle than he did with his own parents.

How safe do you feel? If you don't feel safe, you're not happy.

Satiation

In simple terms, satiation means being full. A happy person is someone who, *at least at this moment,* is full. She has had enough of something (or things) she values.

You may be asking yourself, "But who decides when you have enough of something?" *You* do. It's just that simple. You, and only you, are the arbiter of how much is enough. If nothing is ever enough for you, your search for happiness is one without end!

Seeking happiness can be like walking on a treadmill. You tell yourself, "If only I had a boyfriend, I'd be happy." Then, after you get the boyfriend, you find yourself thinking, "If only we were married, I'd be happy." After you get married, you think, "If only I had kids, I'd be happy." In other words, happiness is always one step away from where you're standing.

Take a minute and ask yourself this question: Which of the things I value in life do I have enough of and which do I not?

When enough isn't enough

Eddie worked hard his whole life and, in the process, amassed a tidy retirement nest egg — several million dollars to be exact. But he's still out there literally killing himself working every day at age 68. At least twice a month, he calls his long-time financial advisor and, in a tone of desperation, says, "Do I have enough money set aside to retire? My wife's on my back, wanting me to stop working and just enjoy our remaining years together."

His advisor — with great exasperation — tells him, "Of course, you do — you can live quite handsomely on the interest the money earns and leave the principal to your kids or whomever you want." Eddie remains unconvinced, and he continues to push himself day after day while his wife travels, enjoys their lovely new home on the lake, and visits with their children and grandchildren. For some reason, Eddie isn't ready yet to say enough is enough — and, he isn't ready to be happy.

It takes real courage to reach a point in life where you declare for all to hear, "Enough is enough!" In other words, it takes courage to let yourself be happy.

No one has everything he wants. You may have enough money, but not enough friends. You may have plenty of friends, but not enough money. You can be happy even if your life isn't 100 percent "full," but you can't be happy if your life is empty.

Perspective

Finding happiness requires that you take a step back from life and reflect on the bigger picture of what your life is all about. That's called perspective — and, in today's hectic world, not many of us have it! We're far too busy climbing or cutting down the trees in front of us to have any sense of the forest as a whole. What we really need is an aerial view of our own lives. Happiness, after all, is not about what you're doing at the moment — it's about the impact of what you're doing on your life, positive or negative. If the impact is positive, happiness follows. If it's negative, unhappiness follows.

What does your forest look like? Is it lush and green, or does it resemble something wrecked and ruined by the logging crew?

Quietude

Happiness cannot find you amidst a lot of noise — it finds you when you're in a quiet place or circumstance. You need a place where you can get in touch with the other three basic elements of achieving happiness, someplace where you can appreciate how safe you feel, where you can see how satiated you are, and where it's not so difficult to achieve some perspective. You have to get off the proverbial treadmill of daily life, stop running with the bulls (the ones that wear suits and ties, not the four-legged kind!), and give it a rest.

You may be able to find quietude in the following places:

- In a library
- In the sanctuary of a church, cathedral, synagogue, temple, or mosque
- On a walking trail through the forest
- At an out-of-the-way table in a small, quiet restaurant
- By the pool, when no one else is around
- On the beach, early in the morning or late in the day
- On the drive home after a long, hard day at the office
- On a long road trip
- In a lovely garden

Here are places where you likely *won't* find quietude:

- ✔ In a noisy restaurant
- ✔ At a popular bar
- ✔ In the middle of a college football stadium on Saturday afternoon
- ✔ At a wedding
- ✔ In a place where you're competing with others
- ✔ At your office
- ✔ Running from place to place in a busy airport
- ✔ Fighting to maintain your place in line for coveted concert tickets
- ✔ In a car with hyperactive kids

 What you're looking for is a place where you can hear yourself think, free of distractions or responsibilities. Ideally, you want to be able to spend at least 20 minutes a day in quietude. It doesn't have to be in the same place every day, though — one day you may find your quietude in your garden, the next it may be at the beach. The important thing isn't where you find the quietude, it's that you find it in the first place, because, without it, you'll have trouble being happy.

The Rest of the Mix

The four ingredients I cover earlier in this chapter are essential to any happiness recipe. But after you've tossed those four ingredients into your mixing bowl, you can choose to add a dash of this or a splash of that. The "this" and the "that" are what I cover in this section.

The perfect happiness recipe would incorporate the four basics plus all five add-ons in this section. You can still experience less complete feelings of happiness, however, with even one or two of these additional ingredients.

Satisfaction

Satisfaction is not the same as satiation (which is one of the four key ingredients). Satiation is feeling that you have enough of the things you value. Satisfaction (some people prefer to think of it as contentment) is the sense of fulfillment or comfort that can, but doesn't always, accompany satiation.

An inspiration

My recently departed mother lived the last 20 years of her life solely on Social Security, which amounted to around $1,000 per month. After paying her bills — which she was faithful about doing — she had only about $75 to $100 of discretionary money. Her bank account wasn't full by any means. But, every time my brothers and I tried to help her out, she politely refused, telling us, in no uncertain terms, "Thanks, but I'll get by." My mother wasn't satiated (she didn't have enough where money was concerned), but she was satisfied (she was happy with what she had).

You can be satiated but not satisfied and you can be satisfied without being satiated. You can be both or you can be neither. They're two very different things.

Ever gone into a restaurant hungry and eaten until your stomach couldn't hold any more? That's an example of satiation — you've had enough food. Now, answer me this: How did you feel when your stomach got that full? If you felt satisfied — content that your stomach was full — you weren't looking for anything more to eat. But, what if your head was telling you, "As full as I am right this minute, I sure could go for a piece of pie"? If that sounds familiar, you may have been satiated (full), but you were far from satisfied.

How *satisfied* are you with your current life situation?

Pleasure

Happiness is a pleasurable experience. It's the feel-good emotion. Generally, you'll have an easier time finding happiness when you're leading a life that pleases you. If you hear someone say, "I'd do this job even if they didn't pay me," you're listening to someone who derives great pleasure in her work. If you look at your husband and think, "I wouldn't trade him for all the money in the world," you're obviously pleased with the person you go to bed with every night and wake up next to each morning.

The pleasures of everyday life come from both *being* and *doing*. Here are some examples of the kind of pleasure that comes from doing:

- Doing a good deed
- Doing a good job when others don't
- Doing something because it's right, not because it's popular
- Doing the difficult things in life, like visiting a sick friend in the hospital or loaning money to a loved one knowing full well that he'll never pay you back

✔ Doing something until it's completed

✔ Doing a favor without being asked

✔ Doing something without being compensated

And here are the kinds of pleasures that come from being:

✔ Being healthy

✔ Being compassionate to those in need

✔ Being true to your word

✔ Being a good friend

✔ Being faithful in intimate relationships

✔ Being articulate and expressing yourself well to others

✔ Being tough or tender depending on the circumstances

Make a list of as many things as you can think of that please you. Now ask yourself this crucial question: When was the last time I was *being* that person or *doing* those things?

Gratitude

If there is one extra ingredient that comes the closest to insuring happiness, it's gratitude. Gratitude is simply the readiness and willingness to show appreciation for those things that bring pleasure into your life. (See how interconnected these ingredients are?) Gratitude is the "thank-you" feeling that some people have throughout the day.

Gratitude is the opposite of entitlement — the idea that you deserve or are owed something from life (see Chapter 22). Entitlement has to do with what you feel is expected (or required) from others; gratitude is your response to the unexpected. When you eat out in a restaurant, do you say "thank you" every time the waiter refills your coffee or tea, or do you simply expect that he'll do that as part of his job and let his behavior go unnoticed?

Helen and Kate are both midlevel managers at the same company. They each earn six-figure salaries. When the year-end bonuses are handed out, each gets a check for $2,500. Kate had expected much more, given how hard she worked throughout the year, so she's disappointed and ungrateful. She tells her boss "thank you," but the tone of her voice and the look on her face convey her true feelings: Kate is very unhappy. Helen, on the other hand, long ago vowed to herself that she would never expect a bonus. So, she's thrilled with the $2,500, thinking of the trip she and her husband can take with the extra money. Who are you more like — Helen or Kate?

Begin each new day of your life with a few minutes of quiet reflection about all the things you have to be grateful for, and then, either silently to yourself or out loud, say thank-you for each item on the list. Trust me, there's no better way to start your day and open yourself up to the possibility of happiness.

Serenity

Serenity has to do with peace of mind. Happiness can't find its way into a mind cluttered by worry, anxieties, anger, stress, and who knows what else. Quietude is about finding a quiet *place;* serenity is about having a quiet *mind.* Of course, you'll have an easier time finding serenity in a place of quietude.

Like most young professionals, Elizabeth isn't able to experience a feeling of serenity the moment she first sets foot on the beach. Because of all the residual clutter in her mind about things left undone at the office and things that will need her urgent attention as soon as she returns from vacation, it typically takes at least three or four days walking the beaches, sleeping late, and enjoying a good novel before she begins to relax and feel a sense of inner peace. Because Elizabeth has learned this about herself, she's smart and allows herself two full weeks at the beach. Before she came to this realization, just about the time she found serenity, it was time to pack up the car and head home.

Meditation is an excellent way to find serenity. Pick up a copy of *Meditation For Dummies,* 2nd Edition, by Stephan Bodian (Wiley), to get started.

Well-being

Common sense will tell you that it's easier to be happy when you're feeling healthy or well than it is to feel happy when you're sick. (Of course, it isn't impossible for human beings to experience happiness when they're not well — it's just more difficult.)

I've spent the last 40 years of my career observing and treating men and women who suffer from one or another type of chronic, unremitting, musculoskeletal pain (for example, chronic back pain). One interesting thing I've learned is that the one area of activity that these folks give up soon after injury is the kind having to do with social and recreational interests. Ironically, they're more apt to continue engaging in household chores (vacuuming, preparing meals, washing clothes — all of which aggravate their pain) than they are to continue visiting family and friends, going to watch their grandkids play sports, or attending church. This leads me to conclude that the real reason that 70 percent of chronic-pain patients suffer from depression is not because of the pain itself, but because they've chosen to terminate all activities that previously brought pleasure into their lives. In our rehabilitation program, we work to help them resume (or find substitutes for) pleasure-giving activities that they can do even in their reduced state of well-being. And guess what? Suddenly, we're surrounded by happy pain patients.

Modern science has proven that peppermint and lavender both serve to increase subjective feelings of well-being, increase feelings of relaxation, and lead to more positive mood states. Tea, anyone?

You may need some professional assistance in order to achieve happiness if you're not well physically or mentally. Don't be afraid to tell your doctor that you're unhappy and ask her to refer you to someone who has a background in health psychology or behavioral medicine (such as a psychologist).

How Close Are You?

If you want to know how close you are to happiness, I've created a little self-assessment you can do. ***Remember:*** Be honest with yourself — otherwise the exercise won't be helpful.

Circle one answer under each of the following questions:

1. **Generally speaking, how safe and secure do you feel in your everyday life?**

    • Not at all: 1

    • A little: 2

    • Fairly safe: 3

    • Very safe: 4

2. **All things considered, do you feel you have enough of what you need to be happy?**

    • Not at all: 1

    • Possibly: 2

    • Probably: 3

    • Absolutely: 4

3. **Do you have moments when you look at the totality of your life rather than just the events of the moment?**

    • Not at all: 1

    • Occasionally: 2

    • Regularly: 3

    • Quite often: 4

4. **How often do you find yourself in a quiet place or circumstance where you can have a moment of true self-reflection?**

   - Never: 1

   - Seldom: 2

   - Occasionally: 3

   - Very often: 4

5. **How satisfied are you with specific things in your life — finances, relationships, career?**

   - Not at all: 1

   - Somewhat: 2

   - Moderately: 3

   - Very much: 4

6. **How pleased are you with your general life situation?**

   - Not at all: 1

   - A little: 2

   - Moderately: 3

   - Very much: 4

7. **How grateful are you for the way your life is turning out?**

   - Not at all: 1

   - Somewhat: 2

   - Moderately: 3

   - Very much: 4

8. **How often do you have a sense of peace of mind?**

   - Never: 1

   - Rarely: 2

   - Occasionally: 3

   - Much of the time: 4

9. **How would you rate your overall state of mental and physical well-being?**

   - Poor: 1

   - Average: 2

   - Above average: 3

   - Excellent: 4

10. How often do you find yourself experiencing a feeling of contentment?

- Never: 1

- Rarely: 2

- Occasionally: 3

- Very often: 4

Add up the scores. If your total score is below 20, you're a long way from being a happy camper. If your score is 35 or above, you're either already happy or you're right on the verge. And if you're in between 20 and 35, you're neither happy nor miserable.

This is a test you should take often, both while you're reading this book and afterward as you employ many of the strategies I offer in these pages. It lets you know whether you're on track or off track when it comes to finding happiness.

Take a minute and more closely examine your individual answers to the ten questions. Focus on those you had a low score on — either a 1 or 2. These are the ingredients that are missing from your recipe for happiness, and they're the ones you need to work on. By focusing on these missing ingredients, you move closer to your objective of being a happier person.

Chapter 3

Knowing What Happiness Isn't

*F*or Jake and Jim, it's the best of times and the worst of times.

Jake is 72 and retired, and he suffers from a chronic back problem that began over 15 years ago. He lives with his wife of 45 years in a modest, albeit paid-for, home. He has some retirement savings but depends a good bit on Social Security. Most days, he piddles around the house with minor fix-it projects or finds himself helping out a friend or neighbor less fortunate than himself. Jake was born poor, had a difficult childhood, and suffered from a learning disability that kept him from completing his education and forced him into a lifetime of blue-collar employment. And, for most of his adult life, he had a bad temper that strained his relationships with his wife and children. And yet, despite all this, Jake is quick to tell anyone who will listen that "This is the happiest time of my life!"

Jim is 68, is in exceptionally good health, and, like Jake, has been married for over 40 years. He graduated from college and has run a very successful business for years, leaving him with a nest egg of several million dollars, a nice getaway cottage in the mountains, a big new home in town, and a Cadillac. By comparison, his life has been easy and uneventful. And he's never had a problem with his temper. But Jim isn't happy.

Why is Jake happy with so little? And why is Jim unhappy with so much? Why is Jim still working as hard as he ever did and worrying incessantly about having enough money? Why hasn't he spent any time at his mountain retreat in the past three years? Why doesn't he travel and do more fun things with his wife, who's enjoying her retirement years?

The richest man I ever met

Most people measure wealth in dollars and cents. In my opinion, another measure of wealth is how many people show up at your funeral.

For years, I had a next-door neighbor, Marion, who would do anything for you. He'd give you the shirt off his back — all you had to do was ask. He was a man of modest means. He never made a great deal of money, but he was still generous. The last years of his life, Marion suffered from progressive heart disease. He dropped dead in the middle of a conversation with friends and family at the beach.

His funeral was truly impressive! There were hundreds of people there — so many that the church couldn't hold them all. When it came time for those in attendance to say a few words about Marion, people couldn't wait to get up and give testimony to how he had impacted their lives in some positive way — people young and old, friends from World War II and recent acquaintances, neighbors like myself and members of his church softball team, dignitaries from Duke University Medical Center, and on and on.

As I sat there listening to their words and quietly remembering this good man, I couldn't help but think, "He's the richest man I ever met."

In this chapter, I answer those questions. If you're like me, you tend to confuse happiness with culturally valued outcomes such as wealth, power, and success. This chapter eliminates that confusion! As the title suggests, it tells you where *not* to look for happiness.

What Money Really Buys

A recent headline in a newspaper says it all: "Market lapse makes way into retirees' homes." The article goes on to say that when the stock market goes down, people on fixed incomes suffer — they forego dinners out, do with less heat in the winter, and buy more store-brand items in the grocery store. Does that mean that they're unhappy? No — but it *does* mean they're less comfortable and less free to live their lives the way they may want to.

I'm not here to tell you that money doesn't matter. It does. But it doesn't buy happiness. In this section, I cover the things that money *does* buy.

Comfort

Money buys physical comfort. That's true for everything from paper products to underwear and furniture. I learned early in my married life that the more comfortable a sofa is, the more it costs. The more comfortable the ambience in a restaurant, the more expensive the entrees. If you've ever slept on silk sheets and overstuffed pillows, worn expensive Italian loafers, or driven a Mercedes, you know what I'm talking about.

But comfort does not equal happiness. If it did, I wouldn't have counseled so many wealthy people — lawyers, doctors, businesspeople — over the last 40 years. Take Martin, for example, a 43-year-old man, who wears $2,000 suits, drives a $75,000 car, and brags about his two vacation homes — yet finds himself hopelessly depressed. Or Emily, who inherited a family fortune early in life only to find herself miserable and without any real friends in her late 50s. They both live very *comfortable* lives — but they aren't happy.

Support

Money also buys you emotional comfort in the form of support during trying times. That's what lawyers, accountants, life coaches, financial advisers, psychotherapists, bartenders, political consultants, publicists, and — if you're a celebrity — "handlers" are all about. In one way or another, they're all paid to help you handle your problems — financial, emotional, or legal. The more support you have at your disposal, obviously the easier it is to navigate the troubles of everyday life.

Here's the kinds of support that money can buy:

- **Emotional support:** A life coach or therapist who is behind you 100 percent and cheers you on through adversity.

- **Informational support:** An accountant who provides you with critical information on how to minimize your tax burden.

- **Tangible support:** Hands-on support, like an attorney who will come down and get you out of jail or a maid to clean your home.

- **Appraisal support:** Your family physician, who levels with you about your odds of having a heart attack if you continue smoking and don't lose weight.

Freedom

Money buys economic freedom:

- Freedom from financial worry
- Freedom to pursue life on your own terms, instead of settling for what comes along

✔ Freedom to take risks — for example, to quit a well-paying job in the corporate world in order to start your own small business, where you give the orders instead of always taking them

✔ Freedom to vacation when and where you want rather than where you can afford

✔ Freedom to live life according to your wants rather than your needs

✔ Freedom to get the best healthcare possible

✔ Freedom to be generous to those you love as well as those in need

✔ Freedom to stand up for your convictions without fear of retribution — for example, losing your job

✔ Freedom to have as many children as you want

✔ Freedom to shop in the best retail shops

✔ Freedom from debt

✔ Freedom from the time constraints of a 9-to-5 job

If you want to know exactly how much economic freedom you have in your life these days, list your assets (everything you own outright) and your liabilities (everything you owe) and come up with your net worth. I can't promise you'll be happy with what you find out, but at least you'll know where you stand.

The Elixirs of Modern-Day Life

An *elixir* is a remedy for what ails you. In modern-day life, that comes down to three things: power, success, and excitement. If you have enough of these, you're bound to be happy, right? Wrong! In this section, I tell you why.

Power

Power means different things to different people. Political power, for example, has to do with influencing the vote at election time or which laws get enacted in your community or state. Economic power is the power of the purse — as is evident when an abusive husband controls his wife's daily life by only allowing her to spend money on the things that *he* values. There's power of attorney, power of the press, police powers, and physical power, which far too many people use to intimidate others. There's social power — often referred to as *status* (which, along with income, separates the "haves" and the "have-nots").

In the end, all forms of power involve having control over the world around you — something we all seek and aspire to, whether we realize it or not. Ironically, however, those with the most power often end up being the least happy. Here's an example:

> The CEO of a local corporation — one that did over $40 million dollars worth of business annually — visited my office a couple of years ago, asking for my help. His problem: "I'm tired of being a referee in physical confrontations between my top executives. Twice in the last month, I've had to get in between two of my vice presidents who were slugging it out in the executive men's room. I don't have time for this crap!"

> The man was perplexed about the boorish behavior of his most powerful employees, given the fact that he paid them each a six-figure salary with all kinds of perks and gave them the kind of freedom to operate not often seen in most companies. He hired me to meet with his entire executive staff for three consecutive Saturday-morning anger-management workshops. What an experience that was — talk about some unhappy people!

> It didn't take a rocket scientist to figure out what their problem was: They were all trying too hard to control each other in the course of everyday business. I gave them all a little test to measure how aggressive they were — both in terms of achieving goals and engaging in demanding or confrontational behavior. I concluded that the odds of any 2 of these 11 executives having an interaction that *wasn't* a power struggle were zero — that's right, zero. These guys were literally trying to kill each other!

The very characteristic that enables people to rise up the corporate ladder to positions of power — aggressiveness — can also lead to their eventual downfall and a lot of unhappiness along the way.

Success

Power and success are two sides of the same coin. Success is a relative concept — it means you're doing better and accomplishing more than the people you're competing with.

The successful salesperson belongs to the Million Dollar Club no matter what she's selling. The successful stock broker makes more money for his clients than all the other brokers. The most successful people in society end up wealthy, famous, on the covers of magazines, and, in a few cases, with the Nobel Prize or Pulitzer Prize on their living room mantles.

What they don't say in the introduction

When I conduct workshops, I always enjoy being introduced by someone who recounts all of my many successes early in my academic career — administrative head of this, founding editor of that, author of this, that, and the other. It's like a stroll down memory lane.

But what they don't tell the audience in the introduction is the price I paid for all that success — a nervous breakdown at age 45 that lasted for five unhappy years. I learned the hard way that too much of anything can be harmful — even success.

Success, however, is sometimes accompanied by misfortune and tragedy. Ernest Hemingway, the American novelist, was without doubt highly successful — and he ended up killing himself. Martha Stewart, one of the most successful business-women of our time, ended up serving a prison sentence. Winston Churchill and Abraham Lincoln — both successful political figures — suffered from chronic depression their whole lives.

In short, success is no antidote to misery and misfortune, nor is it a guarantee of happiness.

Excitement

You want excitement, go to Las Vegas, New York, Paris, London, Hong Kong, Hollywood . . . anyplace where there's lots of action, brouhaha, energy, commotion, enthusiasm, tension, and passion. Go with whatever turns on your nervous system and pumps your body full of adrenaline and your brain full of dopamine. Gamble until you're broke, shop 'til you drop, eat until your stomach is in pain, dance until your feet lose all feeling.

Problem is, excitement can create the *illusion* of happiness. My wife and I love to visit Las Vegas, even though neither of us gambles. While we're there, I always enjoy listening to people on the streets, late at night, laughing and telling each other how much fun they had losing all their money: "Did you see me at the blackjack table? I lost over $600! Can you believe that? I'm gonna hate myself in the morning, but damn that was fun!" Excited? Yes. Happy? No.

Make a list of ten things that excite you. Referring to the definition of happiness in Chapter 2, ask yourself how happy you feel after doing each of these things — how grateful you feel, how satisfied you are, how much contentment and serenity you feel.

The Problem with the Abundant Life

Between 1957 and 2005, the average income of Americans rose by a whopping 278 percent, yet the percentage of those who described themselves as "very happy" remained virtually the same — around 30 percent. This finding alone has convinced happiness researchers that a lifestyle of increased income has little effect on how positive a person feels.

There are three possible explanations for this:

✔ **The hedonic treadmill effect:** Each time you reach a new level of achievement, you adjust your *level of neutrality* — the point at which you feel neither positive nor negative about the world around you. And, then it takes something *more* to make you happy. In effect, you're comparing what you have today with what you had yesterday, and it's the *change* that leads to happiness, not the absolute level.

If you make $30,000 a year, a $5,000 raise makes you happy — but only for a while. You quickly get used to making $35,000 per year, and now you won't be happy until you get bumped up to $43,000. And so it goes, on and on and on. People on the hedonic treadmill are never truly happy with what they have — they always want more. And there is always more to want.

✔ **Relative deprivation:** People are constantly comparing themselves to other people — typically those who have more than they do — and they come away with a feeling of being *relatively deprived* when it comes to those things they think make them happy.

For example, instead of being satisfied and grateful (see Chapter 2) that you live in a house twice the size of the one you grew up in and that your parents still live in, you end up feeling unhappy because your house is smaller than your neighbor's.

If you find yourself often making comparisons between your lifestyle and other people's lifestyles, make sure you spend as much time comparing your situation to those *less* well off than you are, too. That way, you'll be much more content and grateful with what you have.

✔ **Escalating needs:** Human beings unfortunately have a shifting and — all too often — escalating sense of what they perceive they need to be satisfied with life. Simply put, the more you get, the more you want! It's not a conscious, deliberate thing — most people are unaware of this aspect of human nature. But it's there in the back of your mind, working on you — and, keeping you from being happy — all the time.

Negative emotions like envy, jealousy, greed, and resentment (see Chapter 22) are the emotional by-products of these types of unhealthy comparisons. It comes down to the fact that, instead of being happy with what you've got, you feel bad toward those who have more than you do. In effect, *their* success makes you feel less successful, *their* power makes you feel powerless, and *their* freedom makes you feel less free. It's all about them!

Economic recession and your health

Believe it or not, Americans actually get healthier as the economy gets worse — during a recession. Economist Christopher J. Ruhm at the University of North Carolina at Greensboro calculated, in fact, that there are 14,000 fewer deaths when unemployment increases by as little as 1 percent.

Why? Because as people have more time on their hands and less money, they lose weight, smoke less, exercise more, drive less — and, thus, have fewer accidents — and have less contact with people who may have the flu.

Happiness Is Not a Life-Transforming Experience

I wish I could tell you that one moment of happiness can transform your life from what it is now to something much better, but I can't. Happiness is an emotion, and emotions are, by definition, short-lived — they come and go like waves on a beach. You're happy, excited, joyful one minute — and the next minute, you're not.

Although happiness doesn't alter your life situation in any significant way, what it does is *define the more prominent and uniquely positive circumstances of your life.*

Each person is happy about different things, and those differences tell us something important about ourselves. For example, here are a few of the happiest moments in my life:

- I remember, as a very small child, rolling an orange around the garage while my mother did the ironing. Something about watching that orange roll and roll or perhaps having my mother all to myself made me happy.

- I was very happy when I was allowed to go to the nearby Catholic school — even though I wasn't Catholic. There was order in the classroom and they taught you more than in the public school. I know because I went to public school first, and it was dreadful!

- I was super-happy when my older brother joined the armed services after graduating from high school — because for the first time in my life I had a bed all to myself.

- I was very happy when a girl I asked out on a date actually said yes! (She wasn't the first one I asked out, just the first one who said yes.)

✔ I was happy when my 11th-grade English teacher read my short story to the whole class, adding, "This young man has a gift."

✔ I was happy when I got engaged to my wife, who's still my partner after 41 years.

✔ I was happy on the days each of my wonderful children were born — something I had to keep in mind when they were going through their teen years!

✔ I've been happy pretty much every day since I quit using alcohol a decade ago.

And here are some things — albeit positive — that *never* made me happy although you could argue that they should have:

✔ Making more money than most of my peers.

✔ Getting a new car.

✔ Belonging to the country club.

✔ Having my 100th article published in a journal. The first one or two made me happy, but after that it was just part of the job.

✔ Getting a promotion.

✔ Watching an upturn in the stock market.

✔ Getting a new cashmere sweater.

Take a quiet moment to yourself, close your eyes, and recall the ten happiest moments of your life. Who were you with? What were you doing? Where were you? Write them down on a piece of paper and then listen to what they tell you about yourself. Then make a second list, a list of positive events or circumstances in your life that you thought would've made you happy but didn't. What does that list tell you? What you're looking for here are what you value, your priorities.

Happiness occurs in moments, not hours, days, weeks, months, or years. Sometimes the experience lasts just a few seconds; other times it lasts as long as a few minutes. But inevitably it disappears. The trick is to enjoy the moment, to relish the experience, and to be mindful that it'll be gone before you know it. What I do in this book is show you how to create and have more of these moments than you ever have before.

Chapter 4

Seeing Happiness as a Sign, Not a Symptom

*J*ust as negative emotions like anger and depression tell you that you're at odds with your surroundings, happiness is your nervous system's way of telling you that you're living a meaningful and healthy life — that you're right with the world.

To say that Matthew wasn't happy was an understatement. It was what you *didn't* see and hear that was most telling. Matthew never smiled and he seldom laughed. There was no energy in his voice and the way he moved suggested an attitude of apathy or indifference. Matthew had a job, but not one that excited him — he sat in a cubicle all day interacting with a computer screen, when what he really wanted to do was be out amongst people promoting himself as well as some product or service that could benefit his fellow man. This was what he dreamed of when he had a few minutes to himself throughout the day. But his job paid well and the benefits were great, so he was "stuck" in his present circumstance. "After all," he rationalized, "why take a chance on doing what I really want to do when I've got a sure thing?"

Matthew wasn't depressed. He didn't exhibit any of the *symptoms* you normally expect with a mood disorder — sleep problems, irritability, sadness. But he clearly was unhappy and that was a *sign* that something important was missing from his life. His nervous system was talking to him, but Matthew wasn't listening.

What are you leaking?

An expert on body language commented recently on a cable news show about how difficult — in fact, impossible — it is for human beings to contain emotion. She explained that whatever we're feeling on the inside sooner or later will *leak out* from behind our social façade for all the world to see.

Examples include the angry man clenching his fist while he smiles and attempts to keep his cool, the anxious woman who wrings her hand at the same time she assures her family and friends that she's okay, or the person whose facial expression suddenly turns sad whenever there's a lull in the conversation.

The good news is that not everyone leaks negative feelings — some people actually leak happiness. It's evident in their smiles, their hardy laughter, and the twinkle in their eyes. What are *you* leaking?

In this chapter, I explain how emotions work and why you need them. I also address the question of whether a person can have too *much* happiness. And, finally, I tell you the four most important questions you'll face in your quest for authentic happiness, the answers to which may literally transform your emotional life forever.

Feedback from Your Nervous System

Most people actually believe that they're in total control of their behavior — that they call the shots and that everything they say and do throughout the day is willful and intentional. Well, I've got news for you: No one has that kind of control over his life.

You don't choose or decide to be hungry or thirsty — those feelings are created by your nervous system, which informs you when it's time to get a drink or grab something to eat. If we didn't experience hunger or thirst, we might never feed and hydrate our bodies, and then we'd die. The nervous system —the *central nervous system* (which includes the brain and spinal cord) and the *autonomic nervous system* (which regulates emotions) — has only one agenda: to help you survive. That's why you need anger and that's why you need to be happy.

Survival depends on feedback between your nervous system and you. If you suddenly find yourself irritated, your nervous system is telling you that you're exposed to some type of unwanted stress or threat — it could be something as simple as being around an annoying person or being in a situation where it's too hot. If you then remove yourself from that irritating circumstance (walk away from the person you find annoying or turn on the air conditioner), this tells your nervous system that it can stop feeling irritated — and, it does.

The same is true for happiness. If you suddenly find yourself feeling satisfied, joyful, and content, that's your nervous system talking to you. What it's saying is: "This is great! This is where you want to be. This is what makes you happy. I like this — let's do more of this."

Emotions provide a means of communication between you and your nervous system that aids in your survival. The healthier the dialogue, the longer you'll live and the better your quality of life. That's what the word *well-being* implies and why it's so often used interchangeably with the concept of happiness.

The "e" in your emotion

Emotion is a two-part word. The *e* stands for energy and *motion* implies movement. Together, emotions — positive or negative — are a source of emotional energy that constantly move you toward and away from various aspects of your environment. If you're not an aggressive person, fear causes you to move away from whatever you're afraid of. On the other hand, if you're aggressive, fear may cause you to confront that same source of emotion. The same is true of anger. An aggressive person will attack when angered, whereas a non-aggressive person will run away from whomever or whatever made her mad.

We're all energized by happiness, too. Happiness makes you want to reach out and hug the world! It connects people and leads to supportive relationships. As I mention in Chapter 2, happiness drives you to satisfy your basic needs for everything from food and shelter to more complex things like social belonging, acceptance, and self-esteem. It drives you to find ways of feeling safe and satiated — to have enough of what it takes to survive.

Sad, mad, and glad

Everyone has a range of emotions. These include everything from generic feelings like upset or nervousness to more specific feelings such as anger, sadness, curiosity, guilt, disgust — and, yes, joy.

Emotions are there for a reason — they're trying to tell you something about the way you're living your life. The question is, what are your emotions trying to tell you? If you're happy when you're broke, maybe it means that money really isn't that important to you after all. If you and your partner don't have children, but you find yourself happy whenever you're around other people's kids, maybe it's time to start your family. Your job is to learn from your happy moments how to live the life you should ideally be living.

Sadness lets you know what you're most attached to. If you don't feel sad when your dog dies, he wasn't really *your* dog. If you feel sad when you move from a community you've lived in for 25 years, then you were *involved* in that community — if you don't feel sad, you just lived there. Emotions tell the story of our lives — the happy years, the sad times, the angry moments — in a way that cannot be captured by words alone.

Take a few minutes and reflect on your emotional life. Ask yourself which emotions seem to stand out most in your memory. Perhaps the feeling that comes easiest to mind is sadness or joy. Now, ask yourself if your life story includes a healthy balance of sad, mad, and glad, or is it skewed toward one of these? If you had to sum it up, would you say you've mostly had a happy life or an angry life? Now, reflect on how you've felt the last three months and ask yourself the same questions. Is there continuity between your long-term and short-term emotional life? If you were happier in the past than you have been recently, why do you think that is? Has something changed? If you're happier now than in the past, what have you started doing that accounts for this positive change?

There's No Such Thing as Too Much Happiness

Negative emotions can be toxic. Prolonged sadness — for example, over the death of a loved one — can lead to a state of depression, which can itself be life-threatening. (Depression is linked to the development of heart disease and is a risk factor for heart attacks.) Too much fear can cause people to become housebound (a condition known as *agoraphobia,* which means "fear of public places"), have unrelenting headaches, and develop ulcers and high blood pressure.

The same is true if you experience too much anger. How much anger is too much? In *Anger Management For Dummies,* I define *toxic anger* as anger that is felt on a daily basis, that is intense (7 or higher on a 10-point scale), and that lasts for more than 25 minutes. Why 25 minutes? Because the majority of people are over their anger by this time.

The good news is that positive emotions, including happiness, aren't toxic. You can't be too happy. So if you find yourself in a happy moment, be thankful for it, and hope it continues beyond 25 minutes!

The next time you find yourself having a happy moment, rate how intense that feeling is on a 10-point scale (where 1 is barely happy and 10 is ecstatic) and time yourself to see how long that feeling lasts. The happier you are, the longer it should last.

Being in Sync with Your Surroundings

Your emotions are affected by the world you live in — your physical and social surroundings. If you're in sync with that world, you have a much better chance of achieving happiness.

Take Eric, for example, a man in his early 20s who was living in New York after graduating from college. Eric was extremely intelligent, and he had managed to land a high-paying job as an economist in a large corporate firm. At first, he enjoyed the excitement that New York had to offer — museums, concerts, Broadway shows. But it wasn't long before he found himself feeling lonely and missing the simplicity of the life he had known back in Virginia. As the months passed, Eric became more and more unhappy, until finally he quit his job and moved back home.

Becky, on the other hand, loves living in a big city. She moved to Washington, D.C., seven years ago and she can't imagine living anywhere else — even with the high cost of living, traffic problems, high crime rate, and tourists clogging up the streets. To her, the city is home!

And then there's Paul, who's somewhere in the middle. He likes the simplicity of the small town in which he lives — very little traffic, no long waits in restaurants, feeling safe walking downtown at night — but he has to admit that there's not much there that interests him. Paul isn't unhappy, but he's bored.

Where do you stand when it comes to being in sync with your surroundings? Would you describe your relationship with the world around you as a tight fit, a loose fit, or no fit at all? In the following sections, I help you answer these questions.

It's not essential that you be in sync with all aspects of your everyday surroundings — place, people, activities, motivation — in order to experience happiness. But, obviously, the more in sync you are, the happier you'll be.

Happiness is a sign that you're in the right place

Physical surroundings are more important than most people realize. The notion that a person can be happy anywhere if he wants to simply isn't true. Place matters — and, by place, I mean things such as:

- The country you live in
- The region you live in (if you live in the United States, this includes the South, the Midwest, the East Coast, the Pacific Northwest, and so on)
- The climate
- The size of the community
- The architecture
- The terrain (for example, mountains, beaches, desert)
- The amount of sunlight you're exposed to
- How close you are to your neighbors
- The type of housing you have (for example, apartment, house, cottage, loft)
- How much noise there is
- How "green" the surroundings are (for example, a concrete jungle or a place with lots of trees and parks)

Think about where you currently live. Now, ask yourself whether you're living in a place where you can be happy. If the answer is yes, then you know that your environment is not the root of your unhappiness. If the answer is no, it might be. If that's the case, you may consider a "geographic cure" — move to that sunny climate you long for during the winter or a city in which you'd be hard pressed to feel bored.

Happiness is a sign that you're with the right people

Happiness is also a by-product of the social world in which you live — the people who surround you. Do you need to live close to family in order to be happy? Do you need to live around people your own age? Are you around enough people day in and day out? Are these people supportive? Do the people you spend most of your time with share your interests — cycling, sports, the arts? Are you in sync intellectually with those around you? Are you a single person in a world where everyone you know seems to be married? Are you a Republican working around a bunch of Democrats or a Democrat working around a bunch of Republicans? The answers to these questions may have a lot to do with how happy you are.

Think about the people who are around you — your neighbors, co-workers, family, and friends. Are you living around people who make you happy? If so, then you know for sure that people aren't the reason you're unhappy. If not, try making some new friends or looking for happiness outside of work or your neighborhood. There's no law that says you can't move back closer to your family if that'll make you happy.

Happiness is a sign that you're doing the right thing

Another part of your surroundings has to do with the activities you engage in every day. These include domestic activities (marriage and family), employment activities, and community activities (like participation in religious activities, sports, civic organizations, and the like).

Think about how you spend your time throughout the course of a week. Generally speaking, are you active enough? Do you find what you do at work meaningful or are you just in it for the paycheck? If you have children, how involved are you in raising them? Do you provide any type of community service — for example, building houses with Habitat for Humanity, helping out in a soup kitchen, or working as a volunteer for the Salvation Army? Do you do things on a regular basis to help your neighbors? Do you serve on city government? Are you a scout leader or a coach for a Little League team? Are you a mentor for kids who are having trouble in school? Or do you spend the majority of your time sitting at home, watching television, and heading to the kitchen every 30 minutes for another beer or bag of chips?

Ask yourself whether you're doing things that make you happy. If you answered yes, then it's a no-brainer: Keep doing those things. If you answered no, try out some new activities — including some of those that I mention in the preceding paragraph.

Happiness is a sign that you're doing things for the right reasons

In order to be happy, you not only have to be doing the right things, in the right place, with the right people — you also have to have the right motives for doing what you do. If the only reason you play golf with friends from work is so you can show them that your game is far superior to theirs — and you couldn't care less about the camaraderie — then my guess is you'll win, but winning won't make you happy. If you show up at your kid's baseball game only because your spouse will be angry with you if you don't, that's not the right reason. If you help a neighbor only because you think that means she'll be obligated to help you out sometime in the future, you're not really a good — or happy — neighbor.

Making change where change counts

I can't tell you how many people I know who've made a dramatic change in their lives only to regret it later on. For example, one morning, Ramon abruptly left his wife of 30 years — he walked out the door, suitcase in hand, saying, "I'm taking some things over to my new apartment now, and I'll be back later this afternoon to get the rest." His wife, unaware that her husband was that unhappy or contemplating divorce, was devastated. Ramon made changes — he dyed his hair, bought an expensive set of golf clubs, grew a mustache, changed his entire wardrobe to look younger, and basically alienated himself from his three grown children.

Was he happy after making all these changes? No, because he wasn't making change where change counts. Ramon's wife wasn't the problem — the problem was that Ramon had a lot of pent-up anger and resentment about failures and losses in his life, he was clearly depressed, and he was lonely. Golf clubs and a mustache can't fix that!

Reading *Happiness For Dummies* can help you decide where you need to make changes in your life in order to be happy. You can begin by focusing on those personality attributes — optimism, hardiness, and conscientiousness — that facilitate a sense of joy and well-being (Chapters 5–7). Then, you can start behaving more in ways that produce happiness — for example, getting in the flow, finding benefit in life's many challenges, and living a coherent and confident lifestyle (Chapters 8–12). Next, you can start re-engineering your life so that it's more balanced in terms of work-play activities, socialization verses solitude, and selfishness versus generosity (Chapters 13–17). These are the changes that really count — the other things are only cosmetic!

Look at what you're doing — all the activities of your life (from work to fun and everything in between) — and ask yourself, "Why?" Are you doing things with and for other people for the right reasons? If you answered yes, there's nothing to change. And if you answered no, you need to come up with another reason for doing the same thing — for example, "I want to go to my kid's ball games so he'll have some positive memories of me when I'm no longer around" or "Golf is a great form of exercise — a lot easier than going to a gym and killing myself on the treadmill."

Never Pass Up an Opportunity

You may not realize it, but life provides you with lots of opportunities for constructive change — the chance to correct things and get it right.

What determines whether change represents an opportunity or a curse is not the change itself, but rather what you do as a result of the change. If you get fired from a job you hate, and you decide to find another job that's more to your liking, your life will be a lot happier. If you choose, instead, to find another job just like the one you lost, you won't be happier. It's really up to you.

Take a few minutes to think about your life and ask yourself, "How many opportunities have I had to change my life for the better?" Try to picture each of these times in your mind and remember exactly how you responded to those opportunities. Were they missed opportunities or did you turn your life in a new direction? Maybe you missed these opportunities because you were too pessimistic about the future (see Chapter 5) or you were thinking of these situations as catastrophes rather than opportunities (see Chapter 6). If you're the type of person who has, in the past, made good use of forced opportunities (ones that you wouldn't have chosen for yourself), then you're in good shape for dealing with whatever comes your way next.

Part II
Personality Attributes That Lead to Happiness

The 5th Wave — By Rich Tennant

In this part . . .

I share with you insights from the emerging field of positive psychology that will help you build toward the experience of happiness. If you want to be happy, it sure helps to be a "glass half-full" type of person — if you *think* you can be happy, you can!

In this part, you discover how to engage in what psychologists and psychiatrists call *transformational coping* (translation: "making a silk purse out of a sow's ear"). And you begin to appreciate how being an ethical, honest, trustworthy person pays off when it comes to happiness. Bottom line: Your emotions — anger or happiness — reflect the kind of character you have and the person you truly are — it's like a reflection in the mirror of life.

If you're starting to realize that you're not an optimistic, hardy, and/or conscientious person, don't worry — it's not too late! The strategies I set forth in these three chapters can help you begin to develop these positive traits.

Chapter 5

Optimism

*H*appy people always see the glass as half-full — they're optimists! No matter what they encounter in their daily lives — disappointment, illness, tragedy — they invariably see the possibilities for a positive future. Optimists expect to solve problems successfully, accomplish their goals, and, most important, expect to be happy.

In this chapter, I show you how to transform your *world view* — the way you perceive and think about your future — from one of cynicism and pessimism ("If something bad can happen, it will!") to a more refreshing, positive outlook full of hope and promise ("Things usually work out the way I want them to").

Why does optimism matter? Because if your *future* looks rosy, being happy in the *present* is easier.

What's So Good about Optimism?

Beyond the simple reality that optimists are happier people (and happiness is what you're striving for), optimism has other benefits as well:

> ✓ **Optimists enjoy a greater degree of academic success than pessimists do.** Because optimistic students think it's possible for them to make a good grade, they study hardier and they study smarter. They manage the setting in which they study (choosing the library over the dorm room) and they seek help from others (fellow students, teachers) when they need it. (Optimism, it turns out, is almost as predictive of how well students do in college as the SAT — another reason not to be discouraged if you didn't knock the socks off the SAT.)

- **Optimists are less likely to become compulsive gamblers than pessimists are.** Optimists are realists and they understand that, when it comes to wagering bets, the odds *always* favor the house. Pessimistic gamblers (which is what most gamblers are) believe in "long shots" more than they do their own ability to achieve success the "old-fashioned way" through hard work and individual initiative. When optimists lose, they quit gambling. Pessimists, on the other hand, dwell on their losses and continue gambling — which actually increases the odds of losing — in an attempt to break even. And it doesn't work!

- **Optimists tend to set more specific goals than pessimists do (for example, "I want to increase my sales by 20 percent this year").** The more specific and concrete your goals are, the more likely you'll be to achieve success. The optimistic student has a goal of making a B+ average this semester; the pessimistic student simply wants to "do well" in school. Similarly, when it comes to achieving happiness, you're better off having goals such as "I want to engineer a better balance between work and play" (Chapter 15) or "I want to double the number of uplifting experiences I have week in and week out" (Chapter 13) than something as non-specific as "I want to be happy."

- **Optimists are more self-confident than pessimists are.** They believe in *themselves* more than fate. (They also bet on themselves more than they bet on the horses!)

- **Optimists are more likely to be problem-solvers than pessimists are.** When pessimistic students get a D on a test, they tend to think things like: "I knew I shouldn't have taken this course. I'm no good at psychology. I'm just wasting my time — and my parents' money." The optimistic student who gets a D says to herself, "I can do better than this. I just didn't study enough for this test. That's something I can remedy. I'll do better next time." And she will!

- **Optimists persist and persevere.** They're not quitters!

- **Optimists are more active in their pursuit of happiness than pessimists are.** Are you waiting for happiness to find you? If so, I'm afraid you're a pessimist. If you know that happiness is out there, somewhere in your future, and you're willing to hunt for it (to use the strategies set forth in *Happiness For Dummies*), you're an optimist. It's as simple as that.

- **Optimists welcome second chances after they fail more than pessimists do.** Optimistic golfers always take a *mulligan* (a redo swing without penalty). Why? Because they expect to achieve a better result the second time around.

- **Optimists are more socially outgoing than pessimists are.** I love that line from the movie *As Good As It Gets,* when Carol Connelly (Helen Hunt) asks Melvin Udall (Jack Nicholson) why he wants a relationship with her, and he says, "You make me want to be a better man." Socially outgoing folks believe that the time they spend with other human beings makes them better in some way — smarter, more interesting, more attractive. Unfortunately, pessimists see little, if any, benefit from venturing out into the social world.

✔ **Optimists are not as lonely as pessimists are.** Because pessimists don't see as much benefit from socializing with others, they have far fewer social and emotional connections in their lives, which is what loneliness is all about. (I make the distinction between being alone and being lonely in Chapter 16.)

✔ **Optimists utilize social support more effectively than pessimists do.** They aren't afraid to reach out in times of need.

✔ **Optimists are less likely to blame others for their misfortune than pessimists are.** When you blame someone else for your troubles, what you're really saying is, "You're the *cause* of my problem and, therefore, you have to be the *solution* as well." Optimists have just as many troubles as pessimists throughout life — they just accept more responsibility for dealing with their misfortune.

✔ **Optimists engage in safer sex than pessimists do.** Studies show that gay men who have an optimistic outlook tend to practice safer sex — fewer partners, condom use — than gay men who are pessimistic (you might say fatalistic) about their chances of contracting and transmitting HIV.

✔ **Optimists cope with stress better than pessimists do.** Pessimists worry, optimists act. A patient with coronary heart disease who is pessimistic "hopes and prays" that he doesn't have another heart attack anytime soon. The optimistic heart patient leaves little to chance — instead, he exercises regularly, practices his meditation exercises, adheres to a low-cholesterol diet, and makes sure he always gets a good night's sleep. (Cardiologists love optimistic patients!)

✔ **Optimists are more likely to engage in preventive healthcare than pessimists are (for example, wearing sunscreen to prevent skin cancer).** Pessimists are always waiting to see how their health turns out, whereas optimists take a more hands-on approach to preventing illness.

✔ **Optimists are less likely to become disabled from chronic pain than pessimists are.** After 40 years of working with patients who have chronic back pain, I've come to realize that if all a patient can see is disability in her future, she behaves as a disabled person in the present. Pain management begins with the optimistic notion that you can have pain without being all that disabled.

✔ **Optimists are more likely to take vitamins than pessimists are.** Optimists stay ahead of the curve as far as health and well-being go.

✔ **Optimists are more likely to follow through with rehab after a heart attack than pessimists are.** If you don't believe rehab is going to do you any good, what's the point? With some patients, you have to first rehabilitate the mind (change to a more optimistic outlook) before you can rehab the body.

Keep on keepin' on

My Aunt Lillian was the poster child for optimism! She had a hard life, but she just kept on keepin' on, always moving forward to the very end. Her parents died when she was a small child and she and her siblings ended up being raised in an orphanage. Lillian was involved in a traumatic car accident when she was in her early 20s, which left her with a crushed knee and a stiff leg. In part because of that, Lillian ended up marrying a man much older than herself and wasn't able to have children.

She had to work her whole life as a secretary — long before women actually wanted to work outside the home — never making much money. Her husband dropped dead one day, from a ruptured aneurysm, so Lillian spent the last 20 years of her life alone. She had a stroke in her mid-70s and ended up living the last ten years of her life in a nursing home, paralyzed on her right side.

Yet, through all that, Lillian never complained about life, always had a captivating smile, never had a negative word for anyone, laughed all the time, and made everyone around her — including me — feel good. I remember the night I had to tell my family that I had failed my PhD exams and might not have been able to continue with my doctoral training. The others looked shocked and depressed, but not Aunt Lillian — she just gave me a big hug and said, "Don't worry, honey. It'll be fine. It'll work out. You'll see." Lillian was right.

- ✔ **Optimists are less likely to suffer from depression or commit suicide than pessimists are.** Optimists — even depressed optimists — can always see the light at the end of the tunnel. Not so for depressed pessimists. As far as they can see, it's all an unending darkness, which is where despair and hopelessness comes from. (A big part of treating depressed people is doing everything you can to help them remain optimistic until you can resolve their mood disorder.)

- ✔ **Optimists have more robust immune systems than pessimists do.** The essence of *health psychology* and *behavioral medicine* is the belief that mind and body are inextricably connected as a result of the way we live our lives. If you live a robust, healthy, and happy life — which is easier to do if you're optimistic — you will have a robust immune system, that invisible shield that keeps you well and/or helps you regain your health when you're get sick. Improved immune function is, without question, one of the consequences of taking vitamins, practicing safer sex, staying socially active, and engaging in health-promotion activities — at least, that's the way optimists see it!

Optimism *rocks* when it comes to . . . well, when it comes to *everything* in life, from your health to your social relationships. Its benefits truly can't be exaggerated or overestimated!

How Optimistic Are You?

Not sure how optimistic you really are? I've devised a little assessment to help you see just how positive you are (or aren't) about your future. ***Remember:*** Be absolutely honest with yourself to get the most out of this exercise.

Circle one answer under each of the following questions:

1. **When you're not certain how things will turn out in the future, you remain hopeful.**

    - Definitely false: 0

    - False: 1

    - True: 2

    - Definitely true: 3

2. **You believe that there are lots of situations in life that do not have a "silver lining."**

    - Definitely true: 0

    - True: 1

    - False: 2

    - Definitely false: 3

3. **You believe that if you have failed in the past, you're likely to fail in the future.**

    - Definitely true: 0

    - True: 1

    - False: 2

    - Definitely false: 3

4. **When you're faced with a challenge in life, your first thought is always a positive one.**

    - Definitely false: 0

    - False: 1

    - True: 2

    - Definitely true: 3

Sixteen years and counting

A former client of mine came in for her first appointment, well dressed and with a smile on her face. We sat down and when I asked her how she was, she instantly broke down in tears and sobbed uncontrollably for the next 20 minutes. I could see that she was in a lot of emotional pain, so I sat quietly and let her cry. When she stopped — with mascara running down her face, her silk blouse wet from all the tears — I asked a second question, "My gosh, how long have you felt like this?"

"Sixteen years," she said, and then she cried for another 20 minutes.

The next question I asked her was, "Why didn't you get some help before now — ten years ago, five years ago — why did you wait until today?"

I never will forget her answer: "I just thought things would get better." This is optimism gone awry. You really *can* have too much of a good thing, and there's no shame in admitting that things are bad and you need help.

5. **Just because people say something is impossible, that doesn't mean that it is.**

   - Definitely false: 0

   - False: 1

   - True: 2

   - Definitely true: 3

6. **You see every day as a welcomed, new opportunity at life.**

   - Definitely false: 0

   - False: 1

   - True: 2

   - Definitely true: 3

Now, add up your scores. If your score is 9 or higher, you definitely have an optimistic outlook. If you scored below 9, you have some work to do on the optimism front. Although these scores tend to be fairly stable throughout life, the good news is you *can* change them with some work.

Believe it or not, it is possible to be *too* optimistic. If you scored between 15 and 18, you may be suffering from *exuberant optimism* — you not only believe that good things *can* happen in your future; you insist they *will*. I hope you're right — but not all problems have a solution and you may not know when to give up and move on. (Don't believe me? Check out the "Sixteen years and counting" sidebar in this chapter.)

Happiness: A Self-Fulfilling Prophecy

Life is not nearly the happenstance we sometimes like to think it is — and, that goes for happiness as well. You'd be better off forgetting about luck, fate, and destiny and instead thinking of your future as a self-fulfilling prophecy. Put simply: The attitudes you have *today* largely determine how things turn out *tomorrow*.

Can't never could

Here's a conversation that Andrew had with his uncle many times while growing up:

> **Uncle:** How are you? How was your day?
>
> **Andrew:** Rough. I'm not sure I'm cut out for this type of work.
>
> **Uncle:** Why not? You're young and healthy. What's the problem?
>
> **Andrew:** It's just hard work — more than I expected, I guess.
>
> **Uncle:** Of course, most things in life are more difficult that we first imagine. But we adapt, get used to it, and then it's not so bad.
>
> **Andrew:** I don't know. I'm thinking about quitting. I just don't think I can do it anymore.
>
> **Uncle:** Son, listen to me carefully. Can't never could!

If Andrew had a penny for every time his uncle said that phrase — *Can't never could!* — he reckons he'd be a wealthy man today. The message was simple, but profound: If you convince yourself that you can't do something, you'll find a way to make sure you can't. The more you think failure, the more you fail — in school, at jobs, in relationships. And the more you actually fail, the more you *expect* to fail. This is the vicious cycle of pessimism. You become your own prophet of doom!

Every morning before you begin your day, stand in front of your bathroom mirror and recite out loud ten times: "I am ready to take on life. Good things will come my way today — I know it. I will overcome any obstacles that I encounter." Then go about your day as usual and see how things go.

Heart happy

Researchers at the Harvard School of Public Health, in a study of over 1,300 healthy men, found that pessimists had twice the risk of developing heart disease over a ten-year period compared to optimists. And this was true even after controlling for traditional risk factors such as smoking. You can bet this made the optimistic men — and their families — happy.

I think I can, I think I can . . .

I believe that some very meaningful psychological lessons are contained in children's books. I use them as therapeutic aides in working with troubled kids and even, in some cases, with my adult clients. One of my all-time favorites is the story of *The Little Engine That Could.* I loved this story as a child and I still find it useful all these years later.

The Little Engine That Could is a story of optimism. It's about how telling yourself "I think I can, I think I can . . ." can lead to success. It also suggests that:

- ✔ Optimism is how you overcome unforeseen obstacles.
- ✔ Optimism is an essential part of helping others in need.
- ✔ Optimism isn't necessary when life is easy — only when it's hard.
- ✔ Optimism comes in handy when no one around you will help you out.
- ✔ Optimism is a great antidote to sadness.
- ✔ Optimism is available even to those who consider themselves unimportant.
- ✔ There are plenty of pessimistic people out there.
- ✔ Optimism is empowering — it provides the energy needed to move mountains.
- ✔ Everyone loves optimists!

Go to your local bookstore and pick up a copy of *The Little Engine That Could.* Put it in some conspicuous place in your home, where you can easily see it, and be sure to read it every day — maybe before you begin your day or the last thing at night. It's a nice positive message to start your day with or sleep on.

Winning the Battle of Negative Expectations

Joe, a middle-aged mental-health professional, is what I like to call a *closet pessimist.* On the outside, Joe looks and sounds like an optimist. He's quick to offer advice to his clients, as well as friends and family, like: "Hey, it'll work out — you'll see" or, "Better times are right around the corner." But when it comes to his own future, Joe is much more pessimistic. He says, "Every time the phone rings, my first thought is 'Oh Lord, what's wrong now?' I hate that, but I can't help it — it's just automatic."

Joe thinks like a pessimist. Like millions of others, he was raised in an alcoholic, abusive home. Joe likes to put it this way, "In our family, we were always just one beer away from chaos. The future was very tentative." As a kid, Joe learned to hope for the best but expect the worst — it's how children of alcoholics survive. The problem is, the pessimism of Joe's past has persisted, and now it just complicates his present mental and emotional life. What was adaptive for the child is now a problem for the adult!

If you see yourself in Joe's story, the good news is that you can *win* the battle of negative expectations. ***Remember:*** Anything that is learned can ultimately be unlearned. You learned to expect the worst, and you can unlearn it, too. Here are five simple rules to help you do just that:

- ✔ **Accept the fact that you're a pessimist at heart.** You don't have to go around sharing that information with just anyone, but you should be honest with yourself about the challenge you face in becoming a more positive-thinking person.

- ✔ **Accept the fact that your first thought is always a negative one — that's just a given.** But don't go with this thought, don't dwell on it, and certainly don't let it guide your behavior at that moment.

- ✔ **Remember that it's the second thought that counts.** Learn to counteract your initial pessimism by substituting an optimistic thought. So, for example, "I'm not sure I can do this" becomes "Wow, what a great opportunity!"

- ✔ **Separate the past from the present (and the future).** Start saying, "That was then; this is now." No longer link the chaos of your early years (or whatever negative experiences you had in the past) with the expectations you have for things that come up in today's world.

- ✔ **Reward yourself for this self-initiated change in thinking.** Give yourself a pat on the back, or head to your local coffee shop for your favorite drink.

Moving Beyond Pessimism

If you've figured out that you're a pessimist, what can you do to change that? Lots! Here are my recommendations:

✔ **Don't fight it — *change* it.** You have to begin by accepting, not resisting, the reality that you always start out with negative thoughts. Resistance is a waste of energy. The more you resist something, the more it persists — try not thinking about the word *elephant* and see what happens. All you can think about now are elephants! The key here is to change the way you think.

✔ **Turn your thoughts around so that you never end with a negative.** For example, instead of thinking, "I can do this, but it's going to be difficult," say to yourself, "It's going to be difficult, but I can do this." You want the last thing your brain hears to be positive.

✔ **Put yourself in the company of optimistic people.** Attitudes are contagious. Who do you know who sees the glass as half-full? That's the person you want to hang with!

✔ **Develop a personal action plan for reconstructing your attitude.** You're stuck in your negative thinking and you need to get unstuck. Here's a method for doing just that:

1. **Identify some important or valued goal — something you want to achieve but have put on hold or been afraid to tackle.**

   I recommend starting with something small — something that will take a minimum of effort, but have a big payoff. It's important to think in terms of evolution — slow, progressive change — not revolution.

   For example, you might say, "I want to take a trip to Wisconsin to see my sister."

2. **Identify the incentives of reaching that goal.**

   This is the reason behind the goal. For example, why do you want to go to Wisconsin to see your sister? You might say, "I want to feel the joy of reconnecting with family. I want a change of scenery. I want to escape the day-to-day routine back home."

3. **Ask yourself, on a scale of 0 to 10, how committed you are to achieving this goal.**

4. **List three things that you would need to do to accomplish this goal.**

   For example, if your goal is to visit your sister in Wisconsin, maybe you need to map out the route you'll take, call your sister and set a definite date to arrive, and rent a reliable, comfortable vehicle.

Exercise and optimism

Some years ago, my colleagues and I conducted a small study of cardiac patients at a local hospital, administering a test of optimism and also seeing how compliant they were with the exercise rehab program to which they had been referred by their cardiologists. Not surprisingly, there was a significant link between the two. Those patients who were the most optimistic exercised the most, and conversely those who exercised the most were the most optimistic. This suggests that, even if you don't start out all that optimistic, you *will* be if you stick to the exercise program.

5. **Ask yourself whether you see any obstacles to accomplishing your goal.**

6. **Ask yourself how confident you are you that you can achieve this goal.**

   You can be committed to something but not necessarily confident that you'll win out. Commitment has more to do with making the effort, confidence more with your belief in yourself.

7. **Start the ball rolling by doing the first thing you listed in Step 4 that you need to do to achieve your goal.**

   After you've completed the first step, reward yourself with a literal or figurative pat on the back or say out loud, "Good for me!"

8. **Do the second thing you listed in Step 4. And then move on to the third thing you listed in Step 4.**

   Don't forget to reward yourself after each step — that keeps you moving forward.

What you're trying to do here is change your pessimistic attitude by changing your *behavior* first. Normally, people think of attitudes as something that *leads* behavior — like a horse pulling a wagon. But I want you to turn that around and think of a change in attitude as something that *follows* behavior — in effect, putting the cart in front of the horse!

This "cart-before-the-horse" approach I'm talking about is the essence of what has come to be called *behavioral medicine,* a new approach to health and well-being that I was privileged to help pioneer, where you literally behave your way into, in this case, happiness.

Chapter 6

Hardiness

Rudy was a fascinating man. Born in the early 1930s in Germany, he became one of millions of Jews caught up in the Nazi Holocaust — a time of unspeakable horror. Rudy was a survivor of Auschwitz-Birkenau, the most notorious of the death camps. What I found most compelling, however, was the fact that he could talk endlessly about his experiences during the war without any trace of bitterness or distress. In one very real sense, he was a victim — but in another sense, he was not. Forty years after the fact, Rudy was a happy man, a successful architect, a loving husband and grandfather, and a good neighbor.

What was his secret? What enabled him to survive the nightmare of Auschwitz and go on with his life? What did he have that others less fortunate did not? The answer can be found in the pioneering work of psychologist Salvatore Maddi who first introduced the idea of the *hardy personality*. According to Dr. Maddi, hardy people are like hardy animals and plants — they are resilient. They survive adversity, weather the storms of everyday life — and in doing so, they grow stronger, more competent, and happier over the course of their lives.

In this chapter, I show you how to tell if you're a hardy personality and, if you aren't yet, how you can become one. Unlike Maddi and his colleagues at the University of Chicago, who were primarily interested in the link between hardiness and physical health, I want you to appreciate how hardiness also impacts on your psychological health.

The Holocaust: Past versus present

A study of 38 Holocaust survivors showed that those who continued to relive the trauma of the past experienced far more mental-health problems — for example, anxiety, phobias, insomnia, depression, crying fits, suicidal thinking, hostility, and feelings of self-hate — in the years since the war than did those who had found a way to become less preoccupied with that dreadful time in their lives. Those non-hardy souls who could not disconnect from the past became perpetual victims of this horrific experience.

The Recipe for Hardiness

Hardiness is a complex personality trait that is comprised of three essential elements. I call them the three Cs: control, commitment, and challenge. No one element is more important than the other — it's the combination that counts.

So what's the difference between hardy people and non-hardy people and how do the three Cs come into play? Hardy people:

- **Want control over their own lives:** Non-hardy people, on the other hand, depend more on luck, fate, chance, and the actions of other people — all things beyond their own control — to make the difference in how their lives go.

- **Are committed to the things and people that matter most to them:** Non-hardy people feel alienated and detached from the world around them. Hardy employees, for example, love their careers, while those lacking in hardiness see work as just a job.

- **Hardy people view life as a series of challenges:** Non-hardy people see life as "one damned thing after another."

In the following sections, I go into more detail on each of these three Cs.

Control

Do you want to be master of your own destiny? Do you feel confident about your ability to deal effectively with whatever life throws at you? Do you believe in that saying, "Success is 10 percent inspiration and 90 percent perspiration"? If people take advantage of you, do you say to yourself, "That's just because I let them"? Do you vote regularly because you believe your vote counts? If you answered yes to these questions, then you're high on what psychologists call *internal control:* You believe that it's what's inside of you — intelligence, courage, creativity — that ultimately determines how happy you are in life.

Bill is high on that internal control scale. When his left lung hemorrhaged at the age of 17, he suddenly found his whole world turned upside-down — he had a major part of his lung removed, had to drop out of school, and spent the next year trying to regain his health. Not one to be a victim, Bill thought to himself, "What can I do to get my life and health back?" The answer was simple: rehabilitation. And not just physical rehabilitation (although that was the place to start), but spiritual, social, and emotional rehabilitation as well. Bill worked out with weights and did strengthening exercises daily; he reconnected with his friends; and he began to spend a lot of his time appreciating life — thinking about how lucky he was to have a second chance. Bill was busy! And it worked. He went on to have a healthy and productive adult life. He's currently alive and kicking at 61.

Believe it or not, Bill's sister, Eugenia, suffered the same fate when she was about the same age. Unfortunately, Eugenia wasn't high on that internal control scale. After having her lung removed, she refused to do anything on her own behalf to get well. Eugenia thought of herself as a fragile person. She felt sorry for herself, and she spent the rest of her life trying to get other people to take care of her in one way or another. Her destiny was literally in the hands of others. Tragically, she died at age 42.

The difference between Bill and Eugenia is a personality difference, not a difference in disease. Both suffered from a severe, chronic lung disorder that manifested itself early in life. The fact that Bill has outlived his sister by 20 years (and counting) is no accident — Bill wanted to be in control of his future and Eugenia did not. It's just that simple!

Take a few minutes, close your eyes, and try to imagine that you're faced with the same health problem as Bill and his sister. Then ask yourself, "How would I respond to that type of adversity? Would I be more like Bill or more like Eugenia?" Finally, think about the long-term consequences of that last answer.

The key to the *control* aspect of hardiness is the word *I* — Bill asked "What can *I* do to help myself?" He told himself "*I* have to lift weights, *I* have to do the strengthening exercises, and *I* have to reconnect with my friends, if *I* want to regain my health and keep on living." His sister only thought about *you* and *me* — "What are *you* going to do to make *me* well?"

Take ownership of your illness — or any other major problem you encounter — and you take ownership of your recovery.

Hardiness and coping

Hardy personalities cope with stress differently than non-hardy people do. The hardier you are:

✔ **The more likely you are to take a problem-focused approach to things that go wrong in your life instead of just reacting to the emotions of the moment.** Better to fix the flat tire than to stand there cussing and kicking the tire.

✔ **The more likely you are to solicit support from others during stressful times.**

✔ **The less likely you are to waste your time wishing that things would get better (as opposed to *making* them better).**

✔ **The less likely you are to go out of your way to avoid thinking about or actually dealing with the problem at hand.**

Commitment

Hardy personalities have a deep sense of emotional commitment. They're players, not spectators. Hardy people are passionate — they get involved in what's going on around them and they begin and end each day with a sense of purpose.

What's your purpose in life? What types of activities give meaning to your life? What are you enthusiastic about? If one type of passion ends, do you find an alternative activity to commit yourself to?

Eleanor was a devoted mother to her two kids. She interrupted her career as a counselor so she could be home for them during their formative years. She cooked, sewed, went to school conferences, chaperoned band trips, cared for her children when they were sick, and made sure she instilled in each of them a set of values that would see them successfully through their adult lives. Eleanor had a passion for motherhood and she was a happy mom!

But eventually Eleanor's kids grew up, left home, moved out of state, and quickly became busily engaged in their own meaningful lives. Eleanor's job as a full-time parent was finished, but she wasn't about to let go of the joys of interacting with and nurturing young people. So, she became involved in an all-volunteer community group that raised scholarship money for outstanding high school girls. Eleanor couldn't possibly imagine that what had started out as a few hours here and there would evolve into a year-round commitment of her energies to this worthy cause. (Chapter 14 discusses the empty nest, which is what Eleanor might have experienced had she not restructured her life with a new set of meaningful activities.)

Which of the following areas of your life are you currently committed to?

- ✔ Intimate relationship
- ✔ Family
- ✔ Career
- ✔ Friends
- ✔ Hobbies or recreation
- ✔ Community
- ✔ Religion
- ✔ Politics

If the answer is "none," you may feel alienated from the world around you. Well, you're not alone, as Robert Putnam, professor of public policy at Harvard, suggests in his national bestseller *Bowling Alone* (Touchstone). Cultural changes in the American culture, he contends, have contributed to a sense of disenfranchisement among the general public. Putnam recommends a revival of communal activism, where ordinary people can regain a feeling of connection — *belonging* — more akin to that experienced by past generations. Specific examples include bringing back the arts into school (for example, choir) and re-engineering the workplace so that it's more "family-friendly and community-congenial." Other ways that alienated people can find a sense of purpose and commitment include radio call-in talk shows (where you can regularly and safely become part of a meaningful dialogue) and Internet chatrooms.

In some instances, alienation has more to do with personality (for example, shyness) and emotional issues (social anxiety), in which case you're better off seeking out the services of a mental-health professional to help you overcome your shyness and social anxiety. If you dive in to activities without strategies in place, you may just face the same anxiety all over again and retreat.

Challenge

Challenge has to do with how you look at stress. Are you one of those people who reacts to all problems and conflicts throughout life as if they're catastrophes, calamities, or crises? That's not the hardy perspective. What you want to do is view these same problems as challenges — in other words, events and circumstances that will test your courage, fortitude, and resourcefulness.

Cubs versus the club

For three years, my friend Rob and I were "den mothers" for eight young Cub Scouts. During that time, we planned a number of father-son excursions, providing an opportunity for dads to spend some quality outdoor time with their sons. To my amazement, not one father ever came along. I remember one occasion when we were going to spend the entire fall day walking through the deep woods surrounding the little village of Appomattox, Virginia, where Robert E. Lee had surrendered to Ulysses S. Grant, effectively ending the Civil War. Father after father dropped their sons off with one excuse or another as to why they wouldn't be joining us.

The last father to arrive walked his son up to me and said, "I appreciate your doing this for my son. I know you'll have a great time. I wish I could come along, but I've got a tennis match at the club." The expression of sadness and disappointment on his son's face sticks in my mind to this day.

Anything worth doing is worth doing well, and that includes being a parent. Being a committed parent isn't just about giving your kids food, shelter, and clothing, and it's not just about buying them the latest video games or toys. It's about being there with them, doing things together, and sometimes giving up the things you want to do in order to do the things your kids want. Think about how committed you are as a parent. If you're committed to nothing else in life, at least be committed to your kids.

Consider the following exchange I had with a young man, Jerry, who had just been blindsided with the news that his work schedule was being drastically changed so that he no longer had any weekends free. When Jerry came in to see me, he was very agitated.

Jerry: This is ridiculous. They can't do this to me. I don't deserve this after all the years I've worked here. I've been a good employee, bending over backwards to help this company, and they stab me in the back. I'm going to quit this damned job.

Me: Quitting is always an option, but first help me understand what you see as the problem with this change in schedule. Exactly how do you feel it's going to change your life?

Jerry: It's going to change *everything*. I won't be able to play golf with my buddies on the weekend. I'll have to get used to working 12-hour days. Just everything!

Me: Do you see any positives here — *any* opportunity — or does it just seem like a catastrophe?

Jerry: Opportunity? Like what?

Think Chinese

In Chinese, the word for conflict has a dual meaning: danger and opportunity. I like that because it gives you a choice both about how you view conflict and how you deal with it. Cultures that think of conflict as a bad thing tend to encourage their members to either avoid conflict or find ways to manage — minimize — it. In other words, they miss the opportunity!

Me: Well, you've talked, for example, about how you wish you could find another job, but you didn't have time during the week to look around. Now you will. We've also talked before about how you might like to take a course or two at the community college, but again most of the classes are during the week. Now you could pursue that possibility. That's what I had in mind.

Jerry: I guess I wasn't looking at it that way. What you say makes sense. I really *would* like to find another job, one with more of a future in terms of pay and advancement. I'm at a dead end where I am.

Me: Right. So even though this came at you out of the blue and isn't something you wanted to happen, maybe you can make this work for you?

Jerry: I guess *so* — it's worth a try.

Me: Absolutely, what have you got to lose?

Can you relate to Jerry and how he initially saw his predicament? Most people start out thinking of stress in all negative terms. All they hear is that little voice in their heads that says, "Oh, my God! This is *awful*." But, eventually, either with some help or on your own, you can start to see that this really isn't the end of the world — it's a challenge, and you'll see what you're made of by how you deal with it.

How Hardy Are You?

Take a minute and answer each of the following questions. *Remember:* Be honest with yourself.

Circle the answer that fits you best.

1. Ordinary work can be exciting.

True

False

2. **Getting what I want in life has nothing to do with luck.**

   True

   False

3. **Citizens are the ones who are responsible for bad government, not politicians.**

   True

   False

4. **When putting something together, I often read the instructions first.**

   True

   False

5. **I'm not one to ask for a lot of advice.**

   True

   False

6. **When I go out to eat, I like to try different types of food.**

   True

   False

7. **I rarely waste time.**

   True

   False

8. **If people don't respect you, it's because you don't deserve it.**

   True

   False

9. **I have a diverse set of friends.**

   True

   False

10. **I enjoy betting on sports.**

    True

    False

11. **I don't believe teachers *give* grades; students *earn* them.**

    True

    False

12. I can't wait to get to work in the morning.

True

False

13. People's misfortunes result from mistakes they make.

True

False

14. I expect to be very busy in my retirement.

True

False

15. When I can't find something in a store, I keep looking until I do.

True

False

Add up the number of times you answered True. If your score is between 0 and 5, you're low on hardiness. If your score is between 6 and 10, you have a moderate degree of hardiness. And if your score is 11 or above, you're high on the hardiness scale. In the following sections, I fill you in on how you can increase your hardiness.

Non-hardy, Type-A personalities: The worst of the worst

You're likely familiar with someone who exhibits all the characteristics of the Type-A personality — the friend who never lets you finish a sentence without saying "Yeah, right" a dozen times, the person who finishes eating long before everyone else, the colleague whose eyes are constantly scanning the room while you're talking to her, the client who's a little bit too serious about life and who has an edge about him all the time. Type-A's are the folks who, medical research has shown, are more likely to have heart attacks and strokes, as well as suffer from an assortment of other illnesses — and they're the same folks who never seem to be happy.

Well, it turns out that if you lack hardiness and you're also a Type A, as far as your health is concerned, you're up the proverbial creek without a paddle. To be specific: People who are low on hardiness and high on Type A are *three times* more likely to become ill (with everything from minor ailments to major diseases) than those who are high on hardiness and low on Type A.

If you think you may be a Type A personality, check out Chapter 15, where I tell you how to set yourself up to be a Type B — the type of person who is easy-going, laid back, patient, nonjudgmental, and would rather walk than drive.

If you scored 11 or above, you may have what I call *exuberant hardiness* — feeling you can (or should) control everything, being overcommitted, and being too eager to take on challenges. Exuberant hardiness is a good way to end up burned out. *Remember:* As with most things in life, balance is key.

Transformational Coping

Hardy people cope differently with stress than non-hardy people do. Hardy people are less apt to take a step backward when confronted with one of life's many curveballs. Instead, they behave in a way that transforms a bad situation into something better — this is known as *transformational coping.* Hardy people are optimistic (more about this in Chapter 5) — they believe that all situations, no matter how difficult, have a potential for a happy ending. And they tackle stress head-on rather than avoiding it.

Hardy is as hardy does

Hardiness is more about actions (doing) than it is about attitude (thinking, feeling). Hardy people *do* the following types of things:

- Volunteer in the community
- Vote
- Show up at municipal government meetings
- Write letters to the editor of the local newspaper
- Get involved in their kids' activities
- Collect things — everything from bottle caps to teddy bears
- Go white-water rafting
- Take classes at the community college, regardless of their age
- Devote themselves to their pets
- Share their opinions about important matters with others
- Look for jobs with new challenges and opportunities
- Become advocates for abused and neglected children
- Help get out the vote for their favorite political candidates
- Run marathons

- ✔ Accept leadership positions
- ✔ Get regular health checkups
- ✔ Spend time with people they love
- ✔ Give to worthy charities
- ✔ Attend religious services regularly
- ✔ Take on the tough challenges in life

This is just a list meant to illustrate the *types* of things hardy people do. You can be a hardy person and not go white-water rafting, or you can be a hardy person and not attend church. The common thread connecting all these types of activities is that you're actively doing them on a regular basis — and not just *thinking* about doing them.

The best and worst of times

Life is full of paradoxes. What often appears to be the worst of times ends up leading to the best of times. Take Roger, for example. Roger's a man in his late 50s, who just found out his job as a midlevel executive had been terminated. "I came in at 8 o'clock and there was a letter in my mailbox telling me I had been let go — and, I needed to be off the premises by 5 o'clock that day," he said. "I couldn't even get angry — I was in such a state of shock."

Hardiness and exercise: The best of both worlds

In 1982, psychologists Suzanne Kobasa, Salvadore Maddi, and Mark Puccetti examined the effects of combined hardiness and exercise in 137 middle- and upper-management employees at a large utility company. Exercise was defined in terms of how many actual hours each employee spent regularly engaged in both strenuous sports and non-sports activities (for example, gardening or home repairs). Employees were also asked to identify any common physical and mental symptoms and/or diseases they had experienced; these included such things as bursitis, hay fever,

psoriasis, depression, hyperventilation, nosebleed, migraine headaches, and gallstones.

What the doctors found was fascinating: Those employees who were low on the hardiness scale and who failed to exercise regularly had nearly *seven times* more illness than their co-workers who were hardy exercisers. Those who either were hardy or who exercised (but who didn't fall into both categories) were somewhere in the middle. Why not combine the two and enjoy the best of both worlds?

Thanks for ~~nothing~~ everything

You may be able to relate to Roger's story. You've suffered some misfortune in life, only to find out later on that it somehow changed your life for the better. Here's a thought: Why not write an overdue thank-you note to the person who created that unfortunate circumstance? Remember: Gratitude is one of the key ingredients to achieving happiness (for a list of the other key ingredients see Chapter 2). Here's an example of such a letter.

Dear Mr. Miller,

I know it's been a while since you fired me, but I wanted you to know what has happened to me since. When it first happened, as you can imagine, I was quite upset — angry even. I hated you for taking my job security and forcing me to look elsewhere for employment. But — and this is really the reason for my note — as it turned out, you did me an enormous favor.

Seriously, I didn't realize just how stressed and unappreciated I was when I worked for you until the job ended. It was only then that I began to appreciate how unhappy I was at work and why. Simply put, I was doing a good job (even though you didn't see it that way!) at the wrong thing. It turns out that I'm a people person and spending all my working days in front of a computer was just not my cup of tea. I'm now doing what I was put on Earth to do: I'm working in retail clothing, where I meet scores of interesting people every day. I literally can't wait to get to work every morning, a feeling that I honestly never had when I worked for you. I know you didn't intend for my life to turn out better when you fired me, but it has — and, I wanted you to know that and to say thank-you for forcing me into a better career fit.

Sincerely,

Jane Doe

Remember: You don't even have to actually mail the letter in order to get the benefit from the exercise — it's the thought that counts!

Roger wanted my advice on what he should do next: "How can I tell my wife that I no longer have a job, and who's going to want to hire a guy my age?" He was clearly distressed.

I thought a minute and then asked, "Didn't you tell me once you had a little business on the side that you enjoyed — something about jewelry?"

He said that, yes, he did sell jewelry — mostly diamonds — to family and friends. "And you find that sort of thing both enjoyable and profitable?" I asked.

"Oh, yes," he replied. "I like how happy people get when they find out that top-quality diamonds can be affordable."

My last question was "And, why was it that you weren't in the jewelry business full-time?"

Roger said, "Because I had a job and could only devote my spare time to it."

I told him, "Well, now you don't have a job, do you? So maybe you should think about starting a new career."

Fast-forward five years, and Roger is the proud owner of a local jewelry store. Today he's making more money than he ever did at his old job — the one that he'd still have if they hadn't let him go — and he's a much happier man. Getting fired is not always a bad thing, but that depends on what you do if and when it happens. Hardy people, more often than not, do the thing that'll turn the worst of times into the best of times.

Using Roger's situation as an example, I want to map out the process by which you can transform a potential disaster into an opportunity:

1. **Clearly define the stressful situation facing you.**

   In Roger's case, he was fired without warning and suddenly unemployed. Even more important was his concern about finding a new job at his age.

2. **Reframe the problem as an opportunity.**

   Roger was understandably focused on what he had lost — his job — rather than on what he might conceivably gain from this unexpected change in circumstance. When faced with a problem that seems overwhelming, ask yourself, "What does this change in circumstance free me up to do that I've been wanting to do, but couldn't?" In other words, did closing one door open another? Most people have unrealized ambitions that only come to light when allowed to by some alteration in their circumstances.

3. **Identify existing resources that can be used in transforming the situation.**

   Roger had strong family support, substantial savings to tide himself over until he could get his new career up and running, and a history of overcoming other difficult situations in his past.

4. **Develop an action plan.**

   After I suggested that Roger use this opportunity to think about changing careers, the rest was up to him. He was the one who put all the pieces of a business plan together — product, financing, mission statement, competition, overhead expenses. Getting from the worst of times to the best of times requires a plan!

5. **Implement the plan.**

   Roger was the one who ended up going to his local banker for a business loan. Roger was the one who met with real-estate agents to find suitable space for his jewelry store. Roger was the one who flew to New York to meet with jewelry suppliers.

6. **Revise the plan as needed.**

   When you're implementing your transition plan, if you find that you need to revise some aspect of it, do it. For example, Roger's new business grew so quickly that he had to hire more associates than he had initially anticipated — definitely a nice problem to have, but one he still needed to solve for.

7. **Celebrate the fact that you turned what looked to be a crisis into a success.**

   It's time to pat yourself on the back!

Chapter 7

Conscientiousness

In their wonderful little book The Roseto Story: An Anatomy of Health (University of Oklahoma Press), Drs. John Bruhn and Stewart Wolf described a small Italian-American community in eastern Pennsylvania called Roseto. The inhabitants of Roseto appeared to be immune from heart attacks despite rampant obesity, a high level of dietary-fat consumption, heavy cigarette smoking, and a sedentary lifestyle. Roseto was founded in 1887 and didn't have its first recorded heart attack until 1971.

So what was the Rosetans secret to health? According to Bruhn and Wolf, it was a set of *protective social forces* that included:

✔ Unusually close family ties

✔ Strong religious beliefs

✔ The fact that Rosetans revered the elderly

✔ An extreme sense of group identity

✔ A reliance on each other atypical of surrounding communities

To illustrate the role that social forces play in protecting Rosetans' health, Bruhn and Wolf offer a case history of a man who died from a heart attack at age 41. The man had spent his whole adult life experiencing chronic unhappiness. He wanted to go to college but didn't because his wife discouraged him and he claimed he didn't have the money for it — so he spent 22 years in a job that he hated. He admittedly disliked living in Roseto — saying, "I don't fit in the town — I'm not like the Rosetans" — but remained there nevertheless. He had few friends and had little to do with family who lived nearby. And he didn't belong to any of the many social and civic organizations that were the cornerstone of Rosetan life. According to Bruhn and Wolf, the man simply "found himself out of the mainstream of Rosetan culture," a situation that they believed ultimately caused his untimely death.

What *I* believe killed this man was that he was *living a lie* his entire life. He claimed to be a devoted family man, yet in truth he had a strained relationship with his wife and he had several extramarital affairs. He could afford to send his son to college and his two brothers paid their own way to college, so why couldn't he afford to go himself? Another lie. He claimed to be "stuck" in his job but appeared to make no effort to find alternative employment. Another lie. All these lies, and the physical and emotional discomfort that accompanied them, he kept to himself. In the end, this was his undoing.

In this chapter, I show you how the truth — not just *telling* the truth, but *living* the truth — leads to happiness. Conscientiousness is about truth, about ethics, morality, being forthright and trustworthy, having integrity. It's also about self-discipline. When you meet a conscientious person, what you see is what you get — there are no hidden agendas and, thus, no burdensome stress. In Chapter 2, I talk about how safety is a prerequisite to happiness. Well, you can never feel totally safe if you're living a lie — you're always on guard that someone will find out the truth.

Are You Living an Honest Life?

It's not always easy to know if you're living an honest, conscientious life. Sometimes you have to ask yourself some tough questions and hope you like the answers. For example:

- **Do you find yourself angry too much of the time?** Anger is often the result of conflict and frustration. If you're experiencing some type of inner conflict — for example, between how you feel and how you act — that can express itself in hostility to others, rudeness, or irritability. Other people keep trying to figure out what they've done wrong and the answer is "nothing" — the source of your anger is you!

- **Do you find yourself feeling tense too much of the time?** The human body is wired to be tense (heart pounding, blood pressure skyrocketing, muscles tightening, stomach knotting) for brief intervals whenever your brain senses some type of threat or danger. But the body is not designed to experience ongoing, chronic tension. That's what causes stress-related illnesses like tension and migraine headaches, high blood pressure, ulcers, and coronary heart disease. Tension is not only a defense against outside threat; it's also a defense against letting others know your true self.

✔ **Do you find yourself apologizing too much of the time?** You may spend a large part of your everyday life apologizing for one thing or another — "I'm sorry I was late," "I'm sorry you don't like what I fixed for dinner," or "I'm sorry I'm not the perfect daughter." I've found that most apologies are made not because the apologetic person has done something wrong — they're simply apologizing for not being what other people want them to be.

✔ **Do you find yourself feeling discouraged, disheartened, and dissatisfied most of the time?** All these *dis–* feelings reflect a chronic state of unhappiness that most likely results from your not being true to yourself and living life on your own terms.

✔ **Do you find yourself avoiding other people too often?** If so, it's most likely because you have some unfinished business with the person you're avoiding.

I loaned some money to a relative once, and he promised to pay me back soon. I would've gladly given him the money, but he insisted on it being a loan — he wasn't looking for charity, just some help. Months went by, and I heard via the family grapevine that he had gotten back on his feet financially and was doing quite well, but he made no attempt to repay the money. We visited our family several times over the next year or two and each time he went to great lengths to avoid seeing us while we were in town — he had one excuse after another. I later found out that he had no intentions of paying me back because he didn't believe you should have to pay family back for loans like you would a bank. I wish he'd just been honest with me and not let a couple of hundred dollars come between us.

✔ **Do you shy away from the truth when it hurts?** A friend of mine told me about when his sister died in her mid-40s from a serious illness. She was in a hospital, wasting away, and death was imminent. In a quiet moment, during what turned out to be their last visit together, she asked him, "Am I going to die?" Either the doctors had not been straightforward with her, or she wanted to hear it from the person she trusted most in this world — her big brother. His heart breaking, he thought a minute and said honestly, "Yes." Then she asked her second question: "Will it be soon?" Choking the tears back, he said, "Yes." A conscientious person tells the truth even when it hurts.

✔ **Is there a part of you that you're not proud of and that you don't want other people to see?** People who live secret lives are duplicitous — they're deceitful, dishonest, and double-dealing. They appear one way to the general public and a very different way in their own private lives. Alcoholics and drug addicts are duplicitous. So are far too many politicians. Husbands cheating on their wives are duplicitous, and so are wives cheating on their husbands. Duplicitous people are never happy because they're afraid someone will discover the truth about them — and, because they make so many other people unhappy.

Making sure you're trustworthy

Are the people you work with, love, and depend on day in and day out trustworthy? Can you rely on them — for example, to keep their word and follow through with commitments? Can you entrust your innermost feelings and thoughts to them without worrying that they'll betray you? And, conversely, can those same people trust you?

Trust is not only essential to intimate relationships (see Chapter 20); it has a lot to do with how long you live. A friend and colleague, Dr. Ilene Siegler at Duke University Medical Center, and her associates studied the effect of trust on longevity in 100 elderly men and women and found that trust — the generalized expectancy that you could depend on others — was associated with:

✔ Better self-rated health

✔ Less illness-related disability

✔ Greater life satisfaction

✔ Fewer negative emotions (such as anger or loneliness)

✔ Longer life span

Study participants who were high on trust had half the mortality risk of those who described themselves as relatively untrusting.

Remember: You can extend the lives of those you love the most by being a more trustworthy person. That should make you and them happy!

If you really want to know if other people view you as trustworthy, ask five of your closest friends and family members to rate you on a 10-point scale of how much they can count on you most days, where 1 is not at all and 10 is completely. Take the average of their scores and that should tell you whether you need to work on this aspect of your personality.

If you aren't living an honest life, you can change. Here are some ways you can begin:

✔ **Stop apologizing for who and what you are.** If you're a scoundrel, admit it. If you're a decent person who fails to live up to someone else's expectations, let that be their problem — not yours.

✔ **Begin living your life as if it were, in fact, your own.** Make your own decisions and accept the consequences that follow. Always be open to advice from others, but don't take that as a mandate for how to live your life. If you do, you'll always blame them when things don't turn out in your favor.

✔ **Make sure your outer self matches up with your inner self.** Otherwise, you're, as they say, a house divided against itself.

✔ **Confess to yourself what's really behind all your anger and dissatisfaction.** In *Anger Management For Dummies,* I explain how easy this is to do.

> ✔ **Stop making excuses for not dealing with the part of life that's difficult or painful.** If you lack the courage to visit a dying friend in the hospital, just be honest and let her know that's how you feel. Don't try to tell yourself that you don't have the time or there are more important things that you need to do. Otherwise, head to the hospital and realize that it's a lot easier to live with your discomfort than it is to be dying.

How Engaged Are You?

Conscientiousness also means being engaged in activities that are personally valued. It's not enough to consider something important or meaningful — you have to do it. If you believe it's important to be charitable, but you can never find the time to spend a few hours in a soup kitchen or working with Habitat for Humanity, you aren't a conscientious person. If you think it's important to be compassionate, but you never put money in the Salvation Army kettle or contribute to the American Heart Association, you're not a conscientious individual. Conscientiousness is not about talk — it's about action!

If you want to measure how conscientious you are in terms of engagement, answer the following three questions:

1. **Does most of what you do everyday seem trivial and unimportant to you?**

   • Very Much: 0

   • Somewhat: 1

   • Not Really: 2

2. **Do you care a lot about the things you do every day?**

   • Not Really: 0

   • Somewhat: 1

   • Very Much: 2

3. **Do you *think* about engaging in meaningful activities more than you actually *do?***

   • Very Much: 0

   • Somewhat: 1

   • Not Really: 2

The closer you are to 6, the more conscientious you are about those activities that give your life meaning. And, how does being engaged benefit you? Studies show that it's linked to higher levels of positive emotion and life satisfaction — two key components to happiness.

If you're someone who's not engaged at all, you need to ask yourself:

- **What do I value in life? What are my goals?** What do I want out of life — good health, wealth, long-lasting relationships? Be specific. There's no right answer here — each of us values different things. Goals give your life a sense of direction, a destination toward which you can proceed. Without them, you're just driving around in circles!

- **How attainable are those goals?** In other words, can you picture yourself getting what you want most out of life? If not, what are the obstacles that keep you from succeeding? For example, if you're a member of an ethnic minority, do you think that this will prevent you from becoming financially independent? If you're born into a poor family, do you believe that you're destined to be poor your entire life? Are there skills you're lacking that, if you acquired them, would greatly enhance your chances of realizing your goals? What could you do to make your goals more attainable? Have you thought about getting more education — for example, at the local community college? Would you be more likely to attain the things you value in life if you asked others for help — or is it more important to you to stand alone?

Substance over form

The word *substance* has many meanings, all of which are positive. When applied to human beings, it refers to being worthwhile, strong, solid, sturdy, impressive, and fundamentally sound. If you make a substantial contribution to the world, your life is said to have both value and impact — and, is looked upon by others with respect.

Form, on the other hand, has to do with appearance — what people see when they look at you. Form can be deceiving, but substance never is.

A lot of unhappiness comes about from realizing that your life may be more form (looks good) than substance (very little impact). In other words, people may give the impression of being happy when, in fact, they're far from it. Happiness comes from within and, if someone has made a substantial contribution to life, she has the full measure of happiness.

Erik Erikson, one of the great American psychologists, noted that we enter old age with either a feeling of *integrity,* having spent our time on Earth being meaningful, or in *despair* over all the things we failed to accomplish and the goals we never reached.

No matter what your age, take a minute and reflect on how you want to feel when you near the end of your life. Better yet, take a minute to reflect on how you want to feel next week! Would you rather look back with a feeling of pride and peace of mind or a feeling of regret? You have a choice! You can alter your future at any point along life's highway. Even today, you can choose to begin a new journey of great joy and fulfillment.

Examining Ethics

A friend of mine is an ethicist — he makes his living educating people about ethics in general and medical ethics in particular. He says that ethics is about behavior that has prescriptive value — in other words those things we *should* do if we want to live a happy and successful life. Ethics is not the same as morality, which more directly distinguishes between right and wrong. There are different forms of ethics. For example, the Puritan work ethic says that if people engage in constant labor for the benefit of society, they'll achieve salvation. In modern times, the prescribed benefit is defined in terms of economic prosperity and materialism.

According to my friend, it's not all that difficult to know whether a person is ethical. If he's doing what he *ought* to do according to society, he's an ethical man; if he isn't, he's not. Ethical students refrain from cheating. Ethical therapists avoid having intimate relationships with their clients. Ethical pro ball players refuse to cork their bats, use steroids, or put foreign substances on the ball to make it do tricks on its way to the plate.

An ethical person lives a coherent lifestyle (see Chapter 10), is more reliable in his dealings with others, and, thus, is more likely to achieve happiness — which can be viewed as a form of emotional salvation. Another sign that you're dealing with an ethical person is the smile on her face (see Chapter 12). Why wouldn't she smile when she's doing what she ought to be doing?

You can become a more ethical person if you:

- **Develop a set of principles to live by that conform to society's expectations.** For example, ascribing to the belief that "two wrongs never make a right" keeps you from answering bad behavior with more bad behavior.

- **Always try to put yourself in the other person's shoes.** If you wouldn't like someone to take advantage of you, then don't take advantage of him. If it upsets you when someone you trust lies to you, remember that when you're thinking about lying to someone else.

- **Deal with others in a straightforward manner.** Say what you think. The other person may not like it, but at least she knows where you stand.

- **Are consistent.** Don't tell one person something in one situation and then tell someone else just the opposite in another situation.

- **Seek to be righteous instead of always being right.** Being *right* means you say or do something that is technically correct. Being *righteous* is a virtue that's synonymous with being honorable, fair, and upstanding. The individual decides if he is right — society decides who is righteous.

Being ethical is not the same as being conscientious, but it is one important ingredient of conscientiousness.

Conformity counts

One aspect of conscientiousness has to do with social conformity — behaving in socially approved ways and espousing attitudes strongly endorsed by society. To conform — in Western society at least — means that you get as much education as you can, you hold down a job, you pay taxes, you vote, you salute the flag, you get married, you care for children, you respect your elders, you pay your bills on time, you stop when the light is red and go when it turns green, you wash your hands before you eat, you keep your dog on a leash, and so on.

One study showed that college students who were high on conformity seemed to do better under stress and were healthier than their counterparts who went their own way. And I bet they were happier, too.

Are You a Conscientious Objector?

To gauge how conscientious you are, take the following test. Be honest with yourself to get the most accurate results.

Circle one answer under each of the following questions:

1. Do you ever feel like you're living a lie?

- No: 0

- Possibly: 1

- Probably: 2

- Definitely: 3

2. Do you have secrets you wouldn't want anyone else — even your loved ones — to know?

- No: 0

- Possibly: 1

- Probably: 2

- Definitely: 3

3. Do other people consider you trustworthy?

- Definitely: 0

- Probably: 1

- Possibly: 2

- No: 3

4. **How engaged are you in things that matter most to you?**

   - Not at all: 3
   - A little: 2
   - Pretty much: 1
   - Very much: 0

5. **Would you agree with the saying "Appearance is everything"?**

   - No: 0
   - Possibly: 1
   - Probably: 2
   - Definitely: 3

6. **Do you always do what you *ought* to do in everyday life?**

   - Definitely: 0
   - Probably: 1
   - Possibly: 2
   - No: 3

7. **Would you cheat on a test if it meant you could pass a course you needed in order to graduate?**

   - No: 0
   - Possibly: 1
   - Probably: 2
   - Definitely: 3

8. **Do you vote in local, state, and/or national elections?**

   - Always: 0
   - Most of the time: 1
   - Occasionally: 2
   - Never: 3

9. **Do you believe it's more important to emphasize your rights than your responsibilities?**

   - No: 0
   - Possibly: 1
   - Probably: 2
   - Definitely: 3

10. **When you reflect on your life, do you ever feel a sense of regret?**

    • No: 0

    • Possibly: 1

    • Probably: 2

    • Definitely: 3

If you scored 15 or less, you're a highly conscientious person — good for you! If you scored 16 or above, you're on the low side, suggesting that you may actually object — whether you realize it or not — to being conscientious. If so, you may be keeping yourself from experiencing happiness.

In this chapter, I suggest a number of different ways to become a more conscientious person. Pick any one of these and make a concerted effort beginning today to change *that* aspect of your behavior. Setting a goal for yourself is one step toward being a more conscientious person.

Part III
Behaving Your Way toward Happiness

The 5th Wave   By Rich Tennant

Paul's PETS

"We've been playing motivational tapes about seeing the world from a different perspective."

In this part . . .

I offer you a range of proven behavioral strategies that will increase your potential for achieving true happiness. The specific happiness tactics that I discuss here are all firmly supported by science, although I present them in understandable, non-jargon terminology.

I give you a simple five-step process for getting in the flow of life and experiencing the joys and pleasure that result. I show you how it's possible to be happy even when you (or someone you love) is suffering from some type of unhappy life circumstance — like disease, unemployment, or post-traumatic stress.

You may also be surprised by how a simple, somewhat paradoxical writing exercise can lead to happiness and how empowering the right kind of smile can be.

Chapter 8

Getting into Flow

. . . .

In This Chapter

▶ Searching for your true self

▶ Finding out what makes you happy

▶ Going on the offense

▶ Making flow a routine experience

▶ Looking back with satisfaction

. . . .

*W*hen Rachael hears her husband say, "I'm going up to the computer room for a while," she knows that his pain has become unbearable. The victim of an industrial accident many years earlier, Don lives in a world of constant pain. The pain that began in his lower back now eclipses his entire body — a harsh reality that has left him unemployed, physically disabled, and, at times, struggling to keep his sanity.

In the early years after his injury, Don relied on his doctors to provide him with pain relief. They tried a variety of painkillers and physical therapy, but nothing worked. Eventually, like millions of fellow pain sufferers, Don was left to manage his pain on his own. And that's when he discovered the miraculous benefit of "getting into flow." Flow, according to Dr. Mihaly Csikszentmihalyi, a Professor of Psychology at Claremont Graduate University in Claremont, California, is a state of positive consciousness that occurs in humans when they find themselves immersed in a challenging activity that is uniquely rewarding. Some people would suggest that flow comes from being able to lose yourself in some meaningful task, but actually it's just the opposite. Flow is about finding yourself — your *true* self — by engaging in activities that make you happy.

If you were to ask Don what happens to his pain when he sits at his computer for an hour or two (prolonged sitting typically aggravates pain), he'd tell you, "I don't have any pain — none. I'm absolutely pain-free. The pain only returns when I stop." The key to Don's pain relief, it seems, has to do with his ability to get *into,* instead of just getting *on,* the computer. Why is Don's pain gone when he's on the computer? Because Don *loves* working on the computer. He loves it so much that he enters a state of *flow* (a trance-like state where nothing else matters and you lose all track of time), which allows his mind to transcend his painful body. Flow works!

Twelve rules for achieving flow despite pain

Don is a happy man despite being in constant, disabling pain. How is that possible? Simple — he lives each day by the following 12 rules:

✔ Remember that you have the right to pursue happiness — no matter what.

✔ Stop being afraid of your pain.

✔ Be selfish — take care of yourself instead of depending on others.

✔ Accept yourself as you are — give yourself a feeling of legitimacy.

✔ Be your own best friend, not your worst enemy — don't do things you know will aggravate your pain.

✔ Fight depression.

✔ Put your anger to good use (for example, in fitness training).

✔ Stay connected both intellectually and socially.

✔ Exert control where you can — be satisfied in controlling the little things.

✔ Look for small victories throughout the day.

✔ Have a focal point other than pain (for example, a hobby, your grandkids, your religion).

✔ Add some adventure back into your life — don't be afraid to take a risk once in a while.

In this chapter, I apply the concept of flow to achieving happiness. I tell you why identifying the best moments of your life is important, and why you shouldn't just settle for what you have in life, but pursue what you want. Finally, I lead you through a step-by-step program for getting into flow.

Where Flow Lives: Identifying the Best Moments of Your Life

If I asked you to identify the ten best moments of your life, could you do it? If it's difficult for you, is that because you haven't had that many "best moments" or because it's been so long since you had one that you can't remember? Are you just too busy trying to survive the modern-day rat race to have the time to think about such a thing?

I surveyed a small group of family and friends about the best moments in their lives — when they were experiencing pleasure that comes from *flow* — and this is what they had to say:

> "A few years ago, I rebuilt a computer-injected spray truck at work. I ripped out all the old wiring, dismantled all the systems, and basically built a new truck. I did it all myself and I had a real sense of accomplishment."

Getting into flow versus going with the flow

Getting into flow is not the same as going with the flow. Going with the flow is about conforming to the mainstream in terms of values, goals, and expectations — blending in, not rocking the boat, and being what other people want you be. As I discuss in Chapter 7, conformity counts when it comes to happiness, but so does marching to your own drum.

"I'm a photographer and I got a call telling me some work I had submitted to a major museum had been accepted for display. When I went there and personally handed off my work to them, it was a moment of great satisfaction."

"I love to sew. That's how I make my living — making women's purses. It's such a creative time for me. Time flies by. I don't eat. I'm just into what I'm doing. The end result is what is so satisfying — each purse is unique."

"I'm happy when I'm working in my garden — things are growing, blooming, and everything looks nice. It also makes me happy when I give away my plants — so that someone else can enjoy them like I do."

"I love to go through old magazines that have stacked up over time. I can spend a whole day, sitting on the floor in my pajamas, leafing through hundreds of magazines, clipping out stories and coupons — all the while, as content as I can be."

"The best moments of my life are the ones spent in my kitchen. I love to cook — preparing old favorites and trying out new, interesting dishes. My mother taught me to cook when I was a young girl. She was a great cook. We didn't have a lot of money, but we ate like royalty."

What do all these "best moments" have in common?

- ✔ **The moments involve activities and experiences that people *want* to have in their lives, rather than ones they feel they *have* to have.** You don't spend your day culling through old magazines because it's one of those chores you need to check off the "have to" list — you choose to do it because it makes you happy.

  Maybe the thought of culling through old magazines sounds about as awful to you as any chore you can think of. The key is that, for that person, it's an activity *she* loves.

- ✔ **The moments require your full attention.** Getting into flow is a mindful thing. You have to be fully immersed in the moment. It's an all-or-nothing experience.

✔ **The moments involve activities that are challenging and creative.** Forget the routine stuff like cleaning the house, washing clothes, and most of the mindless things you do at work.

✔ **The moments provide an immediate sense of reward.** It's the pleasure of the moment that makes it special. It's not about delayed gratification, although some of that can be a good thing too.

✔ **The moments involve *doing* something.** Flow comes from utilizing skills — musical, mechanical, culinary — that you've developed throughout your life. The more highly skilled you are, the easier it is to get into flow.

✔ **The moments can occur anywhere** — a tennis court, under the hood of a truck, or in your kitchen.

✔ **The moments come from knowing yourself.** Flow isn't about losing yourself, escaping — it's about finding yourself, your true or authentic self, your happy self. That's why each person has a different "best moment."

 What's important is not what types of activities provide *flow* for my family and friends, but rather which activities in *your* life can serve in that regard. Take a sheet of paper and across the top write each of the following common elements of *flow*:

✔ Activities *I Want* to Do

✔ Activities I Can *Become Absorbed* In

✔ Activities I Find *Challenging and Creative*

✔ Activities That Provide an Immediate Feeling of Gratification

Now, in the left-hand margin, list activities you engage in at work and in your non-work life (leisure and relationship activities) that you think might possibly create *flow*. If you're a teacher who loves what she does, you could list, "preparing lesson plans." If you're a collector, you could list, "checking out flea markets to see if I can find a new treasure to add to my collection." Put a checkmark next to each of those activities indicating which, if any, of the *flow* criteria apply. Those activities that fit three or more of the criteria listed on top are ones that you should do more often if you want to experience the happiness that comes from *flow*. (Keep in mind that *flow* is only one source of happiness — many other sources are discussed throughout this book.)

Understanding Who You Really Are

One of the prerequisites of getting into flow has to do with knowing yourself. By that, I don't just mean name, rank, and serial number: "I'm Doyle Gentry, a psychologist, with a wife and two kids." I mean something much more than that:

> ✔ What makes you tick?
>
> ✔ What makes you unique?
>
> ✔ What satisfies you and makes you happy?
>
> ✔ What gives your life a sense of purpose?

These are not easy questions to answer for some readers. In part, the difficulty lies in the fact that you may be too caught up in the daily "rat race" to have the time for some healthy introspection (examining one's inner self). Also, if you're one of those co-dependent personalities I talk about in Chapter 17, you're more aware of what makes other people tick, what makes them unique, what makes them happy, and what gives their life a sense of purpose than you're aware of these things in your own life.

I pose these questions now so that it will be easier for you to work your way through the four-step process of "Getting into Flow" outlined later in this chapter.

It doesn't take a lifetime to understand what's unique about yourself. Some 20-year-olds already have a clear sense of who they are — and can answer these questions without hesitation — whereas others who find themselves in the second half of life still don't have a clue.

Every experience you encounter in life — good or bad — shapes and ulti-mately defines who you are. Your job is to learn from each of those experi-ences and progress, slowly but surely, toward what the eminent American psychologist Abraham Maslow called a state of *self-actualization*. According to Maslow, you can only get to this point when your biological needs are ade-quately and consistently satisfied, when you feel secure, when you feel loved and supported by significant others, and when you have developed a sense of mastery over life — again, you don't have to wait for the end of life's journey to be self-actualized, and some never make it no matter how long they live. (For more about Maslow, check out Chapter 1.)

Some of the understanding of who you really are — what satisfies you and gives your life a sense of purpose — comes from experimenting with employ-ment opportunities. That same understanding can also head off a midlife crisis. Both of these issues are addressed in the next two sections.

The importance of taking a bad job

Dr. Csikszentmihalyi noted that, contrary to what you might imagine, people experience more opportunities for *flow* at work than they typically do in their free time. But, that depends, of course, on whether you like what you do for a living or not. My wife and I encouraged our kids to get jobs from the time they were old enough to be responsible, beginning in the ninth grade, not just to make money or learn a work ethic, but so they could begin to discover which types of work suited them – and led to enjoyment - and which did not. Because you're going to spend most of your waking life working in some capacity, you're better off working at something that gives your life a sense of purpose and pleasure — something that allows you to utilize your strong points every day.

With each new job, including ones they had in college as well as after they graduated, we often heard them say, "This job sucks. I thought I would like it, but I don't. The money is good, but I'm bored out of my skull — and, I'm getting depressed." My answer was always the same: "Well, good, I'm glad to hear it!" Of course, my kids wanted to know what was so good about realizing that they didn't like their jobs. And I always said, "It's good because now you know one more thing you *don't* want to spend your life doing — a job that will never bring you happiness. That frees you up to go out searching for something you're better suited for."

If you find yourself in a job or other experience that is making you miserable, think of it as one more piece of evidence that tells you what you *don't* want to be doing. In other words, every time you find a job you hate, you're one step closer to finding the job you'll love.

Life is an experiment and, as with all experiments, you're seeking truth — in this case, the truth about who you really are and what makes you happy. The way science works is that each time an experiment fails, it brings you closer to the truth. And so it is with life. The important thing is to keep on experimenting!

How to avoid a midlife crisis

Knowing who you really are not only helps you stay in *flow,* it will also keep you from experiencing the dreaded midlife crisis we hear so much about.

The notion that a midlife crisis is inevitable as soon as you turn 40 years of age is untrue. If you reach your 40s and you haven't yet begun to live life on your own terms, you could experience a crisis. The good news is it doesn't have to be this way.

Consider this exchange between myself and a 47-year-old man who came to me in a highly depressed, agitated state:

> **Client:** I'm just so sick and tired of always doing what other people want. I never get to do what *I* want — it's always "You need to do this; you need to do that; go here; go there." There's no end to it.

> **Gentry:** So, tell me what you want to do this coming weekend.

> **Client:** I have to go to my son's baseball game on Saturday, and my wife wants. . . .

Gentry: (Interrupting) Excuse me, but I asked you what *you* wanted to do, not what *they* wanted you to do. Isn't that what you're complaining about — that no one asks about or cares what you want to do? Well, I'm asking.

Client: (Silent and looking more agitated)

Gentry: You seem to be having trouble answering my question. How do you feel right now?

Client: I'm upset — angry — because I don't know what to say.

Gentry: Precisely. I can see you're angry — your face is red and your fists are all balled up. Now, try to look at this from my perspective. You're a middle-aged man who has done everything that life has asked or demanded of you. You're a real boy scout! And, you're successful as far as the material things of life go. But you can't tell me how you want to spend one day of your life without referring to everybody else's needs rather than your own. Does that seem right to you?

Client: (looking very sad and tearful) No, it doesn't.

Gentry: Well, we're agreed on that. Now all we have to do is help you find the answer to that question and maybe then you'll start enjoying life for a change.

This man was in crisis not because of his age, not because he made a lot of money at his job, not because he had a lovely wife and three great kids — he was in crisis because he had made it halfway through his life and he had no clue about who he really was.

The time to deal with a midlife crisis is before it happens. Don't wait for all the wheels to fall off — psychologically speaking — at the same time! The vast majority of folks actually enter midlife feeling pretty good about the way their life is going. They're in *flow* enough to make life worthwhile and fun. And that's what will sustain them during the second half of life. However, if you're not one of those fortunate people, then you'll definitely want to take steps to engineer more *flow* in your life, which I get to later in the chapter.

Being Happy Today — Not Next Week, Next Month, or Next Year

When it comes to flow, let your motto be: Procrastination be gone! Make today a happy day — don't wait for tomorrow. Be proactive. Flow activities don't always present themselves; you have to *create* them.

Imagine if the young woman earlier in this chapter had decided not to "waste time" going through old magazines. Imagine if the young man had decided it was too much trouble submitting his photographs for display in the prestigious museum. Imagine staying out of the kitchen, when you're an excellent cook, because it's cheaper to eat out when there's only the two of you. In the absence of all these experiences, these folks would have a hard time being happy.

The dessert theory of happiness

Some people ascribe to the dessert theory of happiness — that is, they believe that their happiness only comes as a by-product of meeting other people's needs. A wife, for example, may think the entree consists of satisfying her husband's needs and wants, as well as those of her children, parents, in-laws, and so forth. If she addresses her own needs, it's an afterthought — a sweet moment at the end of a long and tiring day. Problem is that by the time she gets to dessert, she's lost her appetite!

Getting into *flow* shouldn't be an afterthought. It should be something you do for yourself periodically throughout the day while you still have the energy necessary to be creative and fully utilize your skills in challenging activities. Reorder your priorities and have your dessert first. Take care of number one before you begin taking care of numbers two, three, and so on.

Waiting for the ship that never came in

You may also be one of those people for whom happiness is a reward that automatically comes as a result of honest, hard work. When I was a kid, my father frequently said that he was "waiting for his ship to come in" — alluding to the fact that the eventual reward for a lifetime spent in hard, honest labor was a little peace, relaxation, and pleasure at the end of life. Toward that end, my father worked tirelessly day in and day out without complaint. Other than when he went fishing, which was his way of getting into flow, I never remember him being happy. He lived a very unbalanced life — all work and no play (see Chapter 15) — and he paid for it by dying much earlier than most of his brothers and sisters. After we buried him and I was driving his old, ramshackle car back to his house, I couldn't help thinking that he waited all his life for the ship that never came in.

Strive to be happy each and every day of your life. It's possible to work hard and be happy at the same time. My father didn't understand that, but I'm hoping you will.

Appreciating the importance of Being Happy Today will hopefully motivate you to take those steps I outline later on in this chapter that lead you into a state of *flow* — and, happiness.

Pursuing What You Want, Not What You Have

If you're like me and millions of other folks, you spend the bulk of your time and energy pursuing what you already have in life rather than what you want. You get up every morning and pursue — continue, maintain, carry on with — the *same* job you've had for years. You pursue the *same* handful of relationships with family and friends that have provided you with comfort and support over the years. You play golf with the *same* foursome, at the *same* course, teeing off at the *same* time on the *same* day week after week. That's what you're doing. My question is: What are you not doing?

Redirecting your life with therapy

Self-discovery — and the happiness that results from it — is not always a planned thing. Nor is it a journey that everyone can take alone. That's where therapy can help.

Sue was clearly skeptical when she was referred to a psychotherapist by her orthopedic surgeon. She was experiencing constant back pain, resulting from an injury at work, and, "How in the world," she asked herself, "can seeing a psychologist help relieve my pain?" The answer — though not evident to Sue at the time — was "by restoring you to a happy and productive life." Like most people suffering from intractable pain, she desperately looking for someone to turn her life around to what it had been before she was injured. A new, *redirected* life was not on her radar screen.

Sue was clinically depressed, hopeless, and on the verge of suicide. "What have I got to look forward to," she asked "but a lifetime of pain and disability? I can never be happy again — doing the things I used to do — so what's the point of going on?" Sue was at a standstill.

What her therapist helped her understand over the months and years ahead was that, when it comes to the human brain, *pleasure always trumps pain.* With the therapist's help, Sue got her smile back (see Chapter 12) and for the first time in a long time she laughed more than she cried. Slowly but surely, Sue substituted new pleasures for old ones. In her prior life, before injury, she got into flow by mowing her 2-acre yard (she fancied herself the greatest, most precise mower of all time with landscape skills comparable to a surgeon). In her reconstructed life, she became the "queen of comics" — spending hours on end searching magazines and newspapers for cartoons, which she then distributed to friends and family (and even her doctors) on a frequent basis. And what was happening to her pain all the while? It had taken a backseat to feelings of joy and contentment and, thus, was no longer dominating her life. Sue is somewhere out there, I feel certain, having one best moment of her life after another — pain or no pain.

Remember: There's no shame in seeking counseling or coaching. It's no different from seeking out your lawyer for legal advice, seeking out a physician when your body tells you there's something wrong with it, or seeking out the clergy when you find yourself wandering in the spiritual desert. It's all about redirection.

You're not challenging yourself. You're not building new skills. And you're not proceeding toward Maslow's final stage of personal growth and development — *self-actualization*, the stage at which humans are most happy. Without realizing it or consciously intending to, you've settled for security and support at the expense of self-discovery. This, quite understandably, eliminates a good bit of the anxiety and uncertainty that accompanies life change.

We're happy when we achieve those things in life — at any stage — that we want. The problem is that as soon as we achieve them and we get used to them, they cease to make us happy. Then we have to find something else that we want in order to be happy once again. It's what's called the *hedonic treadmill*.

If you're no longer happy with the status quo, here's what you need to do:

- **Explore life.** Don't be afraid to try new things — new foods, new vacation spots, or new types of reading material (the Wall Street Journal in place of your home town newspaper). Take your mind and body to places they've never been before.

- **Question life.** If you're listening to the world news, don't just passively accept what the commentator says — question it: "Do I agree with what she's saying about the war in Iraq or not?"

- **Examine life.** Pay greater attention to what's going on around you and put all those meaningful issues in your life under your own microscope. Abortion, racism, affirmative action, gay parenting, and government-sponsored health insurance — none of these are simple issues and they need to be examined more closely before you decide how you feel about them.

- **Judge life.** Don't be afraid to make your own judgments about what constitutes right and wrong, fair and unfair, just and unjust, what will make you happy and unhappy — it's your right.

- **Ponder life's possibilities.** Don't just settle for life as they way it is — consider, "What if things were different?" Open your mind to alternative possibilities no matter what aspect of life you're dealing with.

- **Experience all of what life has to offer.** I had a lapel pin once that read "This is not a dress rehearsal." How true!

- **Let yourself feel — even when what you feel is uncomfortable.** You're wired to have lots of different emotions — joy, anger, fear, sadness. As I point out in Chapter 4, emotions are your nervous system's way of communicating with you without using words. If you shut off the feelings, you shut off the messages behind them.

- **Learn to trust your feelings.** Intuition is a good thing. Your brain is telling you, "I've been in a similar situation before and here's what I think you should do right now."

✔ **Start looking at life as a glass half-full rather than half-empty (see Chapter 5).** Optimism always leads to hope; pessimism all too often leads to despair.

✔ **Seek diversity in all things.** Understanding diversity is really about understanding how each of us is unique.

✔ **Let curiosity reign.** Curiosity is the emotion that makes it easy for us to explore, question, examine, and ponder all of what life has to offer.

✔ **Quit holding back on passion.** If something makes you happy, let the world know it.

✔ **Stretch, moving beyond your usual comfort zone.** Every once in a while, try something unfamiliar, something more challenging than you're used to, or something without a predictable outcome.

Getting into Flow: A Four-Step Process

So you're sold on the concept of flow and now you want to get into flow in your life. But how? You've come to the right section. Here, I lead you through a step-by-step process that will help you get involved in something so deeply that nothing else will seem to matter.

Step 1: Identifying your sources of flow

Flow is the end result when you apply a set of skills to a challenging situation.

If you have skills but they're unchallenged, the best you can hope for is a feeling of relaxation that quickly turns to boredom. An example is someone with landscaping skills who is simply mowing the lawn.

If you find yourself in a challenging situation, but you lack the skills necessary to deal with the situation effectively, you end up anxious or angry.

If you lack skills *and* challenge, you end up disinterested, apathetic, and dissatisfied.

You're never too old to follow your dream

Even as a child, I had aspirations of being a writer. I dreamed of writing novels and being well-known like Hawthorne, Poe, Hemingway, and Michener. Writing came easy to me and my teachers often told me I had a "gift." I was always happy when I was writing something — even my doctoral dissertation, if you can believe that! And, yet, I never even thought about writing as a career.

In college, I started out studying to be a chemist, quickly switched to economics, then to sociology, and finally to psychology — but I never gave a thought to being an English major. In my early academic career, I had no problem with academic writing — for many of my colleagues, writing was a chore, but not for me.

Only toward the end of my career did I finally allow myself to embrace the identity of a writer. I joined a literary guild and told my children, "After I'm dead and people ask you what your father did for a living, tell them he was a writer." So, as I write *Happiness For Dummies*, I can honestly say I'm a happy man. My only regret is that I took 55 years to take the plunge.

If there's something you've always wanted to do, now's the time to do it! You're never too old — I can attest to that!

Start with a list of skills you possess that have to do with sports, hobbies, career, socializing, and artistic endeavors. Examples include

- ✔ Writing poetry
- ✔ Golfing
- ✔ Organizing social events at work and in the community
- ✔ Writing fiction or nonfiction
- ✔ Playing tennis
- ✔ Fly-fishing
- ✔ Coin or stamp collecting
- ✔ Participating in Civil War reenactments
- ✔ Painting
- ✔ Gardening
- ✔ All types of crafts — pottery, basket-making, jewelry
- ✔ Cooking
- ✔ Playing cards
- ✔ Wine-making
- ✔ Volunteering for political campaigns

After you've identified your skills, ask yourself three questions:

- ✔ When is the last time I did any of those things?
- ✔ Are there activities that I haven't gotten involved with before, but that I'd like to do?
- ✔ Am I letting my skills atrophy by not challenging them?

If you're a bridge player, have you ever signed up for a bridge tournament? How about trying out a new — and more difficult — golf course next time you play? If you're a writer and you're not ready to tackle the challenge of writing a book, why not submit an article to a magazine? (Either way you get your name in print!)

Step 2: Taking the plunge

Getting into flow is a process, and like any other process it has to have a beginning before it can have a middle and an end. Earlier in this chapter, I cover the importance of pursuing what you want rather than just settling for what you have, as well as the risks associated with procrastinating. Now is the time for action! Don't spend the rest of your life standing on the edge of the diving board being afraid to take the plunge — go ahead and make a splash!

I often hear people — including myself — say, "I don't have time to write, to play golf, to go cycling with a group of my friends in the mountains." But the reality is, you have the same 24 hours you had on the day you were born and that you'll have on the day you die — no more, no less. Getting into flow is not a question of how much time you have; it's a question of how you choose to use it. Why not start using your time in ways that make you happy?

Step 3: Giving yourself enough time

Flow is a timeless state, but it does take a certain amount of time to get there. It's not something that you can hurry up.

I had a client who came to me for help in stress management. I gave him an audiotape of a standard 20-minute relaxation exercise and suggested that he listen to it daily. When he returned the next week, I asked him about the tape and he said, "I haven't had time to listen to it and, besides, you said it takes 20 minutes — don't you have anything shorter?" Instead of challenging him, I gave him a 10-minute tape. The next week it was the same thing, "I really didn't have time to listen to the second tape — do you have one that's shorter, maybe four or five minutes?" You see how foolish this sounds. Telling yourself to hurry up and relax is just as senseless as telling yourself to hurry up and get into flow.

The irony is that after you get into flow, time no longer matters. You're not even conscious of it. Time only matters *before* and *after*.

Flow is about being so highly engaged in an activity that you lose track of time. Take off your watch when you're trying to get into flow — it only makes it easier to lose track of time when you don't know what time it is. (You can find more about this in Chapter 15.)

Step 4: Making flow a regular part of your day

People make all kinds of other things part of their regular day — including negative things like anger outbursts, substance abuse, a tedious and boring job, and hot-button relationships. Why not add in opportunities for getting into flow, being grateful, and doing things you enjoy doing?

Jason used to come home from the office every day exhausted and in an irritable mood. More often than he would like, he ended up barking at his wife and kids over the least little thing. Evenings at home were not idyllic and not something he looked forward to. Then he changed his routine to include stopping off at a nearby school to walk on the track. He quickly developed a proficiency at walking and managed to cover between 3 and 5 miles without effort. The whole time he was walking, he was in a zone, oblivious to anything and anyone around him. He was in flow. When Jason finally arrived at home, he was in a positive, receptive mood and there was no more complaining. He was a happy man and so was his family.

How can you enrich your day and get into flow? If you rarely or never experience flow, start by trying to make flow a part of your week. When you're getting into flow once a week, try upping it to three or four times a week. And then try making it a part of every day.

Looking back — with regret or satisfaction

The eminent American psychologist Erik Erikson cautions that, at the end of life, human beings reflect on the kind of people they've been and the type of lives they've lived. If you've lived the right kind of life — one that made you happy — you're left with a sense of satisfaction and integrity; otherwise, you end your days with regret and despair. And as you face death, you'll be comforted by all those best moments of your life that will easily come to mind.

Chapter 9

Finding Benefit in Life's Challenges

*I*n this chapter, I explain how to make sense out of adversity — it's called benefit-finding. Benefit-finding is about finding the good in the bad. Not only can finding a silver lining in an otherwise bad situation ease your suffering, it can produce a greater appreciation of what life offers, an increased connection with your inner self, and a heightened sense of compassion — all of which can lead to happiness.

An antidote to demoralization

Health psychologist Roger Katz and his colleagues at the University of the Pacific studied how patients with cancer and lupus coped with their illness. To their surprise, patients were more likely to report some benefit coming from their illness than they were to feel demoralized — helpless, cynical, defensive.

They acknowledged, for example, that being ill helped them communicate more openly with their families and helped them be better friends. Benefit-finding was also associated with less pain and suffering — including anger, depression, and fatigue.

A picture of illness

In a class I was teaching on health psychology, I asked students to draw a picture of illness. I wanted them to depict in visual terms how they perceived the idea of being ill — and how they would act if they were ill.

After they were done with their drawings, we had show-and-tell, where each student had to come before the class and explain his drawing. Virtually everyone produced negative drawings. Illness, as they saw it, was gloomy, sad, limiting, and an experience that greatly diminished their life. No one wants to be sick. Illness sucks! But,

if people expect to handle illness badly, they usually do. It's one thing to experience physical pain — from cancer or arthritis — but it's another to suffer emotional pain — bitterness, frustration, depression — which is what happens when people give in to illness and accept disability as an inevitability.

This is the point Mitch Albom makes in his powerful book *Tuesdays with Morrie* (Time Warner): It's possible to die a horrible death without losing your sense of optimism, good humor, and zest for life.

I asked Tom, a relative of mine who had a massive heart attack at age 45, if he thought that his life was in any way better off afterward. Tom said:

> Oh, absolutely. It gave me a chance to reflect on my life — to look at where I was before and where I am now. Before the attack, I was working long hours and under lots of stress. I love my family, but I took them for granted. I realized that I wasn't there for them except in a material sense, and I missed a lot. So, I shifted my priorities — now family comes first and work second. I'm part of their lives now, not just a stranger who comes home every night and puts food on the table.

> The heart attack also changed how I treat people at work. I cut back my hours and began to let my employees and my partner take on more responsibility. I didn't take back any of the stuff I had relinquished while I was in the hospital and during my recovery. And, I learned that I could trust them to get the job done right — something I hadn't felt before. You might say we're more like a family at work now, too. We depend on each other more than we ever have.

> Something that happens so unexpectedly forces you to ask yourself what is really important in life. I know it did me. Truthfully, and this is going to sound funny, if I hadn't had that heart attack six years ago, I'd be dead now.

Tom was presented with a challenge, and he's found the benefit in it. Being able to do that in your own life will help you be a happier person. In this chapter, I show you how.

Having the Right Perspective

Unlike other animals, humans have the gift of perspective, and perspective is about choice! As I discuss in Chapter 5, you can choose to see life as a glass half-full (optimistic) or a glass half-empty (pessimistic). Similarly, in Chapter 6, I discuss the difference between a hardy person and a non-hardy person — it all comes down to whether you define problems as challenges or crises. Having the right perspective is a key to achieving happiness. In this section, I show you how to get perspective on the challenges you face.

Asking yourself whether the sky really is falling

When tragedy strikes, most people initially feel as if there's no tomorrow. This response is nothing to be ashamed of — it just means we're human. The key is moving beyond that initial response and getting some perspective on the situation. To accomplish that, it helps to:

- ✔ **Think of what you've done in similar crisis situations in life.** Similar doesn't necessarily mean the same. For example, if you find yourself grappling with the bad news that you have prostate cancer, you might ask yourself "What did I do when I got fired from that job I had years ago – that I loved?" or "What did I do when my wife up and left me saying she didn't love me anymore?" After all, a crisis is a crisis — if the sky didn't fall the last time, it won't fall this time.

- ✔ **Recall what others have done in this same situation.** How did your brother react when he found out that he had cancer? If you're not sure, by all means call him up and ask him how he kept from panicking. Try looking at the sky from his perspective.

- ✔ **Think in non-catastrophic terms.** Instead of thinking "This is awful, terrible, horrible," say to yourself "This is bad — certainly not something I wanted to hear." Remember: Your brain listens to what you think as well as what you say — if you think the sky is falling, your brain will act as if it is and you will end up feeling overwhelmed.

When something bad happens to me, I too think of some of the worst times in my life and then ask myself if what is going on right now is that bad. Invariably, the answer is a resounding no. I tell myself, "Hey, if you survived the worst times in your life and went on to better times, the same thing will happen in this case." And it does. If you're younger than me (and most people are – I'm 64) and you haven't had all that many crises in your life yet, adopting a non-catastrophic perspective may be difficult. It might help if you talked to someone older about the challenge you're facing and see what they think. Parents can be helpful here along with life coaches, counselors, and clergy (especially if you're dealing with a spiritual crisis).

Being optimistic

Benefit-finding is greatly aided by having an optimistic attitude. Optimists don't *deny* that bad things happen in life — they just refuse to dwell exclusively on the negative. They leave open the possibility of finding the good in the bad.

Nancy, a young woman in her late 30s who had hurt her back while working as a nurse, was an optimist. "At first I was disheartened. I loved being a nurse and I hated losing my job. But I couldn't continue to work with all this pain," she said "Eventually, I decided to look on the bright side of things: Being unemployed — while not my choice — did allow me to be a stay-at-home mom to my three kids while they were growing up. We're a lot closer, I'm sure, than we would have been otherwise. At least I have that to be thankful for."

Ben, also in his 30s and a victim of chronic pain, was not an optimist. Ben could only see the negatives of what life had to offer following his injury — loss of income, no longer having contact with his buddies at work, and a perception of himself as being of no use to anyone. He was an angry man, bitter, and resistant to any notion that life could still be meaningful in some way. Sadly, Ben died of a heart attack at the age of 41, and even his cardiologist admitted it was the result of a broken heart.

Optimists rebound faster!

A study published in the journal *Health Psychology* by researchers at the University of Helsinki looked at the effect of optimism and pessimism on how quickly 5,000 employees rebounded from a major stress — death or severe illness in a family member. Employees high on optimism had fewer sick days as a result of this type of stress than did their counterparts who were low on optimism. Whether employees were high or low on pessimism appeared to make no difference whatsoever.

Bottom line: Pessimism may not hurt you, but an optimistic outlook sure helps.

There are some definite advantages to having an optimistic outlook. Here's the short list (see Chapter 5 for a more extensive list):

- ✔ Optimists are more self-confident.

- ✔ Optimists are more likely to be problem-solvers.

- ✔ Optimists persist despite adversity — they're not quitters.

- ✔ Optimists welcome second chances at life.

- ✔ Optimists are less likely to assign blame for their misfortunes.

Asking the Right Questions

Benefit-finding is the result of asking yourself the right questions about the impact of tragedy on your life. It requires some introspection, some self-analysis, and a connection with your inner self. You have to decide if there is something beneficial about a negative life situation — others can't do that for you.

What can I do now that I couldn't do before?

Loss, tragedy, and adversity leave people changed in some way. So when tragedy strikes, the first question you need to ask yourself is: What can I do now that I couldn't do before?

Tom, my cousin who suffered a heart attack, found that he could do a number of things he couldn't do before:

- ✔ He learned that he could delegate responsibility more at work and still run a highly successful business.

- ✔ For the first time in his life he was able to trust in someone other than himself.

- ✔ He was a better husband and parent, because he knew that it wasn't just about being a provider and a care-taker.

- ✔ He was able to communicate more openly with family and friends.

- ✔ He was more emotional — he hugged more, cried more, and laughed more.

- ✔ He was able to reset his priorities, making his family number one and putting work in second.

When you add it all up, Tom's answer to the question "What can I do now that I couldn't do before?" was simple: "I can be a loving human being!"

Think about some misfortune you've encountered in your life and ask the same question of yourself. Give it some serious thought before you answer. If you're not sure, ask someone close to you if she's noticed any positive change in you since that event. The changes may be there — you just may not be aware of them.

Why have 1 been given this opportunity?

At this point, you're probably saying to yourself, "Opportunity? What opportunity? How do tragedies and challenges give me opportunity?" Perspective is all about choice. And with choice comes opportunity — opportunity to choose how to respond.

The question is why you and why now? These questions are not simple. Sure, people say, "God doesn't give you anything he doesn't think you can't handle," but my guess is it's more complicated than that. Maybe Tom got the opportunity to rethink how he was living his life at age 45 because, by that time, he had lived long enough to appreciate the patterns in his life that were destroying him. Patterns — good or bad — take time to emerge. Maybe his opportunity came then because he was still young enough and otherwise healthy enough to survive the event, whereas, as he himself suggested, had it occurred later on he would have died. Or, it could be that he's been given this opportunity because there is some greater purpose to his life — something out in front of him — that he has not yet discovered.

You don't have to believe in God or fate or destiny to believe that you've been given this opportunity for a reason. All you have to do is decide on what that reason is — you get to choose.

Coping: What works and what doesn't

Research has shown that people who cope most effectively with life stresses, ranging from the minor hassles to the major catastrophes, do so by adopting a problem-solving approach to whatever they're up against and utilizing the support of those around them. On the other hand, people who cope *ineffectively* with these same stresses tend to engage in wishful thinking ("I wish this hadn't happened"), impulsive behavior (throwing a temper tantrum), denial ("Problem? What problem?"), and blame ("It's their damn fault!"). The choice is yours.

Am I up to the challenge?

My years of clinical practice tell me that most ordinary people are capable of surviving difficult — even monumental — challenges. Most people are much tougher and hardier than they realize. **Remember:** Hardy people have a strong sense of internal control (What can I do to benefit from this experience?) and they are actively committed to life before tragedy strikes. They're also more likely to be happy than less-hardy people are.

Past history can be a clue to the future. When faced with some bad circumstance, ask yourself: How have I dealt with other misfortunes in the past? I managed to survive, didn't I? (If not, you wouldn't be sitting here reading *Happiness For Dummies.*) What did I do to cope that helped? Can I use those same tools now?

Making Sure You Realize the Benefit

Benefit-finding is not an automatic thing. You don't suddenly think in the midst of some unfortunate circumstance in life, "Wow, this isn't that bad after all." Benefit-finding is a process — one that takes *energy,* requires that you forge *closer ties* to those around you, involves several stages of *readjustment,* and requires that you develop a *concrete plan* as to how you plan to change your life for the better.

Redirecting your energies

Dealing with adversity takes a lot of energy — physical and psychological — especially when you see your circumstances as beyond your control. Initially, what little energy you have can easily end up being channeled into negative thoughts, feelings, and actions, which keep you from moving forward with your life.

Ben, the pessimistic young man with the bad back, is a good example. He stayed angry for 11 years between the time of his disabling accident and his death. His wife wasn't surprised that he dropped dead in the middle of an angry conversation on the phone one morning — she had been waiting for that day to come for a long time. As an expression of his never-ending anger, Ben had refused to associate with any of his former coworkers, rebuking them even when they reached out in compassion: "I don't need people feeling sorry for me!" That mantle of anger finally became too heavy for his heart to bear.

Mind over matter

A study of 136 patients who had suffered rheumatoid arthritis (RA) for an average of sixteen years revealed that those who acknowledged some type of interpersonal benefit from their illness were less physically disabled — walking, dressing themselves — than those who viewed RA as an all-negative experience.

Too much of Ben's energy was focused on his past and all the losses he had suffered because of his injury. A lot of his energy was also directed at ways to just survive the day — venting his anger on anyone who would listen in an effort to relieve built-up tension, moving back and forth from the recliner to the bed seeking comfort, and resisting efforts by family and friends to do something productive with his life. Ben loved children and he had been a baseball player in his youth, so he was repeatedly invited to coach his son's little league team. His answer was always the same — no!

So, how can you redeploy your energy so that you don't end up demoralized — feeling hopeless and helpless — by a challenge? How can you put the challenge to good use? Better yet, how can you use it to achieve some measure of happiness? Simple, you have to:

- ✔ **Shift your time frame.** The benefit you're seeking has to do with the future, not the past. Sitting around ruminating or sulking about the past will only keep you "stuck" where you are – in a state of perpetual distress. Make sure your mind stays focused on the days, weeks, and months ahead – "I'm going to run some errands for my wife this afternoon. I'm looking forward to spending time with my grandson later this week — I'll take him to the zoo. Next month is when we're going to the beach for a week — when I get down there, I don't seem to hurt as much."

- ✔ **Focus on what you can control, not what you can't.** Ben can't control his pain or get back all the things he lost because of it. What he could do instead is think about all the countless things he still can do which he's not because he's mired down in self-pity and regret (which are understandable, but nevertheless unproductive). Think *ability* rather than *disability* and, trust me, you'll feel a whole lot better!

- ✔ **Be productive in both thought and deed.** Reliving a trauma that happened to you years ago day after day is counter-productive if you're looking for a way to achieve a moment of happiness — all it does is bring back pain. Resisting all efforts to get you back into the mainstream of life is also counterproductive. Better to think "What can I do?" and then do it.

Forging closer ties to those around you

The vast majority of benefit that people find in the aftermath of misfortune comes from their interpersonal relationships — their connections to other people. People end up forging closer ties to those around them. How do they do that? They do it by taking the following advice:

- **When loved ones offer you support, accept it with appreciation instead of pushing it away.** This is no time for foolish pride which only keeps people at a distance. People want to help, so let them. And, always remember to say "thanks."

- **When others offer compassion and empathy, respond in kind.** Remember: You're not the only one in the world who's hurting in some way. People need you as much as you need them.

- **Educate others about your problem.** You have to tell your story in a way that helps those around you understand all of what you're going through and why you're meeting the challenge the way you are. Don't whine — educate!

- **Discover the kindness of strangers.** Friends often start out as strangers who want to help and the relationship evolves from there. If you turn away the kindness, you offend the person on the other end.

- **Foster better relationships with professionals whose help you need**. Doctors and lawyers (and, yes, psychologists) are human beings too — it never hurts to ask them "How are things with you? How's your son doing — I heard he was in an automobile accident?"

Making the necessary adjustments

When human beings face life-altering challenges, they have to make adjustments. In doing so, they must do three things:

- They evaluate the situation. "What just happened? How bad is it?"

- They make judgments about the situation. "I really don't think I can handle this." "This will work out."

- They react to the situation. "I'm going to make someone pay for this."

But, these evaluations, judgments, and reactions are subject to change over time. The changes are predictable and follow a rather specific pattern or sequence (known as *stages of adjustment*).

The first stage I call *turnaround* because what you really want initially is to believe that your misfortune can be fixed or reversed. The problem is that the kind of challenges we're talking about in this chapter — cancer, lupus, arthritis, loss of a child, severe depression — can't be undone.

Fighting spirit

Cancer patients who exhibit a "fighting spirit" — who accept the verdict of having a terminal disease, but who are determined to fight back by living a full life to the end — survive longer than patients who resign themselves to their fate or who appear overwhelmed by the bad news. The fighting spirit is about taking charge of every aspect of your daily life and dealing with illness on your own terms. It's not about being angry — it's about being the boss of your own life!

The second stage has to do with *survival,* which typically involves a roller coaster of emotions — anger, sadness, fear — which is anything but enjoyable.

If you're lucky (or get the right kind of help), you progress to the third stage — *reconstruction.* This final stage I like to think about as the "good news," stage and this is where benefit-finding comes into play. As you begin to move beyond survival, you start to behave in ways that increasingly bring joy back into your life.

Which of the following three statements best describes your current attitude about significant challenges in your life?

> ✔ Maybe if I don't think about it, it'll go away.
>
> ✔ Why get up in the morning? I just want to hide in my warm, safe bed.
>
> ✔ My life has changed and I've changed with it — and, it's not so bad.

If you chose the first statement, you're in the turnaround stage. If you said the second statement, that suggests that you're just surviving. And if you chose the third statement, that means you've entered into the world of personal reconstruction.

Making a revised life plan

Major life challenges involving trauma and loss disrupt your life and force you to redirect your energies, interests, and commitments. But how do you do that? It's not easy to revise your life and move into a positive, more satisfying future. But these steps can get you moving in the right direction:

1. **Create a positive mindset by sitting quietly with your eyes closed while opening your mind to the possibility of hope, optimism, and creative behavioral change.**

Take ten exaggerated breaths, breathing in through your nose and out through your mouth while silently repeating the word *relax* each time you exhale.

2. Identify a short list of valued life goals — for example, being closer to your family, becoming a more spiritual person, reconnecting with old friends.

Goals give you a sense of direction in terms of the changes you want to make. Basically, you're deciding what you want your life to stand for *from this point on.*

3. Decide what the incentives are for you to reach these goals.

What's the end game? Will you have greater peace of mind? Will you be happier? Will you live longer? Will you feel less alone with your suffering? Will you have a new lease on life? Be specific.

4. Ask yourself how committed you are to achieving each goal.

The more committed you are — the more successful you'll be.

5. Ask yourself how *confident* you are about making these changes.

Commitment and confidence are not the same. You can be committed, but not all that confident — or, the other way around.

6. Consider what specific things you would need to realize each goal.

Where would you start? How much support do you need? If you have several goals, which one do you begin with? Make it easy on yourself — start with the smallest, easiest thing and work your way up to the big changes.

7. Identify any obstacles to meet your objectives.

Do you have physical limitations that might interfere? Is depression a problem? Are other people's attitudes holding you back?

8. Decide how you're going to overcome those obstacles.

For example, get professional help for your depression.

9. Begin — just start.

It doesn't matter what you do; the important thing is that you just do something.

Change takes effort so you have to persist, even when the going gets tough. There's no easy way to accomplish change.

Change also takes time, so be patient. As the saying goes, "Rome wasn't built in a day." And neither is a reconstructed life. Focus on the destination, but enjoy the journey.

10. Reward yourself for whatever changes you make no matter how small.

If change is rewarding, you keep at it — if it isn't, you quit. It's just that simple!

My own benefit-finding

Try as I might, I haven't been able to find any way of reconciling or making sense out of my nephew's death from leukemia. Allen was a great kid. He was easy-going, intelligent, and a good-natured soul. He never gave his parents a minute of worry, he was well-mannered, and I never saw him angry. Everybody loved him — for good reason. And then, one day shortly after he turned 13, he was diagnosed with cancer.

For three years, his doctors kept him alive — resurrecting him from death on more than one occasion. And, all the while, he remained hopeful, cheerful, and optimistic, shaved head and all, about his chances for a long and healthy life. He died at the young age of 16, and his family was devastated. To make matters even worse, his mother — my sister — died tragically three years later at age 42. Her doctors said it was because of chronic lung disease, but I think she died from a broken heart.

I was numb for a while and then angry, and then somewhere along the line I accepted the finality and futility of the whole thing. The tragedy made me appreciate how lucky I was to have two healthy kids and reminded me that I needed to take better care of myself. I made the choice to give thanks for my kids and to take care of my body, and that was a positive outcome from an incredibly tragic series of events.

Chapter 10

Living a Coherent Lifestyle

The dictionary defines coherence as an experience that is logical, consistent, and easily followed, and one in which the various parts stick together to form a whole. Psychologist Aaron Antonovsky defined coherence as an orientation — a way of thinking about the world — that leaves you with a pervasive and enduring feeling of confidence. Dr. Antonovsky suggested that you have a sense of coherence whenever you:

✔ Deal with life in a structured and predictable way.

✔ Have enough resources to meet the demands of everyday life.

✔ See these demands as both challenging and meaningful.

Careers provide some people with a sense of coherence; other people depend on marriage, family, or religion. What makes life coherent, in other words, varies with the individual.

In his book *Unraveling the Mystery of Health: How People Manage Stress and Stay Well* (Jossey-Bass), Antonovsky argued that coherence is linked to well-being, one component of which is happiness. This is true, he says, even in the most adverse of life circumstances — for example, in a concentration camp. (Antonovosky studied how people survived in concentration camps.)

In this chapter, I show you how to achieve an abiding sense of coherence in good times and bad. I also offer strategies for dealing with periodic disruptions in coherence and a way for you to assess how weak or strong your sense of coherence is at this very moment.

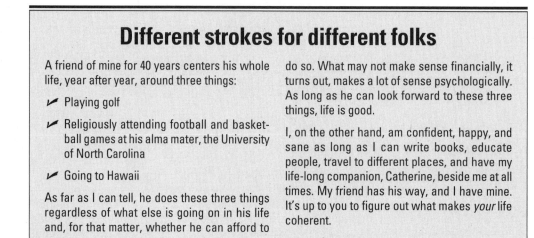

Different strokes for different folks

A friend of mine for 40 years centers his whole life, year after year, around three things:

- ✔ Playing golf

- ✔ Religiously attending football and basket-ball games at his alma mater, the University of North Carolina

- ✔ Going to Hawaii

As far as I can tell, he does these three things regardless of what else is going on in his life and, for that matter, whether he can afford to do so. What may not make sense financially, it turns out, makes a lot of sense psychologically. As long as he can look forward to these three things, life is good.

I, on the other hand, am confident, happy, and sane as long as I can write books, educate people, travel to different places, and have my life-long companion, Catherine, beside me at all times. My friend has his way, and I have mine. It's up to you to figure out what makes *your* life coherent.

Coherence = Confidence

A sense of coherence leaves you feeling confident about the life you're living. That confidence comes from your ability to view the happenings in your life as *comprehensible* (that is, they make sense), *manageable* (you're up to the task), and *meaningful* (they're worthy of your time and effort).

James and Larry were both recently diagnosed as having chronic obstructive pulmonary disease (COPD). James took the news well. The diagnosis was no surprise to him, because he had been dealing with lung problems since he was a child — in fact, he had part of a lung removed when he was only 16. James understands that his COPD is the result of a disease, which tends to run in his family, and not because he was a smoker or worked in an environment laden with asbestos. He understands why (comprehensibility) he is ill, but then again illness has always been an integral part of his life.

He also believes he can manage his COPD (manageability) in a way that will provide him with quality of life for some years to come – again, he's been managing his health for years. He was pleased when his doctor referred him to pulmonary rehab, and he's optimistic that the twice daily inhalant therapy will improve his lung capacity (hence, the treatment is meaningful). He's working hard gaining back the weight he lost over the past year — weight loss is common in patients with COPD.

James is living a successful, meaningful life and he's not about to let that be cut short if he can help it. On his last check-up, his physician remarked, "You have an incredibly positive attitude about all this. You're really an exceptional patient!"

Larry, on the other hand, did not take the news well. It's been months and he still hasn't told his family or friends that he's sick — a fact that he plans to keep secret as long as he can. It makes no sense to Larry that he has COPD – it's incomprehensible. Sure, he's been a smoker all his life, but he quit a couple of years ago and, besides, he's always been healthy and robust. He's been a successful businessman, an active husband and father, and he's enjoyed physical recreation — skiing, tennis, cycling — for as long as he can remember. The idea that his lungs won't continue to support such activity in the years ahead leaves him bewildered and depressed. Larry has entered a brave new world and he hasn't got his footing yet. He doesn't see how he can manage to do what it takes to remain in relatively good health – he hasn't developed any skills over the years that will come in handy now.

When asked about pulmonary rehab, Larry said, "I can't take time for that and run my business at the same time." In other words, Larry is not up to the task (manageability) and does not consider rehab literally worth his time (meaningfulness). Although Larry has lived a meaningful life, the prospects of declining health and a curtailment of his normal, pre-COPD lifestyle leave him questioning whether he wants to fight the good fight or just give up. Larry isn't too confident about his future in terms of health, finances, or just plain old happiness.

The difference in these two men isn't their illness — it has to do with their sense of coherence. That, more than anything, will determine the future course of their health and well-being. For James, COPD is just the latest challenge in his life-long effort to deal with chronic illness – for Larry, it's an entirely new ballgame, one in which he's forced to play for the first time. Most likely, he'll eventually get the hang of it, but it'll take some time and some assistance along the way.

Put yourself in their shoes: Your doctor has just delivered some bad news — you have breast cancer, a chronic and incurable pain disorder, or diabetes. How will you react? Will you handle it pretty well (like James) or be devastated (like Larry)? Which of the three components of coherence — comprehensibility, manageability, or meaningfulness — would you have the most trouble with? When you look down the road, past the initial diagnosis, do you see yourself ever being happy again? Or is that part of your emotional life over? Think about these questions before you get a difficult diagnosis, and you'll be better prepared to handle bad news of any kind when it arrives.

Coherence Isn't One Thing, It's Many

For most people, finding one thing in life that gives them the sense of confidence they need to continue embracing life with all its twists and turns is easy. Some people discover early on how valuable education is, and they spend their entire lives continuing to learn everything they can about the world around them. For others, making money or going to work is the most important thing.

But there's a problem with having only one source of coherence in your life: What if something comes along that takes that one thing away? What happens to your confidence then?

The trick is to diversify — to have multiple sources of coherence in your life at all times — and to always be looking ahead to retool your sense of coherence to fit the particular demands of whatever stage of life you find yourself in.

Diversifying your life

Stock brokers have one word for their clients — diversify, diversify, diversify! It's the mantra of any successful investor and it should be the mantra for all of us when it comes to developing a sense of coherence.

What you need is a network of people and things in your life that collectively create a sense of confidence and satisfaction. The dictionary definition of *coherence* refers to various parts that stick together to form a whole. So, what are some of those possible parts? Consider the following:

- ✔ Engaging in intellectual pursuits, such as reading *The Wall Street Journal* every day or taking courses at your local community college
- ✔ Spending time with family
- ✔ Developing long-term friendships
- ✔ Building a career (as opposed to having a series of jobs)
- ✔ Fostering a spiritual faith
- ✔ Attending religious services
- ✔ Participating in civic organizations
- ✔ Volunteering
- ✔ Doing hobbies
- ✔ Caring for pets
- ✔ Working as a missionary
- ✔ Doing routine recreational activities such as golfing every Saturday morning with your friends
- ✔ Joining a book club
- ✔ Getting involved with your alumni association, such as tailgating at football games or doing fund-raising for your alma mater
- ✔ Participating in community government
- ✔ Working on your marriage

✔ Participating in a prayer group

✔ Getting regular exercise — jogging, walking, cycling, swimming, aerobics

✔ Meditating

✔ Attending AA meetings or other support groups

Review this list and count the number of these activities that make up your day-to-day life. A healthy recipe for coherence would include at least five such activities carried out on a weekly basis.

The more of these, or similar, activities you engage in on a consistent basis, the stronger your sense of coherence.

Understanding how coherence changes with age

Erik Erikson, one of the world's most well-known psychologists, talked about how each of the various stages of life — childhood, adolescence, adulthood — is made up of different personal and interpersonal agendas. For example, as children grow up, they first learn to trust the world around them, then exercise free will, make choices and become interested in different things, and finally develop an appetite for learning everything they can about the world around them. Adolescence is all about forming an identity — how you're different from others — and seeking independence. Young adults are all trying to build a social and economic life and deal with lots of "firsts" — first marriage, first job, first mortgage, first car. Middle-age adults are consolidating their gains — things they achieved as young adults — and working hard to maintain families, careers, and their health. And, the elderly spend a lot of time reflecting back on life and deciding whether their lives were meaningful.

Meditation, stress, and health

Studies have repeatedly shown that people who practice meditation exercises on a regular basis enjoy better health over a lifetime, manage stress better, and live longer. In one study of 154 New York Telephone Company employees, those who practiced mediation routinely over a period of 5½ months showed significant decreases in depression, anxiety, hostility, and paranoia when compared to those who were non-practitioners. It was also suggested that meditation led to better coping, improved efficiency at work, and greater satisfaction with life. Not a bad deal for something that can take as few as two or three minutes of your time!

If you're interested in meditation, check out *Meditation For Dummies,* 2nd Edition, by Stephan Bodia (Wiley).

Coherence — understanding life, managing life well, and feeling as if your life has value — changes as people age. To understand coherence in children, you have to be able to see the world through a child's eyes. Parents are a child's major, if not exclusive, source of coherence. Teenagers, on the other hand, make sense of the crazy, emotional world in which they live primarily through peer relationships and this, unfortunately, drives some parents nuts. Young adults rely on other young adults for coherence. And, somewhere in middle age, we begin to be the source of our own coherence. That's the beauty of growing old!

The specific pursuits and activities that we rely on for a feeling of coherence at each of these life stages (see the preceding section) vary considerably and tend to be age-appropriate. It's safe to say that few children belong to alumni associations or book clubs, but their parents can certainly enroll them in Sunday school classes and make sure they are a fully participating member of the family unit. Coherence is not a *static* experience, but rather something that changes and evolves over time.

What to Do When Coherence Is Disrupted

Most of us have a plan for how we want to live our lives and we spend the majority of our time executing that plan. Sometimes, if you're lucky, life cooperates with your plan, but not always. And, your sense of coherence — which is a by-product of that plan — is either temporarily or permanently disrupted. Common disruptions include such things as:

- The death of a loved one
- The loss of a job
- Divorce
- Life-changing accidents or illness
- Bankruptcy
- War
- Severe economic losses
- Natural disasters — floods, hurricanes, tornadoes, wildfires
- Identity theft
- Winning the lottery
- Imprisonment
- Outsourcing of jobs overseas

- ✔ The death of an industry — coal mining, steel mills, farming
- ✔ Having a special-needs child
- ✔ Being forced into early retirement

Life suddenly gets off track and the confidence that was so much a part of your life is shaken. During those times, you're anything but happy. So how do you get back on track and regain your confidence? In the following sections, I show you.

Have a heart-to-heart with a higher power

The peace and tranquility that comes from a belief in a power greater than oneself is an antidote to unhappiness and the doubt and uncertainty that accompanies unexpected, unwanted changes in life. The nature of that higher power is not as important as the meaningful social tie (see Chapter 16) you have to that entity.

Duncan was a successful and happy man until he had a nervous breakdown. Suddenly, overnight, he was reduced to a shell of a man — unsure about his own self-worth and viability as a husband, provider, parent, and friend. He found himself on an emotional roller coaster, elated one minute and in utter despair the next. Duncan had lost confidence in everyone and everything around him, as well as himself, and there was no one else to turn to for hope but God. Duncan was in an emotional freefall and God was his safety net. So, he began a dialogue — prayer — with his higher power. God became the lifeline that helped Duncan maintain some sense of coherence in an otherwise chaotic world.

In order for prayer to work, you need to be honest in your conversation with your higher power. This is not the time to hold back. Admit your fears, your anger, your feeling of vulnerability, and ask for help. Recognize that you're a human being — no more, no less — and not some invincible, superpower who can handle everything that life throws at you. This is what humility is all about.

Prayer is an act of faith and faith can be a weapon that helps you survive unhappy times. Take a few minutes each day and have a quiet conversation with a higher power. The nature of the prayer doesn't matter. It can be a prayer of uncertainty ("Lord, I've lost my sense of direction and don't know where to go from here"), a prayer of solicitation ("God, please grant me the courage to see this through"), or a prayer of desperation ("God, I feel so lost and alone"). The simple act of having faith is what's empowering.

Hardiness and prayer

Studies show a link between participation in religious services and hardiness (see Chapter 6). Hardiness involves a sense of internal control, an active commitment to life, and the ability to view adversity as a challenge rather than a catastrophe. This is akin to what most religions teach when it comes to issues of faith, commitment, and responsibility for one's actions. Whether prayer leads to a hardy attitude or vice versa, the two seem inextricably connected.

Set aside the unanswerable questions of life

You are, by definition, rational, logical, and thoughtful. Why? Because you're human, and humans are the only animal on the planet that have the immense brain capacity to interact with the world around them in a questioning manner. Other animals lack the ability to question life; they simply act on instinct.

But the human need to ask questions and have them answered to our satisfaction can also be a problem. Not all questions in life have an answer, and that can leave people at a loss.

When my 16-year-old nephew died of leukemia, I sat in the church watching my poor sister and her family devastated by grief thinking, "This is stupid! It makes absolutely no sense. He was a great kid. What was God thinking anyway?" I wanted answers — something to satisfy the anger and confusion I felt at that moment — and was hopeful that the minister would provide those answers. And then a truly miraculous thing happened. The minister said, "I'm not going to stand here and try to explain why this wonderful young man's life was cut short because I don't know myself. What I'm going to tell you is that some things in life just don't make sense and never will, in this life at least — and, that's just something that you and I are going to have to live with. So, instead of sitting there asking the unanswerable questions, 'Why this boy? Why this disease? Why now?', I suggest we all set those questions aside and pray a prayer of gratitude for having had this young man in our lives for these few years and for all the ways he touched us all." I found that very comforting.

What unanswerable questions are *you* struggling with? If you've asked questions for which you still haven't gotten a satisfactory answer, maybe it's time to set them aside. By the way, I think you'll find that you rarely, if ever, seek answers to questions that have to do with things that are going right in your life — Why am I so good looking? Why am I more successful than most other people my age? What did I do to deserve this wonderful woman I've been married to for over a quarter of a century? The unanswerable questions only come when our lives get off track.

Know how to begin and end each day

Coherence comes from structure and when that structure — those routine, meaningful activities that make you feel like you're on top of life — is disturbed, you must slowly but surely replace that structure, not always an easy task.

It takes time to rebuild a life after the loss of a spouse to whom you've been happily married for decades. Finding another job that will provide you with as much satisfaction as the one you just lost can take a lot of effort. And readjusting to civilian life after serving an extended tour of active combat during a war can be difficult. Daily routines that felt all too natural are now a thing of the past.

New routines are best developed by concentrating on the beginning and end of each day. Let the middle of the day take care of itself. Focus on tasks that meet the three M's test — that is, something that makes sense, is manageable (within your power to do), and is meaningful. And keep it simple!

Here are some ways you may want to start and end your day:

- ✓ Spending a few minutes in quiet prayer
- ✓ Doing 20 minutes of light exercise
- ✓ Taking your dog for a walk
- ✓ Having breakfast at a restaurant where you're considered a regular
- ✓ Sending e-mails to close friends and wishing them a pleasant day
- ✓ Spending 15 minutes in meditation
- ✓ Feeding the birds in your yard
- ✓ Having a neighbor over for coffee
- ✓ Having a conversation with someone who cares about you

Start and end your day the same way every day. These routines can be the building blocks for a renewed sense of coherence.

Count your opportunities and blessings

In an effort to achieve a more positive, confident mindset as you go through the day, be aware of all the opportunities life offers you as well as the blessings that come your way.

I once heard a Baptist preacher say, "Folks, there are two kinds of people in this world. The first kind gets up in the morning, gets out of bed, walks across the floor, looks out the window and says 'Good morning, God.' The second kind gets up in the morning, gets out of bed, walks across the floor, looks out the window, and says 'Good God, morning.'" Same three words, only with entirely different meanings. The first welcomes the opportunities and promises offered by each new day, whereas the latter can only see the problems of the past. If you think about it, just having another day to make something meaningful of your life is, in itself, a blessing.

Begin and end each day reminding yourself of at least ten ways in which your life has been blessed. Do you feel blessed with good health? Are you blessed by having people in your life who love and care for you? Are you blessed with certain talents and skills that not everyone else has? Are you blessed with children who are good citizens and are succeeding at life? Everyone has something in his life he can be thankful for.

Opportunities don't always coming knocking on your door — sometimes you have to create them. Ask yourself what you can do today to create some new opportunity in your life.

Making Sense of Life: The Core Components

There are three core components to a coherent life, without which it's difficult, if not impossible, to achieve happiness. These components are order, affiliation, and meaning. Each of these components is important in its own right, but it's the combination of the three that determines where you fall on the continuum of coherence. I cover these core components in the following sections.

Order

Imagine living in a land where there were no rules, no laws, no customs, no rituals, no agreed-upon ways of relating to other people, no responsibilities, no expectations, and no consequences for your actions. That would be the land of chaos! Now, imagine how unhappy you would be.

To be happy, there has to be some rhyme or reason to everyday life, which means order. Order not only tells you how to behave and what to expect today, it tells you what tomorrow will be like.

The concept of civilization implies a sense of order. Some cultures operate under the so-called *rule of law,* which means that citizens learn to behave in certain prescribed ways that have legal consequences. Other cultures operate under the *rule of force,* which means the citizens live seemingly ordered lives out of fear. In either case, removing those rules inevitably leads to chaos.

How ordered is your life? Are you clear about what your world expects from you today? Can you tell what you'll be doing tomorrow? Do you have a plan for today that you'll follow no matter what? How many times during the course of your day do you answer specific questions by saying "I'm not sure," "We'll see," or "It depends"? Is every day of your life a mystery?

If your life is more chaos than order, set down some rules you can live by (Do onto others as you would have them do unto you), be clear what it is you expect from yourself today and tomorrow (I'm attending community college or I have a job to go to), and don't just be satisfied with living "one day at a time" – that sounds good, but it's not too practical.

Affiliation

Humans are happiest when they are attached to and connected with the lives of others. (The opposite — to be detached or disconnected —is to be alienated.) Affiliation is a positive thing; alienation is negative. Much of your sense of coherence comes from being a member of a family, a social or civic organization, a workforce, a political party, a religious community, and the like. It gives you a feeling of belonging and shared identity.

Affiliation is a vital part of the definition of who you are and what your life stands for. When someone meets you for the first time and asks, "I don't believe we've met. I'm _____. And who are you?", you answer by saying, "I'm _____. I just moved here from _____. I work at _____," or, "I'm _____, the host's brother-in-law," or "Nice to meet you. I'm _____. I just moved in next door."

If I asked you "Who are you?", what would you say? If you're not sure, it's time you started filling in the blanks. Align yourself with some group at work, for example, they guys who play golf on Saturday or the bowling team. Join a volunteer organization where you can feel a part of a group effort — for example, Habitat for Humanity. Make a concerted effort to reconnect with your family of origin — most likely, they'll welcome you back with open arms. Organize a small group to eat together every Friday night — something you (and they) can look forward to. The possibilities are endless.

In Chapter 16, I explain the difference between being alone and being lonely. Affiliation is about never being lonely, even if you're alone.

Meaning

Viktor Frankl's wonderful book *Man's Search for Meaning* (Washington Square Press) makes a cogent argument for how a person can only achieve happiness through a life with purpose. That sense of purpose, he suggests, can come from one of three sources:

- ✔ Some type of creative or constructive work or deed
- ✔ Intimate, loving relationships
- ✔ Rising above some tragic life circumstance (in Frankl's case, the horrors of life in a German concentration camp)

A life that includes none of these three elements is, according to Frankl, empty and meaningless. And it is a life rife with unhappiness in the form of depression, violence, and addiction.

How have you managed to find meaning in your life? Today is a good day to start creating your meaning in life. Here's how: Find an activity where you can forget about yourself and focus more on the needs of others — for example, becoming involved in the Big Brother/Big Sister program and doing what you can to enhance the life of a child. Find an activity that has more to do with your character — compassionate, entertaining — than your profession or career — psychologist, electrician. Think of someone you admire and start doing some of those things they do. Look around for things that everyone agrees should be done, but no one wants to do — and, you be the one to do them. All of us look at the trash littering our highways and think "I wish somebody would pick that stuff up." Why don't you be that somebody and make the rest of us happy?

Chapter 11

Making a Daily Confession

*Y*ou're probably saying to yourself, "I thought confession was about confiding in someone the things that I've done wrong — my transgressions, my sins, my shortcomings." Traditionally, confession has been about confessing the bad stuff, but there's no law that says you can't confess the good stuff, too.

I'm not suggesting that you get in line at your local church and confess to a priest — although some people find the Catholic confession a vital part of their lives. What I'm suggesting is that you use a technique called *emotional journaling,* in which you spend time every day focusing on and writing about all your positive thoughts, feelings, and events. Journaling about the good stuff can lead to increased happiness.

No penance required

In the Catholic faith, when you go to confession, you invariably end up performing some sort of penance — for example, praying the rosary five times, doing the stations of the cross, or reciting "Forgive me Father for I have sinned" over and over. The penance is the price you pay for sinning.

But in the case of positive confessions, there is no sin. So, there's no need for penance. Instead of being told "Go forth and sin no more," what you need to tell yourself is "Good for you! You deserve it! Keep it up!" Forget penance — reward yourself for having the good sense to do what it takes to achieve true happiness. And that will add another layer of joy to what you already have!

Aaron spent most of his life asking God for things. He prayed that he would get the job he applied for. He prayed that nothing bad would happen to his two lovely children. He prayed for promotions, prayed that he and his wife would get along better, and prayed that he'd remain healthy.

Asking for what he wanted was the nature of Aaron's relationship with his higher power. But that began to change, not all at once but gradually. Instead of asking God to *give* him things, he began *thanking* God for all the many blessings that had already come his way. He switched from a prayer of *supplication* to one of *gratitude.* He started and ended each day by spending a few quiet minutes reviewing all the things he had to be thankful for — not only that day but all the days of his life. He thanked God for his happy marriage, for his healthy children, for his parents, and for his friends. He thanked God for his intellectual ability, his ability to make a good living, and all the success he had enjoyed in his career. But most of all, he thanked God for the opportunities that came his way — things that he hadn't engineered, didn't expect, and was pleasantly surprised by, things he attributed to that force greater than himself.

When Aaron asked for things in his prayers, it meant that he felt empty, that something was missing. But when he started routinely thanking God for what he already had, it left Aaron with a full feeling, a feeling of satiation, which is one of the primary ingredients to achieving happiness (see Chapter 2).

On the other end of a confession

Recently, I met a wonderful young woman I know at the restaurant where I always eat breakfast. We were both leaving at the same time and we spent a few minutes in the parking lot, where she told me about all the good things that were happening in her life, including being accepted into graduate school in a new and exciting field. The more she confessed how good her life was, the happier I felt. The next thing I knew, I was recounting all the things *I* have to be grateful for in my own life. We were feeding off each other in a very positive, natural, and spontaneous way.

The next time someone shares some bad news with you, listen for a while and be supportive — but then share some good news about your own life. You may worry that your good news will make the other person feel worse, knowing that you're happy while they aren't, but trust me, it won't. What your good news will do is give that person a sense of hope — hope that maybe, just maybe, one day soon she'll also have some good news to share with you. Think of your good-news confession as a lifeline to someone who's swimming in troubled waters.

Everybody wants things — more time with the people they love, more money, more clothes, more vacation time, a better car, a better house. But the key is to shift your focus from what you don't have to what you do. You don't have to be religious or even believe in God to be thankful for what you have. The key is just to be thankful, period.

Confessing the Good Stuff: Thoughts, Feelings, and Actions

Psychology in general concerns itself with how and what human beings think, how they feel, and how and why they behave the way they do. Positive psychology does the same thing — only it focuses on *positive* thoughts, *positive* emotions, and *positive* ways of acting toward others. In making your daily confession — it needs to be daily to get the real benefit — you need to pay attention to the good stuff. Think about what went right rather than what went wrong. Look at that part of the glass that's half full, rather than the half that's empty.

Get in touch with positive feelings — love, compassion, gratitude — not feelings like anger, dissatisfaction, and despair. Ask yourself, "What have I done today that's positive, that made someone else's life easier or better, or that made me a healthier and happier person?"

By simply paying more attention to the positive things you say and do each day, you'll become a much more positive person — and, thus, happier.

Positive thoughts

Over the years, a lot has been written and said about the power of positive thinking. All of it is based on the premise that what's in your head — positive thoughts — inevitably influence what's in your heart as well as how you behave. The golfer who stands on the tee and thinks to himself "What a beautiful hole — I'm going to put this sucker (meaning the ball) right out there in the middle of the fairway" most likely will be happier with his shot that his friend who's standing next to him thinking "Oh God, I hope I don't hit it into the trees on the left." I know because I used to be like his friend and that's why I eventually gave up golf.

Here are some examples of the kind of positive thoughts that can lead to happiness:

- ✔ What a lovely day this is.
- ✔ There really are nice people in the world — like the driver who let me pull in front of him so that I could turn at the light.
- ✔ My partner is such a thoughtful person.
- ✔ I'm not rich, but I'm thankful that I have enough to pay my bills.
- ✔ I'm a very healthy person for my age.
- ✔ I'd rather have my friends than a million bucks!
- ✔ I am so much better off than a lot of people I see every day.
- ✔ I love the smile on that woman's face at the checkout counter.
- ✔ I love it when I hear the birds start to sing — it means spring is on the way.
- ✔ That massage felt wonderful!
- ✔ It's always great to hear from my kids — even when they have a problem.
- ✔ I'm glad I found that nail in my tire before it went completely flat!
- ✔ If I could live my life all over again, I wouldn't change a thing.

I must confess . . .

If you want to have a happy relationship (Chapter 20), be happy in your work (Chapter 18), and have a happy family (Chapter 19), you have to let the people closest to you know how much happiness they bring to your life. Happiness should never be taken for granted — it needs to be shared.

A husband needs to tell his wife regularly — not just on Valentine's Day — how happy he is that she's his partner in life. How hard can it be to tell her, "At least once a day, I realize just how lucky I am that you married me"?

Parents need to tell their children how much they enjoy them despite the growing pains that inevitably come from raising kids. How difficult is it to say, "You're one of the best things that ever happened to me"?

And, it never hurts to tell your employer how much you enjoy working there. Most people find it much easier to talk about what they *don't* like about their jobs than what they *do* like. I know when I was in the business of managing a group of psychologists, I didn't mind their criticism nearly as much if they also confided in me what they liked about how things were run.

Starting today, make a point of telling someone you know "I must confess how much happi-

Take a piece of paper and write down 15 positive thoughts that would help me understand what's in your half-full glass. If this exercise seems difficult and you have a hard time coming up with 15 happy thoughts, you're probably spending too much time focusing on the negative. Don't worry — if you keep up this exercise regularly, eventually you'll be able to come up with 15 positives.

Carry a notebook with you and write down every positive thought you have in a given day. Sometimes at the end of a long day it's hard to remember all the positives you experienced, but if you write them down throughout the day, you'll be able to reread your list before you go to bed and remind yourself that the day was actually pretty good.

Positive feelings

Happiness is not just about feeling joyful. It comes from other positive feelings that you and I experience in the course of everyday life as well. In essence, one good feeling leads to another. If you have enough of these other positive emotions, you can't help but be happy.

What positive feelings have you experienced lately? Here are some examples:

- ✔ Awed
- ✔ Content
- ✔ Comfortable
- ✔ Compassionate
- ✔ Connected (as opposed to lonely)
- ✔ Generous
- ✔ Grateful
- ✔ Excited
- ✔ Humble
- ✔ Optimistic
- ✔ Relieved
- ✔ Righteous (for example, for having done a good deed)
- ✔ Satisfied
- ✔ Serene
- ✔ Upbeat

Use this list as a starting point, and write down any *positive* feelings you've had in the past 24 hours. If you have trouble identifying very many positive feelings, that's a heads-up that you may be paying too much attention to the negative emotions or, in fact, that you simply aren't feeling anything positive. Doing this exercise daily will help you become more aware of positive feelings that are there — just unnoticed. If you aren't having any positive feelings at all, day after day, then you probably need to get some professional help in figuring out why not — even mildly depressed people can feel upbeat and excited.

I didn't include "happy" in this list, because happiness is really the composite of a lot of other positive emotions.

Positive actions

It's not always what you think and feel that makes you happy as much as it is what you actually *do* in the course of a given day. When you're making your daily confession, try to think of all the positive things you did in the past 24 hours.

Here are some examples of positive actions:

- ✔ Held the door open for an elderly person at the post office.
- ✔ Slammed on the brakes to keep from running over a dog in the road.
- ✔ Picked up litter along the roadside.
- ✔ Returned a wallet I found in parking lot to its rightful owner.
- ✔ Sent a get-well card to an ailing friend.
- ✔ Took my dogs for a walk.
- ✔ Did the dishes so that my partner wouldn't have to do them after work.
- ✔ Took a day off from work to sit with a friend who was undergoing chemotherapy.
- ✔ Said "thank you" to everyone who helped me throughout the day.
- ✔ Took time to go to the gym to exercise.
- ✔ Stopped to talk to a neighbor I knew was having a hard time with depression.
- ✔ Treated a friend to lunch.
- ✔ Went to bed early and got a good night's sleep for a change.
- ✔ Smiled at everyone I came into contact with.
- ✔ Bought my partner some flowers.

Confidant = confident

If you have a special person in your life, someone you can reveal anything to — good or bad — then you know what a confidant is. A *confidant* is someone with whom you have an intimate, one-on-one relationship that goes well beyond that of an acquaintance or even what most people think of when they use the word *friend*. Having a confidant means having someone to whom you can confess your true self — your feelings, thoughts, ambitions — without risking judgment or some form of social censure. It's the most trusting relationship that humans have.

Remember: Having a confidant is healthy. Heart patients who could identify a confidant lived three times longer than those who could not. And if you're a pregnant mother, having a confidant increases the odds that your fetus will be born healthy by three times.

Be sure to share the good news with your confidant, too. Sharing news about how well things are going in your life builds self-confidence. After all, you're listening to yourself as you talk to that other person and you're being reminded that things are going well. Your positive confessions end up enhancing your own sense of self-esteem.

Try to come up with 10 examples of positive actions you took that made you feel good in the past 24 hours. If you can't come up with 10 things you did in the past 24 hours, make a list of 15 things you'll do in the *next* 24 hours, and carry the list with you so you can make sure to do them. Eventually, these positive actions will become a part of your routine, and you won't have to think about them consciously in order to incorporate them in your life.

Positive confessions need to start with the words: I *thought*, I *felt*, and I *did*.

Putting It Down on Paper

If you take just 15 or 20 minutes a day and write down everything positive you can think of that happened during the day, you'll see on a daily basis how much you have to be thankful for. This journal is for your eyes only, to remind you of what you have to be thankful for or happy about.

Don't think of this as a diary — you're not going to keep it after you're done. Here are some things to keep in mind as you write your happiness journal:

Confessing with a card

During the five years I was depressed, I received greeting cards from a man I affectionately think of as Uncle Bert — he's slightly older than I am in years and centuries older than I am in wisdom, and he's been a mentor throughout my career. The cards always seemed to arrive at one of my low points — moments of true despair — and they had the desired healing effect that Bert constantly referred to in his handwritten notes.

The cards were joyous looking, brightly colored, and full of hope. What Bert wrote inside each card also brought joy to my suffering heart. Not only did he confess his concern for my well-being and his appreciation for our friendship, he also shared his appreciation of the support I had offered him in the past. He consistently reminded me of what he called my "unique contributions" not just to the profession of psychology, but to the world at large. As he put it in one card, "You are realizing the poet/poem within."

You can imagine how this cheered my sagging spirit and helped me slowly-but-surely reconnect with a feeling of happiness.

Remember: You don't have to wait until someone is ill or there's some special occasion to send someone you care about a greeting card. You can make any day you choose the anniversary of your friendship, a celebration of your relationship, or simply a reminder — to them and to you — of what an important part he plays in your life. Why not let the people you care about know how you feel today?

✔ **Make yourself the audience.** You're writing this to yourself. It's a private conversation — you're not trying to impress anyone or to make someone else feel better. Fill the pages with self-references — words like *I* and *me*. Writing in the first person makes it a *personal* conversation between you and yourself, as opposed to a conversation between you and someone else. It also makes *you* responsible for the positive thoughts, emotions, and actions you write about.

✔ **Forget the grammar.** This is one writing exercise where grammar doesn't matter. You don't have to be an English major to confess how good you feel at the end of the day. Just write from the heart. Write without thinking too much — let your writing be spontaneous. No one is going to grade you, so you can forget the rules.

✔ **Write until time's up.** Give yourself the full 15 to 20 minutes to complete this exercise. Don't be in a hurry to make your confession. Enjoy it! The exercise itself should make you feel better, so make it last. If it helps, set a kitchen timer and write until you hear the bell — and, then just stop even if you're in the middle of a sentence.

✔ **After you're done writing, read what you wrote.** Circle all the positive feelings you wrote about — like *happy, excited,* and *relaxed.* Underline all of the positive *thoughts* you wrote down (for example, "I reminded myself how fortunate I was to have a college education"). Put a check-mark next to each positive *action* you took during the day. Now add up all those notations. Paying attention to the positive feelings, thoughts, and actions you wrote about will give you a sense of whether you're getting a good balance of all three in your day.

This daily exercise serves as an active reminder of the fact that you're probably having a better day than you realize.

Engaging in Group Confessions

When my wife and I get together for dinner with our Friday night friends, we don't sit around and complain about all our problems. Instead, we share all the positive things that are going on in our lives. We confess to each other the good news, not just the bad. We try to uplift one another (see Chapter 13) in order to end the week on a positive note. I announce that "We finally sold our office building and now I can retire." A younger member of our group, who has recently started a business of his own, tells us about a new contract he's landed that will earn him a lot of money. His wife, who makes handbags for a living, talks about the successful show she had in a nearby city the past weekend. Another member of the group updates us on how well her daughter is doing in law school and how much she enjoys living in Florida. And so it goes. (Don't get me wrong: If someone has a problem, of course, everyone will hear them out and offer support. It's just that we don't want Friday night to become a group therapy experience.)

If you're not already involved in a regular group meeting with family and friends, where the conversation is upbeat and focuses on the good stuff, start your own group. The size of the group isn't important — what matters is the character of the people (you want to choose optimists over pessimists) and the content of the conversation.

If you're going to gossip about other people, make sure it's positive gossip. Say *good* things behind their backs! For example, "Did you hear about Sally? She got that job she applied for? Isn't that wonderful. I'm so happy for her." Sally won't know what you said, but *you* will.

What pain?

I have conducted a bi-weekly men's pain group for several years for male clients who suffer from chronic, disabling pain disorders. Many of these men have been attending these sessions religiously for a long time and it's been interesting to hear how the essence of what they talk about has changed.

In the beginning, the focus of their confessions was the horrors of living in constant pain, the anger they had toward the medical profession for failing to fix them, their struggles with the insurance companies, and the strain that all this had put on their families. Now, years later, the same people spend virtually all their time talking about how positive life is despite ongoing pain. One talks about having a new home built — a dream that he thought he had lost because of

his disability and loss of employment. Another talks about his recent fishing trip to the North Carolina coast and how much he enjoys the pain relief he gets when he goes fishing. A third talks about how pleased he is that his son has a good job and is happily married.

These men seldom refer to the word *pain* and they no longer look unhappy. They laugh, smile, tell jokes, and enjoy each other's successes. If you ask them why they continue coming to these group sessions year after year, they'll tell you it's because they feel so much better when they leave and that good feelings seem to carry over into their everyday lives. They've long ago learned all there is to know about living with chronic pain — what they're learning now is how to be a happy pain patient.

Chapter 12

Putting On a Happy Face

● ●

In This Chapter

▶ Smiling worldwide

▶ Smiling for the right reasons

▶ Projecting a positive image

▶ Smiling as a means to an end

● ●

According to psychologist Daniel Goleman, author of the popular book Emotional Intelligence (Bantam), being able to read other people's emotions is part of what makes human beings smart. And what exactly is it that we're supposed to read? Their faces, of course. There's the sad face, the angry face, the depressed face, the curious face, the hostile face, the kind and considerate face, the compassionate face, and the happy face.

How do you know a happy face when you see one? Simple: It has a smile. Not just any old smile, but a natural, unforced, authentic smile unlike any other.

In this chapter, I show you how to interpret the meaning and motives behind a variety of smiles, point out how empowering a smile can be, and tell you how intentionally putting on a happy face can brighten your spirits. I also tell you how to get your smile back if you've lost it.

Smiling: The Universal Language

Forty years ago, psychologist Paul Ekman, professor emeritus at the University of California Medical School in San Francisco, embarked on a psychological adventure to discover the origin of human emotions. He began his journey in New Guinea, where he quickly discovered that the preliterate South Fore people had the same emotions as people in modern, civilized cultures throughout the world. Unlike most psychologists, who study how people think and feel through spoken language, Ekman relied on people's recognition of facial expressions of different emotions, and he took pictures of their faces.

Reading the students' faces

My favorite part of teaching in college is watching the faces of students when they take a test. Some have looks of sheer terror ("Oh my God! Where did these questions come from?"). Others have blank expressions, which probably mirrors what's going on in their minds. Far too many, unfortunately, have frowns ("I could kick myself for not studying for this test!"). And then there are the smiling faces, the ones that let me know how well-prepared these students are and point to how happy they'll be when they get their grades. The looks on my students' faces tell me all I need to know.

What he learned by studying the South Fore people as well as countless other groups of people around the globe — from Broadway to Borneo — left him convinced that six basic emotions are universal among all cultures:

- ✔ Anger
- ✔ Contempt
- ✔ Disgust
- ✔ Fear
- ✔ Happiness
- ✔ Sadness
- ✔ Surprise

Think of these as the primary colors of your emotional life. All other feelings — disgruntled, confused, curious — are spin-off or secondary emotions.

The fact that emotions are universal and not bound to any specific culture means that they're built in to the human nervous system. In other words, you don't have to learn to be happy when you're born — you come into the world already equipped to experience happiness. Infants smile and so do the elderly and that, in and of itself, is the language of happiness.

From Cradle to Grave

Emotions reflect a person's temperament. *Temperament* is an inherited style of experiencing and expressing emotion — it controls both the tone and direction of your feelings. If you're an ill-tempered individual, you move against the world in an angry, aggressive manner. (For more on this,

Caution: Smiling can be contagious

It's a proven fact that human beings tend to mimic each other's emotional behavior. Professor Aron Wolfe Siegman, at the University of Maryland–Baltimore County, noted that in a two-person exchange one person's verbal expression of anger led to an increase in the other person's anger. This reciprocal "in kind" response serves to escalate anger to the point where it's difficult to control. The exact same thing happens with sadness.

I love that scene from the movie *The Odd Couple* where Felix Unger (Jack Lemmon) is left alone with two happy young women and, before you know it, everyone ends up in tears. It works the same with happiness. Hence the saying, "Smile and the whole world smiles with you." The point is that positive emotions are no less contagious than negative ones.

Smile at the next ten people you see and pay attention to how many smile back at you. Don't say anything, just smile. Then frown at ten people in a row and see how many smile at you. I bet you'll notice a difference.

check out *Anger Management For Dummies* [Wiley]). If you have an easygoing, affable, good-natured temperament, you move toward the world, in a positive, cheerful way, with a smile on your face.

Temperament is defined during childhood and is fairly consistent over your lifetime. If you were a happy 8-year-old, you can expect to be a relatively happy 80-year-old — you'll be the guy in the nursing home who all the nurses love! And if you were a whiney, difficult child, that may well be how you'll end up in old age — unless you decide otherwise and you make a concerted effort to change. (Isn't that one reason you purchased *Happiness For Dummies*?).

Continuity of temperament occurs for two reasons:

- ✔ **People tend to seek out people whose temperament is just like theirs.** The kids in my school-based anger management classes, for example, are all alike — irritable, fidgety, and ill-tempered. The temperament of the boys in my son's Cub Scout den was quite different — relaxed and cooperative.

- ✔ **People with similar temperament reinforce each other's style of emotional behavior.** The end result: "I'm happy, you're happy, we're all happy — or not!"

If you aren't by nature a positive person, make sure you hang around with others who are. Let their good-natured ways rub off on you. Emotions can be contagious.

You don't choose your temperament, but you *can* choose your companions.

Interpreting the Smiles of Others

A smile can communicate all sorts of things, not just happiness. Behind every smile there's a reason, a motive, some type of nonverbal message. When someone smiles at you, you immediately translate that facial expression into an idea to which you then respond — for example, "She likes me. She approves of what I'm doing. She's my friend." Or, you could take it a totally different way: "He's being condescending. He thinks he's better than me. I'll show him." The person who's smiling is the messenger — your job is to figure out what the message is.

There are a variety of types of smiles, and I cover them in the following sections.

The lying smile

What underlies some people's smile is a lie. They're smiling and saying one thing, but thinking and feeling just the opposite.

Politicians are often guilty of the lying smile. I love it when a politician smiles and says that his adversary is a "good friend, someone I can work with across the aisle, and someone I truly respect," when you and I both know that he really wishes his opponent would drop dead.

The stereotypical used-car salesman is often guilty of the lying smile, too. With a smile on his face, he says, "This car is a gem. It was owned by a little old lady who only drove it to and from her doctor's office. You don't have to worry about having to put any money into this baby." Are you convinced?

Many people use lying smiles to be polite and avoid unnecessary conflict, particularly with those closest to us. They think it's better to lie than hurt other people's feelings.

Lying smiles are *intentional* — the person deliberately smiles to misdirect you from the fact that she's lying. And, unfortunately, for some people, lying smiles are also *habitual* — the person uses them all the time.

The angry smile

Ironically, sometimes a smile tells you that a person's angry. Their smile is actually an attempt to disarm you so that they can catch you off-guard with their anger. Angry smiles are most often found in conflict situations — where two people disagree or someone has failed to live up to another person's expectations. One of the more obvious situations is in the workplace, where an employee has been summoned by his boss for a little one-on-one dialogue. Don't be deceived by the smile on her face as she welcomes you into her office and shuts the door — what comes next most likely won't be pleasant!

An angry smile is often accompanied by hostility and sarcasm — "Well, I'm pleased you could find the time in your busy day to wait on our customers. After all, they do pay your salary."

The masking smile

Judy, a 40-year-old with chronic back pain, sat in my office with her husband. As I reviewed my impressions of the initial interview with Judy and the various test findings — both of which clearly diagnosed the fact that she was severely depressed — she began to smile and laugh at the very idea that she was upset about her physical health. The more I talked, the louder she laughed — until finally her husband turned to her and said, "Stop it. What are you doing? You're being inappropriate. This man is trying to help you and you're acting like this is all a joke or something." Judy broke down in tears. Her happy façade had been penetrated. Judy suffered from what mental health counselors call "masked depression." And, her condition had now been unmasked.

Misdiagnosing myself

My sister died tragically at the age of 42, after a long siege of chronic illness. For a year and a half before her death, I visited with her almost every week, trying to comfort her and give her some sense of hope that things would get better, even though I knew they wouldn't.

When she died, I was eerily calm — relieved that her suffering was over. I felt no profound sense of sadness and, like a good psychologist, I told myself that I had no doubt dealt with her death by *anticipatory grieving* (literally grieving in anticipation of a loss). For months, I went about business as usual, keeping busy with both my practice and my family obligations. I thought I was happy — by all accounts, my life was in a good place, despite this traumatic loss.

Then Christmas came, and I took a few days off to celebrate the end of a "good" year and relax a little before the upcoming one. It didn't take long to realize that I had completely misread my own emotions. The first morning I had off, after my wife and kids left for the day, I found myself weeping like a baby "for no apparent reason." I tried everything I could to get a grip on my emotions. Finally, I called a psychiatrist friend of mine, who quickly assessed that I was in a rather fragile state. That, it turned out, was the beginning of a bout of severe depression that lasted for five years. And, here I thought I was so happy.

Charisma and heart health

One study showed that charismatic Type A's — those who were more emotionally expressive — were healthier than non-charismatic Type A's. Interestingly, those who smiled more had less evidence of peripheral artery disease. It was the tight-lipped Type A's who were most at risk. This may, at least in part, explain why the vast majority of Type A's do *not* have heart attacks — they're protected by their smiles.

The outward appearance of happiness — a smile — often masks negative emotions such as fear, sadness, and uncertainty, all of which are either *suppressed* (you're aware of the feelings but don't want to openly express them) or *repressed* (even *you* are unaware of your true feelings).

The charismatic smile

Some people have a smile that lights up the room. They have a smile that attracts others around them much like a flame attracts moths. It's simply irresistible. You can't turn away from it and you find yourself caught up in their emotion.

These people have *charisma* — the ability to inspire others. Charisma is an admirable trait, something everyone would like to have, but few of us do. You can usually spot charisma in political leaders — everyone from John Kennedy to Winston Churchill had charisma. The prophets of the Old Testament were charismatic, as were Jesus and Mohammed. Social reformers like Martin Luther King, Jr., and Mahatma Gandhi were charismatic, as was Mother Teresa.

We're hooked by charismatic people the minute they walk into our world. Even before they speak, their facial expressions (always a smile, never a frown) convey an abiding sense of self-confidence, enthusiasm, personal magnetism, positive energy, and spiritedness. Charismatic individuals express emotions in such a way that it excites others. Their smile becomes your smile; their joy becomes your joy.

If you want to know if you're charismatic, answer the following questions yes or no:

- When you laugh, do you laugh with abandonment — loudly and freely?
- Are you outgoing around strangers?
- Does your facial expression tell it all?

 ✔ Are you comfortable being the center of attention?

 ✔ Are you a hugger — especially when you like someone?

 ✔ Do people often tell you they're "touched" by things you say?

 ✔ Do you have trouble keeping still when the music starts playing?

 ✔ Has anyone ever told you that you'd be a good actor?

The more questions you answered yes to, the more charisma you have.

The contemptuous smile

The contemptuous smile is, without doubt, the most destructive type. It conveys both anger and, even more important, the message that the person on the other end of the smile is worthless and disgusting. It's the type of smile a person uses to put someone else in his place and to remind him just how lowly and disrespected he is.

Brandon's subordinates are all too familiar with the contemptuous smile — they see it every day. Brandon is the classic Type A personality. He's impatient, hard-driving, and isn't satisfied unless things are done perfectly. Problem is: Brandon sees himself as superior and everyone else as fools. To say that other employees who work with him loathe him would be putting it mildly. Brandon doesn't verbally criticize his fellow workers — it's the look on his face that tells them how he feels.

This is also the type of smile that goes a long way toward destroying marriages (see Chapter 20).

The real deal

The Duchenne (pronounced doo-*shen*) smile tells you when a person is really happy. It's the real deal — natural, unforced, authentic, unrehearsed, automatic, involuntary, spontaneous, and always signaling a feeling of joy. With this smile, not only do the muscles around the mouth turn upward in the shape of a grin but the muscles around the eyes contract as well — your eyelids droop and there is a wrinkling around your eyes. These changes around the eyes are what distinguish the Duchenne smile from all others.

As early as 6 months of age, infants display the Duchenne smile. Typically, it appears when they're interacting with familiar people — for example, parents — and is not seen when they're in contact with strangers. A mother's

Deciding what you want others to see

During a sabbatical year in the Netherlands, I got to know a medical psychologist who had made a life study of the history of medicine in Europe. The way he went about it was intriguing. He found that the earliest hospitals had a scene carved in stone in the transom over the front door that depicted, in exact detail, what you would see if you went inside. By dating these stone structures, he could then trace the development of hospital life over time.

Your smile does the same thing. It shows others what's going on inside you. If you have an angry smile, you're obviously full of anger, hostility, and resentment. A lying smile means you're chock-full of half-truths and outright lies. A contemptuous smile means that in your mind, you feel superior to everyone else around you — you're important, they're not. A Duchenne smile says to the world, "I'm full of joy!"

Decide how you want others to see you. Do you want to be seen as a liar, a contemptuous jerk, or someone who is conceited? Or do you want to be seen as someone with charisma and who is genuinely enjoying life?

The way to eliminate the negative smiles is to change what's going on inside of you. If you're angry, you need to find a way to deal with your anger — check out *Anger Management For Dummies* (Wiley). If you're depressed, try *Depression For Dummies,* by Laura L. Smith, PhD, and Charles H. Elliott, PhD (Wiley).

voice or the mere sight of her face will elicit this type of smile, signaling that the child feels a sense of pleasure and contentment. Parents smile back, thus beginning the process of attachment or emotional bonding that is not only crucial for early survival but also serves as a foundation for the development of a healthy personality.

The next time you see someone smiling, look at her eyes and decide for yourself if this is a genuinely happy smile or not. It's the only true test.

Empowering Yourself: Smiling Because You Want To

Think about what a smile does for you. It attracts people. It says to the world "I'm a happy, confident, competent, satisfied person." It makes it easier to build a support network — people who will rally to your side when adversity strikes. It helps you transcend difficult times. It lets others know at a glance that you're optimistic (Chapter 5) and conscientious (Chapter 7). It conveys a feeling of power — potency, vitality, and hardiness (Chapter 6).

If you portray false smiles — lying smiles, angry smiles, smiles that try to hide how miserable you feel — you do so because you *have to* in order to keep dealing with the world in a dishonest way. These types of smiles, in effect, disempower you because the world can never know your true self. Instead, smile because you *want to* because of all the positive benefits that will come your way.

If you have a family, one of the shared benefits of a smile is that it says without words, "We're in this together," which is the mantra of a happy family (Chapter 19).

Identifying who or what makes you smile

I don't want to say that most people are clueless when it comes to knowing who and what makes them happy, but it *is* true that people's understanding of the relationship between life circumstances and positive emotion is not as precise as it should be.

One simple, easy way to identify your particular sources of happiness is to rummage through old photographs and cull out the ones where you're smiling. Some of those will no doubt be pictures of family gatherings where everyone is posing for the camera — looking happy for the camera's sake whether you feel that way or not. But other pictures may capture moments of genuine happiness, as evidenced by the Duchenne smile on your face.

Examine those photographs carefully and ask yourself what the common threads are that connect them. For example, maybe whenever you're in the company of certain people or whenever you're engaged in some particular activity, you're smiling. What you're looking for here is a pattern — something that repeats itself. (In every picture where I'm with my wife, my children, my dogs, or special friends, I have a smile on my face — except for those years where I was struggling with depression, and then nothing made me smile.)

These pictures may come in handy in another way. If you have them scattered throughout your home or office, each time you look at them you'll momentarily reconnect with the memory of those happy occasions — and, that will bring a smile to your face.

When you review your life through personal photographs, you may not find many, if any, photographs where you're smiling — posed or otherwise. Over the years, I've had more than a few clients come in for therapy when they looked at all their friends and saw them happy and enjoying life, and realized that they've never felt that way. They're hoping I can tell them why.

And, usually I can. To begin with I check to see of any of those roadblocks to happiness I list in Chapter 22 are present — for example, are they a vindictive type person or do they have a positive history of drug abuse? We explore the issue of temperament and talk about whether their parents were happy people. And, one-by-one, we address all the other issues covered in this book to see where they're falling short. (To be honest, I'd much rather work with a client who's short on happiness than one that is long on anger — it's easier and more fun!)

Face-making 101: Start with a smile and go from there

People are trained to think that emotions lead to actions — in other words, the outward expression of those inner feelings. And that's true. But it's equally true that actions can lead to emotions. An irritated individual who starts yelling and flailing about like a wild man will quickly find himself experiencing much more intense anger. If he doesn't want to accelerate to the point of rage, he needs to talk in a reasonable tone of voice without all the aggressive gestures. Talking about something sad that has happened to another person can bring on a spontaneous feeling of sadness within yourself. And, believe it or not, you can make yourself happy simply by making a happy face.

Put a smile on your face and hold it for 20 or 30 seconds and then relax your face. Repeat this smiling exercise 10 to 20 times and see if you don't suddenly feel more positive. Better yet, do this exercise in front of a mirror so that you can experience what psychologists call *facial feedback* — that is, your emotions begin to conform to your facial features. Assume that somewhere in your psyche there is this thing called happiness; the smile you're putting on your face is just a way of letting it out.

The smile exercise is no different than any other form of exercise. The more you do it, the easier it gets. What begins as contrived eventually becomes natural.

Nobody in my family gets angry

A young man in his late 30s came to counseling and when I asked him what his problem was, he said, "I don't really know. I just don't seem to feel anything. I have lots of success in my life, a pretty girlfriend, a nice car, but nothing excites me. I'm just sort of blah!"

Without much to go on, I asked some questions about his early childhood and his parents — for example, "What were your mom and dad like when they got angry?" His answer surprised me: "Oh, they never got angry." Before I could ask another question, he said, "They might go for days not speaking to one another, sometimes weeks, but I never saw them angry." In other words, his parents were so angry that they literally couldn't speak to one another. He had grown up in a house of silence — where it turned out no one showed even the slightest trace of emotion, positive or negative. He never saw his parents openly angry and he never saw them happy.

No wonder he didn't feel anything as he went about his day-to-day adult life. No one had taught him how to feel, how to be an emotional creature. So, that's what I did. In the beginning, I had to show him a variety of emotional faces and ask him to pick out the one(s) that fit whatever situation he and I were talking about. Each facial expression signified a different type feeling. In effect, I was teaching him emotional fluency — using words to describe emotions — something his parents had failed to do long ago. Later on, we began to explore why he felt the emotions he did, so that he could begin to relate emotional experiences to the people and things around him. I taught him not to be judgmental about his feelings — there's no right or wrong about happiness or sadness. I taught him how to use all this information about himself to navigate his way through life just like his friends. In the end, he was anything but blah.

Part IV
Striking the Right Balance

The 5th Wave   By Rich Tennant

"Smile or lose the 'Life is good' shirt."

In this part . . .

I tackle the challenge of finding a happy medium along five dimensions of your lifestyle. The overriding message in this part is that happiness is never found at the extremes of life — it involves a healthy balance, for example, between work and play, structure and freedom, or selfishness and generosity. The emphasis is on ways to behave.

This is not one of those mind-over-matter discussions you often find in self-help books — suggesting, for example, that you can literally *think* your way into happiness. You can't! What you *can* do are things such as generate some uplifting experiences to offset the hassles, engineer some positive rituals in your daily routine, work toward becoming more Type B, discover how not to be lonely even when you find yourself alone, and become less codependent.

A cautionary note: If you start doing the things outlined in this part of the book, you may begin to appreciate just how unique a personality you are, how much fun life can be when you make yourself part of the equation, and how reenergized and reinvigorated you feel as a result. Are you ready for that? If so, read on!

Chapter 13

Hassles versus Uplifts

· ·

In This Chapter

▶ Knowing when to sweat the small stuff

▶ Understanding the difference between major and minor stress

▶ Discovering why uplifts are so important

▶ Calculating your uplifts-to-hassles ratio

▶ Avoiding depression

· ·

*J*onathan woke up looking forward to a relaxed, productive day puttering around his apartment. He didn't expect to be hassled or end up in a foul mood, but he was. No sooner had he awakened than his wife announced that it was sleeting rain outside and he would have to take her to work because she'd forgotten to fill up her gas tank the night before. Jonathan said, "Fine," thinking he would still have plenty of time to get to his 9 a.m. massage appointment, which he was really looking forward to. What he couldn't anticipate was that he would get stuck in a traffic jam for over 40 minutes. He arrived late for the massage only to learn that the massage therapist had left for the day. As if that wasn't enough, on the way out of the gym he noticed that one of his tires was almost flat. It was only 10:30 a.m. and already Jonathan concluded, "I don't think this is going to be a good day!"

What Jonathan needed was an *uplift* — some small pleasure in life to offset the multitude of stresses he had encountered. He soon found it when he stopped at his favorite local restaurant, had his morning coffee, and was happily greeted by staff and customers alike. "The world is right again," he thought to himself as he lingered over his newspaper enjoying one last cup of java.

In this chapter, I not only emphasize how the small stresses of everyday life can transform our mood and affect your health, but more important, I show you what you can do to balance out this stress and actually end up in a happy frame of mind.

Knowing When to Sweat the Small Stuff and When to Let It Go

Most people make two mistakes when it comes to being *hassled* — experiencing the small, micro-stresses that come their way each and every day just as surely as the sun rises in the east and sets in the west:

- ✔ **Because these stresses are not catastrophic, earth-shaking, life-altering events and circumstances, people think of them as unimportant and not worthy of their time or attention.** I mean, after all, no one dies from a flat tire or a missed appointment — right?

- ✔ **People treat these minor stresses the same as *major* stresses (such as being fired from a job, getting a divorce, learning that a friend has cancer).** In the end, they see stress as stress, no matter what the magnitude.

The truth, it turns out, is somewhere in the middle, and finding that balance between these two extremes is how you get to true happiness.

Sweating the small stuff

Contrary to conventional wisdom, the big stresses in your life are *not* what keep you from finding happiness — the little stresses are what do that, not individually, but collectively. Little stresses pile up and, at some point, they begin to take their toll. This piling up of small stresses happens easily, because most people ignore the potential for hassles to do harm. They absorb the small hassles like a sponge, until they can't hold anymore. Think of this as death by a thousand paper cuts.

The other reason people don't sweat the small stuff is that the small stuff is part of their daily lives, not some unusual circumstance that infrequently comes their way. In effect, people consider these micro-stresses normal — just part of life.

But guess what? Medical research has shown that the impact of little, petty annoyances in the long run is far greater than that of the occasional big stress. And the more hassled you are, the less happy you tend to be.

The worst kind of hassles are those that are chronic — ones you experience repeatedly as part of an otherwise routine day. The grouchy neighbor who gives you the evil eye every day when you walk your dog past her house. The secretary whose first words to you when you come to work each morning are, "Have you seen the obituaries — so-and-so died of cancer?" Or the friend you regularly eat lunch with who always find some way to get you to pick up the check. Sound familiar?

In the "Looking at How Hassled and Uplifted You Are" section, later in this chapter, I show you how to calculate when you're in what I call the "red zone" as far as hassles go.

Letting the small stuff go

You can't let go of the events that stress you, but you can let go of the physical and psychological *impact* that these events have on you. For example, in the introduction to this chapter, I tell the story of Jonathan. Jonathan couldn't do anything about the sleet or the flat tire, but he was able to let go of his initial negative thought — "I don't think this is going to be a good day" — and replace it with a more positive thought: "The world is right again."

Uplifting experiences lessen the impact of stress. They do this by transforming:

- Tension into relaxation
- Negative thoughts into positive thoughts
- Pessimism into optimism (see Chapter 5)
- Agitation into calm
- Displeasure into pleasure
- Anger into love
- Sadness into joy
- Alienation into a feeling of being connected
- Chaos into harmony

Looking at How Hassled and Uplifted You Are

I'm betting you don't realize just how hassled you are, partly because you tend to ignore and trivialize the small stuff, but, even more important, because you have no way to measure how much stress you're under. Well, that all changes now.

Look over the following list of minor stresses (or hassles) that people commonly experience and circle any of those that you've experienced *within the past two weeks.*

- ✔ I misplaced or lost something important.
- ✔ I didn't have enough money to pay a bill on time.
- ✔ I felt like I had too many responsibilities.
- ✔ I was interrupted while I was working on something important.
- ✔ I had to wait in line at a store or bank.
- ✔ Unexpected company showed up on my doorstep.
- ✔ I had to fill out a lot of bureaucratic forms.
- ✔ I had a cold.
- ✔ Unexpected bad weather hit my town.
- ✔ My car had trouble starting first thing in the morning.
- ✔ My neighbors were noisy.
- ✔ I got poor service in a restaurant.
- ✔ I was late for an important meeting.
- ✔ A friend forgot our planned lunch date.
- ✔ I spilled something on my clothes.
- ✔ I found gum stuck to the bottom of my shoe.
- ✔ I forgot my doggy bag in a restaurant.
- ✔ I forgot my computer password.
- ✔ I forgot a haircut appointment.
- ✔ I didn't have change for a parking meter.

How many hassles did you circle? Your hassle score should be between 0 and 20. (The odds of your getting a 0 are remote — no one lives a totally stress-free life!) Write down your hassle score here:

My hassle score = _____

Now, do the same thing for uplifts. Look at the following list of events and circumstances that typically bring peace, joy, happiness, and satisfaction to most people and circle any of those that you've experienced *within the past two weeks.*

✔ I received an unexpected compliment.

✔ A friendly neighbor visited.

✔ I heard from an old friend I hadn't talked to in a while.

✔ I found something I thought I had lost.

✔ I found something I really wanted on sale.

✔ I unexpectedly had some free time on my hands.

✔ A friend treated me to lunch.

✔ I spent a few quiet moments in a church, temple, or mosque.

✔ I spent quality time with my pet.

✔ I received a bouquet of flowers from an admirer.

✔ I got a hug.

✔ I found something unique to add to my collectibles.

✔ I beat my best friend at our favorite sport.

✔ I finished a project ahead of time.

✔ I started a new hobby.

✔ I worked in my flower garden.

✔ I saw a great movie.

✔ I went to the latest exhibit at the local art museum.

✔ I socialized with friends and family.

✔ Someone wishes me a "blessed day."

How many uplifts did you circle? Your uplifts score should be between 0 and 20. Write down your uplift score here:

My uplift score = _____

It goes without saying that people have their own idea of what constitutes a hassle and uplift. One person may find "unexpected company" a hassle, but it could be your idea of a lot of fun. The lists I've used here are typical of those used by psychologists, but you can make your own lists if you want. Write down all the hassles — minor irritants - that have happened to you in the past two weeks and do the same for uplifts — little pleasures. How many of each did you come up with?

Life is always in flux. Some days, weeks, and months are more hassle-free than others, and uplifting experiences tend to come and go. That's why it's good to recheck your scores from time to time to see how you're doing.

What's crucial to finding happiness is not how hassled or uplifted you are, but rather the balance between the two. This balance I call your *Uplifted-to-Hassles Ratio* (UHR). To calculate your UHR, all you need to do is take your uplifts score and divide it by your hassles score. For example, if your uplifts score is a 4 and your hassles score is a 10, your UHR would be 4 ÷ 10 = 0.40. If your uplifts score is 12 and your hassles score is 6, your UHR is 12 ÷ 6 = 2. The higher your U-HR score, the better. (You can make this calculation whether you're using the scores you obtained from the lists I provided or your own self-generated lists — it's all the same.) Generally speaking, any UHR score less than 1 is a problem, because it suggests that you're definitely *not* at a happy medium when it comes to hassles versus uplifts.

Avoiding hassles is difficult. The easiest way to up your UHR score is to increase your uplifts.

How do you increase your uplifts? Simple: You do little things that bring you pleasure. You don't just wait passively to be uplifted — you make it happen! For example, you can lift your spirits by:

- Treating yourself to a delicious dessert in the middle of the afternoon.
- Spending your lunch hour sunning yourself on a park bench.
- Taking 20 minutes to meditate.
- Taking time to feed the birds who visit your yard before going off to work.
- Watching children at play.
- Daydreaming about positive experiences you've had in the past.
- Giving yourself permission to have that extra cup of coffee before you join the "rat race."
- Enjoying a glass of wine at an outdoor café.
- Listening to some of your favorite songs while you drive from point A to point B.
- Reading a magazine article about something that interests you.

These are all things that you can initiate. They don't depend on what other people are willing or able to do that might please you. They're things that you have control over.

One of the things I liked most about the year I spent in Holland was the way the Dutch people celebrate birthdays. When it's your birthday, you get up in the morning and announce to everyone "Today's my birthday!" And,

Uplifts and major stress

Both in their early 40s, Mattie and her husband, Sam, found themselves sandwiched between the normal duties of working and raising two children and at the same time being caretakers for Mattie's mother, who was in a nearby nursing home paralyzed from a stroke. Mattie was an only child, so the burdensome responsibility of trying to reduce her mother's suffering fell squarely on her shoulders. She and her husband were religious in their efforts to minister to her mother each evening after they had worked all day, fed the kids, and left them home to do their homework and entertain themselves. They tried to be in good spirits despite the depressing nursing home environment and they reminded themselves (and each other) that this was a labor of love. But, the days were long and they found themselves exhausted as they headed from the nursing home to their own home — where they would then have to pick up their responsibilities as parents before finally heading for bed.

"It was a tough grind for those four months before mother died," admitted Mattie, "but we have no regrets. What helped us most was the fact that we stopped along the way home each night and got ourselves an ice cream cone at the mall." That simple little pleasure (or uplift) went a long way toward helping these two nice people keep their sanity through one of the more difficult times of their lives. Sam summed it up best when he said, "Don't underestimate the power of an ice cream cone!"

If you're not yet convinced of the survival value of life's everyday pleasures, read Viktor Frankl's masterful book *Man's Search For Meaning,* in which he describes how a few small pleasures — an extra scrap of food, a beautiful skyline — helped him survive the Holocaust in a concentration camp and actually granted him a few blissful moments of happiness. You'll find all the proof you need in this small but powerful book.

you keep doing that throughout the entire day everywhere you go. Also, you bring your own sweets to the office to let everyone share in your day of celebration. It's not like here in America, where we depend on others — family, friends, and co-workers — to remember what day it is and to make sure we enjoy it. The Dutch leave nothing to chance — they make sure their birthday is an uplifting experience for one and all.

Another way you can enhance your UHR score is to do something to uplift the lives of others. Instead of waiting for someone to hug you, go find someone to hug. Instead of hoping that your friendly neighbor will drop over, be the friendly neighbor and pay her a visit. Sure, you'll feel good if a friend buys you lunch — but you'll also feel good if you treat him. Any kindness you extend elevates your UHR score.

Uplifts and depression

A study at Texas Tech University revealed that students' hassle scores were positively correlated with scores on a standardized test of depression — the more hassles a person reported, the greater the degree of depression. Interestingly, they found no link between uplifts scores and depression. In other words, having lots of little pleasures in your life won't *by itself* prevent depression. However, when these investigators examined the relationship between the *ratio* of hassles and uplifts to depression, they noted that uplifts seem to play a protective role in keeping depression symptoms at a minimum — in other words, uplifts don't cause you to be happy; they buffer you from unhappiness.

Here's a case in point: Alex had been seriously depressed for some time now and he was doing everything he could think of to improve his mental health. He was taking the antidepressant drug his psychiatrist had prescribed and he never missed his weekly therapy appointment, but his mood remained steadfastly negative. He felt useless, hopeless, and grossly inadequate when it came to coping with all the challenges in his life — those associated with running a business, being a husband, having two children, taking care of elderly parents, and so on. To say that Alex was unhappy would be an understatement!

One day, as he was reviewing all the distressful circumstances of the previous week, his therapist interrupted (something he rarely did) to inquire about what Alex planned to do the following weekend. Without thinking, Alex began to check off all the stressful obligations he had to his family — errands that needed to be run, chores around the house, attending his kids' sports events — all the while looking sad and lacking in energy. His therapist interrupted again, suggesting that he wasn't really interested in what Alex had planned to do for all these other people — he wanted to know what Alex planned to do for himself over the weekend.

Alex went silent. He couldn't answer immediately because he wasn't used to thinking about himself — his needs — and things he could do to bring pleasure into his life directly without first bringing pleasure into someone else's life. His therapist said, "Maybe one of the many reasons you find yourself so depressed is that your life is out of balance — all stress and no pleasure. You know, Alex, the human brain needs a little pleasure once in a while, just like your physical body needs oxygen, food, and water."

Alex thought about what his therapist said and realized it made a lot of sense, at least as much sense as taking a pill for depression every day. So, he began — on his own — to seek out the little pleasures of everyday life that he has long forgotten. He started making opportunities to meet a friend for lunch, volunteered in his community, and went back to church (ever since he was a child, Alex had always found Sunday sermons comforting and uplifting).

Alex was learning that therapy isn't so much about healing the mind as it is about helping people get back on the right track — the one that leads to happiness and peace of mind. The more Alex fed his brain these little bits of pleasure, the better he felt, and the better he felt the more he wanted to uplift his own life as well as the lives of others. He was now in a positive cycle that would go a long way toward unwinding him from a devastating mood disorder.

Remember: Depression is a serious medical condition. If you've been diagnosed with depression, be sure to talk to your doctor about your treatment, and *never* stop taking a medication you've been prescribed without consulting with your doctor first.

Not sure if you may be suffering from depression? Here are some common signs and symptoms:

✔ Persistent feelings of sadness

✔ Spontaneous crying spells (or feeling like you need to cry but can't)

✔ Loss of appetite

✔ Feeling alone even in the company of others

✔ Thoughts of harming yourself

✔ Waking up in the middle of the night and being unable to get back to sleep

✔ Increased irritability

✔ Difficulty concentrating or remembering things

✔ Fatigue unrelated to activity

✔ A declining disinterest in sexual activity

If you've experienced four or more of these elements of depression, talk to your doctor or a mental-health professional. Depression is treatable, and there's no reason to delay seeking help.

Chapter 14

Structure versus Freedom

● ●

In This Chapter

▶ Moving on with your life

▶ Enjoying doing nothing

▶ Understanding the importance of rituals

▶ Planning and un-planning

▶ Maintaining a sense of purpose

● ●

*T*here is no question that human beings need structure — somewhere to go and something to do — throughout their lives, but it is equally true that they need a certain measure of freedom as well. Too much or too little of either makes for an unhappy life.

Consider the story of Brad. Before he was injured at the age of 46, Brad was a happy man. He enjoyed working — so much so that he always had two or more jobs at one time. He was a union steward, enjoying the respect of his fellow employees, and a highly skilled tradesman. With only a high school education, he had raised four healthy children, who were now married with families of their own. He was in exceptionally good health for his age, still married to his high school sweetheart, and debt free. Brad had a lot to be grateful for and he knew it. But then he injured his back, and all that changed in a heartbeat.

His doctors were unable to restore him to a pain-free life. Everything that had meant anything to Brad — that had given him a sense of purpose and identity — was gone, leaving him bitter and depressed. At his lowest point, Brad seriously considered suicide, but he decided otherwise. He also decided at that critical moment to find a way to once again enjoy life, to be productive, and to reconnect with the world around him. Twenty years later, Brad finds himself what I would call a "happy pain patient."

He gradually restructured his life — building a new house, traveling, developing new hobbies, and hosting a weekly poker game for the guys — so that he now has less free time to sit around and dwell on his pain and more opportunity to make a positive impact on the world around him. And that's what this chapter is all about.

Living a Life of Purpose

The subtitle of Rick Warren's best-selling book *The Purpose Driven Life: What on Earth Am I Here For?* begs a question that is key to achieving happiness. What is the point of your existence? What is your purpose? What are you called to do? How is the world better off for your being here? What will the world miss when you're gone?

Living a purposeful life doesn't necessarily mean that life is static, unchanging. In other words, your purpose — why you're here — stays the same, but the way you spend your time can change dramatically.

For example, at the beginning of my career, I was a dedicated academician, heavily involved in training students, and I was conducting research projects to enlighten the world about the relationships between psychology and medicine. I often spoke at national conferences and I was a prolific author. Then one day I quit all that and entered the world of private practice where I spent my time trying to ease the suffering of troubled souls within my community. No more white coats, no more entourage of students following me like little ducklings, no more applause at scientific meetings — just me, my clients, and the sanctuary of my small office. And now I spend most of my time writing self-help books and flying around the country conducting workshops for all sorts of professionals interested in things like stress, anger, and happiness. The activities and structure of my professional life have changed over the years, but the purpose has not: I am an educator — first, last, and always.

What is *your* purpose in life? Do you have one yet or are you still looking? Instead of searching for something — some task, activity, career — that you think will make you happy, turn it around and think about those times when you're the happiest and ask yourself, "What was I doing at the time?"

Restructuring Your Life after a Major Life Change

The journey of life has many twists and turns. One minute you think you know what your purpose in life is, and then everything changes. You get comfortable with one type of structure — having a career, being a parent — and suddenly you're out of a job. Then what do you do? Basically, you have two choices: You can sit and mourn for the rest of your life, or you can restructure your life into something different yet meaningful. The choice is yours.

Moving on after graduation

When I was a kid, moving on after graduation from high school was easier than it is today — your choices were limited. Parents didn't invite their kids to hang around for a year or two while they were trying to find themselves. Nowadays, that's all changed. Psychologists suggest that there's even a new stage of development now called *emerging adulthood,* which is basically somewhere between adolescence and adulthood. In effect, it's growing up but not moving on.

Assuming that you might be one of those many young people who, after graduating college, finds herself back home with your parents, here are some suggestions for restructuring your life:

- ✔ **Be clear what it is that you expect of yourself now that you are back at home.** Do you expect to act the same as you did when you last lived there? Or, do you see yourself as someone who is capable of living a more independent life now than when you finished high school? *Remember:* The more you expect of yourself, the less your parents have to expect of you.

- ✔ **Talk with your parents about what you (and they) see as obstacles to you moving on with your life.** Are economics an issue? Are there sufficient opportunities for employment in your home community? Do you feel like your parents expect you to be their "child" again just because you're back home?

- ✔ **Imagine that you're living on your own and set up a daily routine that you would follow were that the case.** Think of your time at home as practice — a dress rehearsal — for what comes next in your life. If you would fix your own meals, do your own laundry, do your own ironing if you were on your own, then do these same things while you're at home.

- ✔ **Assume as much responsibility as possible.** If you're working, help out with the household expenses — buy some groceries, offer to pay a little rent, and chip in on the utilities. Also think about ways to help out that don't cost anything, for example, mowing the lawn, washing your mom's car, taking the family pet for a walk.

- ✔ **Set a specific time limit for how long you plan to remain at home.** Better to say to yourself (and your parents) "It'll help if I can stay with you for the next six months" than "I plan to be here for a while." The more vague your time limit, the greater the chances that you'll be with your folks longer than you (or they) want you to be.

- ✔ **Set some specific goals for yourself that will move you forward.** For example, decide where you want to live once you leave home for good. Do you plan to live in the same town only have a place of your own?

> Or, do you see yourself living elsewhere? Start checking out housing possibilities so you have some concrete idea of what's available and what it's likely to cost you. Do a computer search of job opportunities in whatever city you're planning to move to eventually. Work on your resume and make contacts with friends from high school or college that live where you're planning to move.
>
> ✓ **Let your parents know that it's important that you move on to the next stage of your life so that they can do the same.** That way you'll both be happy!

Filling the empty nest

Another major life change occurs when children grow up and leave home for good. Parents who have devoted the lion's share of their time and energy to their kids suddenly find themselves with a big empty space in their lives. Some handle that change well — others do not.

Kay is lost without her daughter, who is 35 years old and lives in another state. If her daughter doesn't call her everyday by 5 p.m., she gets anxious and begins calling her daughter's friends to see where she is. Rather than be embarrassed, her daughter has learned to check in with mom — hardly what she expected life to be like when she left home three years ago.

Kay is suffering from *empty nest syndrome.* For more than two decades, her daughter was her life — and now that life is gone forever, and Kay has done nothing to replace it.

Missy, too, has a daughter in her 30s living out of state. She doesn't see her as much as she'd like, but Missy is happy that she's enjoying the fact that her daughter is independent. When Missy doesn't hear from her daughter, she assumes she's busy and Missy understands. And what's Missy doing in between phone calls from her daughter? She's busy with her own interests — she does things with her friends, she travels. . . . In fact, Missy's daughter sometimes has trouble getting in touch with her, and Missy tells her daughter, "Honey, your father and I have our own life now — get used to it!"

If you're a parent like Kay, who needs to restructure your life, here are a few tips on how to proceed:

> ✓ **Remind yourself that the real purpose of being a parent is to do everything you can to ensure that your child will grow into an independent adult and them recognize that you've actually accomplished that.**
>
> ✓ **Reconnect with friends your own age that you may have lost contact with all those years you were busy parenting.** See if you can plug back into some activities — golf foursome, bridge group — that involve having fun but don't involve kids.

✔ **If you weren't working while you raised your children, find yourself a job — doesn't have to be full-time; part-time will do.** And, don't be afraid to try something new — if you used to be a nurse, but haven't done that for years, maybe you'd enjoy working in retail for a change.

✔ **If you're married, get reacquainted with your spouse. Start dating again, in effect.** Go off on some long weekends or vacations to places you haven't been to in years, but used to enjoy, or better yet some place you've both always wanted to go but couldn't because of the kids.

✔ **Develop some new interests that you can share with your kids when you see them.** Surprise them — let them know that they're not the only ones who are growing and moving on in life.

✔ **Find someone else to (unofficially) parent.** My wife and I spend a lot of time with several young couples about the same ages of our children. They seem to enjoy having some older folks around to seek advice from and encourage them during times when things aren't going smoothly — and, we enjoy being around all that youthful energy.

Ensuring a happy retirement

A 62-year-old man came to see me for counseling, and our conversation went like this:

Gentry: Why are you here? How can I help you?

Client: My wife and my doctor thought I needed to talk to someone. I'm having trouble getting out of bed in the morning and starting my day, and I'm also having some periodic chest pain.

Gentry: Okay. Tell me a little about yourself.

Client: Well, I'm retired. I got a buyout package last year that was too good to pass up. That's pretty much it. My wife and I get along, our house is paid off, and I'm in pretty good health.

Gentry: I see. Had you planned to retire early?

Client: No. I'd planned to work until I was 65, but this came up unexpectedly.

Gentry: So, what are you doing with yourself now?

Client: I told you — I'm retired!

Gentry: I heard that, but what I want to know is what exactly do you do with your time? You know, activities.

Client: I play golf three day a week.

Gentry: Anything else?

Client: I play tennis with some guys twice a week.

Gentry: Anything else?

Client: Not really. I read the paper every morning, but otherwise just tennis and golf. And occasionally we go out to eat with a group of friends.

I met with the man four or five times, explaining to him that he was showing signs of an impending depression and that he needed to get more involved in life. All he would say each time I made a suggestion was, "But I'm retired!"

After those first four or five visits, he disappeared, only to reappear on my appointment book several months later. Once again, he came in because his wife and doctor felt he needed counseling. He was beginning to experience intermittent panic attacks and his unexplained chest pain continued. When I asked him what was going on in his life, again he said simply, "I'm retired — a little golf and tennis and that's about it." I repeated what I had told him before about restructuring his life, he resisted, and again he disappeared after a few visits.

A few months later, he came in to see me again. As soon as he sat down on my couch, I said "Look, if we're going to have the same conversation we did the last two times you were here, why don't you just get up and leave now?" To my surprise, he wanted to stay and talk about what he needed to do to be happier. The good news: Today, he's busy spending a lot of time with his grandchildren, traveling with his wife, and participating in a citizens group that loves to go to city hall and bug the town fathers — along with playing golf and tennis. He looks forward to getting up in the morning and there's no more chest pain.

A healthy retirement should be a time of *structured freedom* — a time when you can live life on your own terms, but where you have somewhere to go and something to do each day.

If you're thinking about retiring, have you considered how you'll spend your free time? Do you have any hobbies or special interests outside of work? Do you have enough projects to keep you busy? Are there things that you and your spouse like to do together — shared interests? How are you fixed for friends? Having free time is one thing; loneliness is quite another (see Chapter 22). These are the kinds of questions you need to be asking yourself *before* you retire.

If you're already retired and are still trying to "find a fit" in this new stage of life, my advice is the same: You have to find somewhere to go, something (meaningful) to do, and someone to do it with. I know a retired engineer who works at a golf course on weekends selling buckets of golf balls at the driving range and making sure everyone sticks to their assigned tee times. And, there's the lawyer who volunteers at the local hospital, wheeling sick patients from place to place. As for me, since I love writing and books, I'm seriously thinking about getting a part-time job in a small, local bookstore after I retire — I can't think of a better way to spend my time.

Recognizing the Importance of Rituals

Much of everyday life is made up of *rituals* — established, predictable, patterned behaviors that structure the day. There are morning rituals (brushing your teeth, showering, reading the newspaper), midday rituals (everything from the so-called "power lunch" to a simple baloney sandwich in your office), and evening rituals (a cocktail or two, dinner at 6 p.m., a few minutes of intimate conversation with your spouse, and — if you're lucky — sex).

Rituals are a form of structure that actually make life flow more easily. They're mindless — you do them without thinking. Perhaps most important of all, they orient you as to where you are and what you should be doing. Rituals are like an invisible watch — if you're taking a shower, it must be morning! Without rituals, every day is a new day full of unpredictability, uncertainty, and the possibility of unhappiness.

Here are some examples of what I'm talking about — rituals you can incorporate into your life (if you haven't already):

- Exercising first thing in the morning
- Having morning coffee with friends at a local restaurant
- Sitting for a few minutes of quiet contemplation, in meditation or prayer
- Getting a professional massage once a month
- Browsing through your favorite bookstore every Saturday morning
- Checking in via e-mail with loved ones once a day
- Enjoying a quiet cup of tea while reading the newspaper
- Taking an afternoon nap
- Enjoying some quality, one-on-one time with your pet
- Writing letters to long-distance friends once a week
- Watching your favorite evening news show on TV
- Attending religious services regularly
- Reading for a few minutes at bedtime
- Spending five minutes every day reflecting on all the things you have to be grateful for

---

No exceptions, please!

A dear friend of mine has been taking friends to college football games for years and everything about the day is a ritual. We leave at the *same* time, stop at the *same* gas station on the way to the game, park in the *same* spot, eat at the *same* restaurant, and stop at the *same* gas station on the way home. Once, he let his friends talk him into eating at a different restaurant and his team lost the game — and that was the last time there was an exception to the rule.

Don't become a slave to rituals — otherwise, they become tedious. If something more interesting comes along at the same time you normally take your afternoon nap, go for it! You can always nap tomorrow.

Knowing When to Plan and When Not To

Lately, it seems as if human beings need a plan for everything. Fewer and fewer people can get through the day without a BlackBerry or PalmPilot. Parents plan for their children's college education when the kids are still in kindergarten. There are retirement planners, travel planners, wedding planners, and even people who — for a fee — will help you plan the perfect birthday party for your 5-year-old.

But as with many things in life, you can have too much of a good thing. Planning becomes excessive or unbalanced when every second is accounted for well in advance, leaving no room whatsoever for the three Ss: surprises, spontaneity, and serendipity:

- **Surprise:** Everyday life seldom goes exactly according to plan. There's always a surprise or two in store for you somewhere along the way. Actually, surprises are what make one day different from the next. If your schedule is jam packed, any surprise — even a happy one — will be seen as an intrusion and will leave you feeling stressed.

- **Spontaneity:** Sometimes it pays to act in the moment without a whole lot of thoughtful consideration. If a friend calls and wants you to meet them at Starbucks for coffee, don't think about whether you should or not, just say YES!

- **Serendipity:** The word *serendipity* literally means "happy accident." You have a moment of serendipity when you run into an old friend on the street, when an appointment is cancelled and you have an hour of free time, or when you get two complimentary tickets to the opening of a new museum at the last minute. You'll always have the plan. The question is, will you ever have this opportunity again?

Allow for the unexpected, unplanned, and unforeseen events, circumstances, and challenges that come your way each day. If you take advantage of the opportunities that fall into your lap, instead of sticking religiously to a schedule, you'll make each day one of surprise, spontaneity, and serendipity — and increase your happiness, too!

Spending More Time Doing Absolutely Nothing

Some people simply can't comprehend the psychological benefit that comes from doing absolutely nothing — nothing that's productive, that is, in a material or tangible sense like building things or making money. On the other hand, when you do nothing, you *produce* a state of relaxation. Funny how that works!

Here are some tips on how to spend more time doing nothing:

- Rent a dozen of your favorite movies and spend the entire weekend watching them. Your kids will love you!

- Get up on Saturday morning and head out for the day without any particular agenda or destination. If something along the road to nowhere catches your eye, stop.

- Waste some time at a flea market. Browse, don't buy.

- When you have an unexpected snow day and can't go anywhere, make sure you don't get dressed, don't work, and don't do any chores. Think of the day as a gift!

- Spend the whole day reading your favorite novel — lose yourself in the author's world.

Just enjoy being

My wife and I have two lovely children, both of whom live out of state. When we first started visiting them, they were always planning lots of activities — eating out in great restaurants, visiting museums, sightseeing trips — to entertain us.

But as time has gone on, they've slowly but surely come to appreciate the fact that my wife and I don't need to be constantly busy. Mostly, we just enjoy *being* with them, since we don't get to see them that much throughout the year. We're perfectly content to just hang around the house with them day or night — doing nothing special and yet having a great feeling of togetherness. That's what makes us happy.

✔ Plan a weekend so that when you go to work on Monday morning and people ask you what you did, you can say, with a smile on your face, "Absolutely nothing!"

✔ Take the advice I give in Chapter 15 and lose your watch. It's much easier to do nothing if you don't know what time it is.

Making Sure Your Life Is Like a Chinese Menu

In some Chinese restaurants, you can still order family style — choosing some items from Column A and others from Column B. Column A has the fancier, higher-priced dishes, and Column B has less costly but still tasty treats. In the end, it's the combination of A and B that made the meal unique and memorable.

That's the way life is, too. Some of your daily experiences are no doubt significant (being told you got a raise or completing a project on time) while other are less so (a stranger letting you go ahead of her in the checkout line at the grocery store). But they're all part of what makes your day positive — they're stepping stones to achieving happiness.

Column A pursuits

What's on your agenda today? What are the have-to's? You have to do this; you have to do that. You have to go here; you have to go there. You have to see him; you have to see her. These are the things you consider essential to your social and economic survival. Most likely, they include some combination of the following:

✔ Going to the grocery store

✔ Picking up the dry cleaning

✔ Straightening up the house

✔ Paying bills

✔ Getting the car serviced

✔ Making a deposit at the bank

✔ Getting a haircut

✔ Feeding the dog

✔ Going to work

✔ Supervising work being done on your home

- ✔ Visiting a friend or family member in the hospital
- ✔ Getting your flu shot
- ✔ Taking your child to school
- ✔ Picking your child up from school
- ✔ Mowing the lawn

The more things you check off the list, the better you feel at the end of the day. You've met the basic necessities of everyday life. You're surviving, but are you *thriving?* Not unless your day also includes some Column B pursuits.

Look over the list of Column A pursuits and check those that are on your to-do list today — and add any others that you have to do but that I haven't listed here. This gives you a picture of just how structured your day is and what that structure looks like. Do you like what you see?

Column B pursuits

Think of Column B pursuits as your hidden agenda. Column B is all about want-to's: You want to do that; you want to go there; you want to see her. Think of this as the icing on the cake. Of course, you can live life without them, but they sure make life a lot sweeter!

Consider the following examples:

- ✔ Sitting quietly and reading the paper before you start your day
- ✔ Filling up the bird-feeder so you can enjoy the comings and goings of your feathered friends
- ✔ Taking a leisurely walk around the block
- ✔ Meeting a friend for lunch
- ✔ Watching children at play
- ✔ Having a quiet moment of prayer
- ✔ Spending some quality time with your child after school
- ✔ Reading the comics
- ✔ Checking out a new clothing store
- ✔ Chatting with your next-door neighbor at the mailbox
- ✔ Taking a catnap

These are the little things that spice up your day. Use them to fill in the cracks between Column A pursuits — for example, meeting a friend for lunch in between picking up the dry cleaning and having the tires rotated.

How many Column B–type things did you do today? Chances are you had fewer Column B experiences than ones that fall under Column A — and that's probably one reason you bought this book. If your life is full of Column A pursuits and short on Column B, restructure your day to make it look more like a Chinese menu — with choices from both columns.

Indulging Your Alternative Self

I believe that each person has two selves:

- **The primary self,** which dominates everyday life and is there for all to see
- **The alternative self,** which is not always free to express itself

Take Wayne, for example. When he's sober, he's a conscientious, hard-working man, the proud father of three children. Most of his friends know him to be a serious man, who always has something intelligent to say on virtually any topic. He's deliberate — thinking before he acts — and not prone to impulsive behavior. He smiles a lot, but rarely laughs.

But when Wayne has a few drinks, he becomes a different person. He's much more relaxed with his surroundings, more outgoing, more entertaining to those around him, more affectionate, sometimes loud and impulsive, and more playful. The problem is that Wayne has to get intoxicated before he can be his alternative self — and that often leaves him embarrassed and regretful the morning after.

Wayne's challenge is: How can he indulge his alternative self without using alcohol? Instead of drinking, Wayne could join a local theater group where he could find a part where he could "play" his alternative self on stage — a lot of famous movie stars are introverts in real life. Or, he could be like my older brother, who used to dress up like a clown and ride around on a mini-cycle to the delight of children who'd come to see the Shrine parade.

Take a pad of paper and make two lists describing both your primary and alternative self. Describe each self by using adjectives — for example, *industrious, cheerful, cynical, happy-go-lucky, adventurous, conservative,* and so on. How different are the two lists? How often do you indulge your alternative self? Does it take something like alcohol to release the side of you that most people don't know? Are you the only one who knows your alternative self — do you only act silly when no one else is around?

Chapter 15

Work versus Play

● ●

In This Chapter

▶ Balancing out your life

▶ Choosing quality over quantity

▶ Becoming more balanced

▶ Playing more

▶ Avoiding burnout

● ●

So many people today are living an imbalanced lifestyle — but not because of a shortage of work. Let's face it: It's a hectic world out there, and you're part of it! Don't get me wrong: I don't have anything against work — work is a good thing. It's just that some people don't know when to give it a rest.

Take Michelle, for example, a young woman in her mid-30s who has already risen to the executive level in a major corporation. She's bright, talented, and a real charmer when it comes to people, but the key to achieving success so early in her life has been the long hours she puts in at work — she averages at least 75 hours per week. Definitely a good deal for her employer, but not such a great deal for Michelle.

When Michelle took her job, she had modest ambitions and was in no rush to advance — she saw it as an opportunity to learn new skills that one day would help her get to the top of the corporate ladder. Her life was more balanced then. She worked about 45 hours a week and got a lot done because of her excellent organizational skills — but she also had plenty of time for socializing, time to run marathons, time to correspond with her many friends, and time for her family. Michelle was happy then.

But life is subject to unexpected change. Suddenly Michelle found herself with a whole new set of opportunities and challenges that she simply could not fit into a normal work week. Something had to go, and guess what it was? If you said family, friends, and exercise, of course, you'd be right. The change wasn't abrupt — it was more insidious, proceeding inconspicuously but with grave effect. Slowly but surely, Michelle became increasingly exhausted and an unhappy woman — successful to be sure, but unhappy nevertheless.

Burnout checklist

Are you burned out at work? Are you like a missile whose fuel is exhausted and is now careening down to Earth in free flight — disorganized, erratic, and inefficient? If six or more of the following statements describe you, you could be suffering from burnout.

- You're accident-prone.
- You're anxious.
- You're agitated.
- You regularly abuse alcohol.
- You're apathetic — you just don't care about much of anything.
- You miss work a lot.
- You're bored.
- You're confused.
- You cry a lot.
- You're cynical.
- You're depressed.
- You have difficulty concentrating.

- You have frequent headaches.
- You have heartburn or indigestion.
- You feel hopeless or helpless.
- You feel hostile toward those around you.
- You can't sleep.
- You don't have any joy in your life.
- You can't seem to bounce back after a weekend off.

If your score suggests burn out, here are three things you might try in an effort to "refuel" yourself:

- Take some time-outs (breaks) during the work day and at regular intervals over time — long weekends, mini-vacations.
- Engage in as many *flow* activities as possible in the course of a work week. (Chapter 8 offers a 5-step process for doing just that.)
- Take as many opportunities as you can to relax — meditate, work out in the gym, sit quietly and read a good book.

If you find that your life mirrors that of Michelle — too much work, too little play — this chapter offers you a way out. Here I give you some tips on how to rebalance your work-play life and, in the process, become more balanced.

Which Is More Important: Your Money or Your (Quality of) Life?

This was the question posed by a leading cardiologist in her keynote speech to a group of medical and behavioral science researchers at a conference I attended many years ago. I'll never forget her first slide — a cartoon showing a well-dressed man standing in an alley at gunpoint, arms raised above his head, with this caption: "Your money or your life?" Needless to say, that cartoon got everyone's attention and set the stage for several days of intelligent discussion about the role that societal demands and stress play in causing heart disease and premature death.

The point the speaker was trying to make was simple: Each one of us makes countless decisions each day that basically come down to this — which is more important, the *quantity* of your material possessions or the *quality* of your life? The answer you come up with speaks volumes, it turns out, about your prospects for a healthy and happy future.

Think about how many times a day you're presented with this choice:

- ✔ You have to decide whether to attend your son's Little League game or stay an extra hour at work.

- ✔ You can play golf with your buddies on Sunday or get a jump-start on the week ahead by going to the office for a couple of hours.

- ✔ You can actually take your vacation this year or not.

- ✔ You can turn down a promotion that will add a little bit to your pocketbook, but will also pile on the stress.

- ✔ You can limit your work hours to the time you're paid for or you can always stay until the job's done.

- ✔ You can take a lunch break — get out of the office, take a walk, spend the time thinking about what you'll do in your off hours — or eat lunch in front of the computer.

What do your choices say about you, your health, and your chances for happiness?

Setting Yourself Up to Be More Balanced

In general, the people who can't seem to pull themselves away from work and are highly stressed are Type-A personalities. And the people who are a bit more laid back and relaxed are Type B's. To understand why Type A's spend so much time working and too little time playing, you have to see the world from their perspective and contrast that with the perspective of Type B's (see Table 15-1).

The 24/7 mindset

At some point in the past century, the mindset of industrialized countries throughout the world changed dramatically from the idea that machines were created to serve human beings (to make our lives more comfortable, more efficient, more productive) to the current notion that human beings are here to serve the machines. And, because machines are capable of working 24 hours a day, 7 days a week, so the thinking goes, you and I should do the same. Hence, the birth of the 24/7 mindset!

The 24/7 mindset originated in the manufacturing sector but has spread to virtually all types of work. Many people are never without their cellphones — they're available to do business or solve work-related problems any time, day or night. To make matters worse, inexpensive and portable office equipment — computers, fax machines, copiers — make it possible to have your office with you wherever you go.

The point of all this? Technology has made it easier than ever to override your life choices with 24/7 work, favoring work over nonwork activities.

Table 15-1	Type A's versus Type B's: Which Are You?
Type A's . . .	*Type B's . . .*
Have a rigid standard for what constitutes satisfactory performance. They're continually striving to meet some illusory goal of perfection.	Demand less from themselves even though they fully intend to meet the requirements of the job. They settle for being a "good employee" rather than striving to be a "perfect employee."
Feel the need to engage in multiple tasks at the same time, giving each task number-one priority.	Are more satisfied completing one task at a time before moving on to the next one. They tend to prioritize tasks, ranking them as more or less important.
Attribute their success at work more to effort than ability. Ironically, they seem less impressed with their own abilities than others are.	Understand that success comes from both effort and ability.
View work as a competitive enterprise. They often initiate competition in noncompetitive situations. The word cooperation isn't in their vocabulary.	Make good team players. They aren't averse to healthy competition but enjoy working collaboratively with others.
Prefer working alone but end up feeling like they carry the burden of getting the job done squarely on their shoulders.	Are quick to share the responsibility of work assignments so that they don't become burdensome.
Seek out "Type A" work environments, which promote a climate of competition and a sense of urgency. Time is money!	Seek out "Type B" settings, where the quality of the work performed is appreciated as much as the quantity of work.

If you see yourself in that Type A column, you can make a few key changes in your life to adopt some more of the Type B tendencies. I fill you in on those changes in the following sections.

Appreciating the arts

I can hear you now, "You want me to waste my time strolling through an art museum when I've got work to do?" My answer: "Absolutely." Music, paintings, sculpture, poetry — these all provide opportunities to enrich the spirit, to appreciate the *beauty* of things rather than their *utility,* and to be inspired by artistic genius. The arts transcend the material world — the world in which your efforts are all-important — into the heart, soul, and mind of the artist.

When you're standing in front of a beautiful painting or reading an awe-inspiring poem, you feel humble — and, humility is a much welcomed antidote to the feelings of superiority and self-importance that so many Type A people have.

Make a point of spending some time at least once a month attending some cultural event — a concert, an art exhibit, a play. Better yet, sign up for a membership at a local fine arts center or museum, and you'll be sure to appreciate the arts — after all, Type A's always get their money's worth!

Expanding your horizons

Type A's are fairly *monolithic* thinkers — they're always thinking about work, work, and more work. Type B's, in contrast, tend to be *global* thinkers — they see beyond the work horizon into a world full of relationship possibilities, hobbies, recreational pastimes, conversation with friends and neighbors, spirituality, community service, patriotism, and an up-close-and-personal relationship with nature. When you think about it, these characteristics make Type B's more interesting to talk to, the sort of people you'd actually want to get to know — and the type of person you'd actually want to *be.*

Imagine you're at a wedding, and you're trying to decide who to strike up a conversation with. There's the successful businessperson in the corner who only wants to talk about work. In the other corner: a modest looking person who's a sculptor and a community activist. Who would you choose? How do you want other people at the same gathering to think about *you* when they're trying to make the same decision?

Type B is very un-American

The United States is in first place when it comes to being Type A and having the greatest potential for developing heart disease. In the following table, positive (+) values indicate more Type A behavior among the citizens of that country; negative (−) values indicate Type B tendencies. Deaths resulting from coronary heart disease are calculated per 100,000 people.

Country	Average Type A/B Score	Prevalence of CHD Deaths
United States	5.3	607
New Zealand	0.5	602
Canada	−0.4	540
England	−1.9	438
Netherlands	−3.2	312
Belgium	−4.7	298
Japanese-Americans living in Hawaii who maintain the "old world" traditions	−7.7	120

Note: These data are compiled from a number of published studies of Type-A behavior in individual countries and collectively for the United States as well as from medical statistics provided by the World Health Organization.

Being curious

Type B's have an abundance of curiosity that leads them to expand their horizons. If you're a Type B, you have an eagerness to know all there is to know about the world around you — not just the work world. You seek a variety of life experiences, a diversity of relationships, and a difference of opinion with others. You're curious about what and how other people think and feel about things of mutual interest. You're not afraid to explore life beyond your own comfort zone, and you have a tolerance for uncertainty that is uncharacteristic of Type A's.

Every so often, go to your local bookstore and buy a book on something you know absolutely nothing about — you may actually learn something new! Join a book club that discusses a wide range of topics. Check your local newspaper to see what's happening in the community this weekend, and go and discover what it's all about.

Putting down the grade book

A Type-B colleague of mine was invited to make a presentation at a prestigious medical conference. When he was done and the applause had died down, a Type-A physician came up to him on the stage and said, "I like what you had to say. I give you an A on your presentation." Instead of taking that as a compliment, my Type-B friend was offended: "*Why do you feel the need to* grade me? If you liked my talk, just say you liked it and leave it at that." The Type-A physician appeared speechless, no doubt thinking to himself "What's wrong with that? I grade everybody — my wife, my kids, people who work for me, even myself." And therein lies the problem. Instead of simply appreciating people for who they are and enjoying the *quality* of whatever it is that they're doing, Type A's tend to quantify another person's behavior by assigning a numerical value.

When you're complimenting or criticizing another person — at work or elsewhere — forgo statements like "I see you brought your A game today" or "You certainly didn't put 100 percent into this one." A simple, "You did a good job" or "I have a feeling you'll do better next time" will suffice.

Losing the watch

One of the core elements of the Type-A personality is their sense of time urgency — what the originators of the Type A concept, Dr. Meyer Friedman and Dr. Ray Rosenman, refer to as *hurry sickness.* Type A's are ruled by their watches. If you don't believe me, ask a Type A you know to surrender his watch for a whole day and see what happens. You may as well be asking him to stop breathing — "Are you serious? I can't go all day without knowing what time it is. I have a schedule and I need to stick to it." The relationship Type B's have with time is much more flexible — they're not plagued throughout the day with thoughts about time passing too fast, not having enough time to complete everything, and time not being on their side.

Most likely it'll be hard for you to relinquish your tie to your watch at first. Start by taking it off and putting it in your pocket or purse (that way you'll know it's close by!) for just half a day. When you get comfortable with that, you can progress to a full day. Who knows, you may even work you way up to the point where you can live without it for a whole weekend.

In Chapter 8, I showed you how to get into *flow* — engaged in an activity that seems timeless, effortless, and completely satisfying. It's easier to get into flow if you're not wearing your watch!

Eating slowly

Type A's do almost everything aggressively and that includes how fast they eat. When you're eating with family or friends, are you the first one to clear your plate? When you're having lunch with colleagues at work, do you eat fast so that you can get on to business? If you finish your meal and the other person is still eating, do you find yourself becoming impatient? If so, you're definitely Type A.

Here are some tips on how to become a Type-B eater:

- **Slow down.** You might try taking a bite of food, putting your silverware down, and counting to 10 before picking up your silverware again. Diet experts suggest taking four to five bites per bite of food before swallowing. Be sure and drink liquid frequently throughout your meal — this will add to the time it takes you to finish eating.

- **Observe the people you're sharing a meal with and try to eat at their pace — unless they're also Type A's!**

- **Whenever possible, don't set a specific time limit for eating.** Let yourself take as much time to finish your meal as you need.

- **Don't eat alone.** People tend to take longer to eat when they're with others, because they're talking as well as eating.

- **Think of eating as a social event.** In many ways, eating is a form of play. Enjoy the experience!

- **Don't eat while you're driving.** Type A's love to do more than one thing at a time. Not only is it too stressful to eat while you drive, but it's dangerous!

- **Stay away from fast-food eateries.** The whole idea behind fast-food restaurants is to get your food fast and to eat it fast. No one goes to McDonald's for a leisurely meal!

- **Relax.** It helps digestion. Try reading your newspaper before and after you eat — or, if you're like me, your daily devotional. It also helps to turn off your cell phone.

Sometimes the smallest change in behavior can pay big dividends in terms of stress reduction. For example, in *Anger Management For Dummies*, I explain how simply lowering the tone of your voice can instantly reduce the intensity of your anger and, similarly, how loosening your grip on the steering wheel can help you combat road rage. Making small changes in how you eat (outlined in this section) can be just as effective in your efforts to move beyond your Type-A tendencies.

Thinking of yourself as a small "i"

Type A's love to talk about themselves. Their conversation is saturated with *I, me,* and *mine.* Rarely do you hear them referring to *we, us,* or *ours.* This tendency toward *self-referencing* is an expression of what psychiatrists call the narcissistic personality. Remember the evil queen in the children's tale "Snow White," who insisted on being the "fairest of them all" and went into a rage after being told otherwise. Well, I can pretty much guarantee she was a Type A.

Type Bs are more humble creatures. They lack the feeling of grandiosity and sense of entitlement that typifies the Type-A personality. They appreciate the truth in the comedian Woody Allen's assessment that "We're all bozos on the same bus." And they think of themselves as a small "i" in the grand scheme of life.

Find activities to engage in where you aren't the center of attention. I once worked backstage on a local theater production, building and painting props, while all the "stars" were rehearsing their lines. I felt wonderfully unimportant — and I loved every minute of it! Serve on the clean-up committee at your church or civic organization when you're hosting some type of event — for example, a pancake or spaghetti supper. Park cars at some large community gathering — it's a lonely job, but somebody's got to do it!

Walking to work — even when you drive

Type A's are always on the run, everywhere they go. I call it *tilting forward* — their head is way out in front (thinking of where they're going next) and their feet are hurrying to catch up. No wonder they're so exhausted at the end of the day.

A simple but effective strategy for slowing down your Type-A engine is to force yourself to walk longer distances to and from work. This was the first tool I used to change my own Type-A behavior years ago. Instead of parking as close as I could to the entrance to Duke University Hospital, so that I could get into work quickly, I intentionally parked several blocks away so that I had to walk through the Duke Gardens in order to get to my office. Walking past all those beautiful flowers and fish ponds literally transformed the tone of my personality and set the stage for a Type-B day. This may sound unlikely, but as I mention earlier, sometimes the smallest change in behavior can pay big dividends in terms of decreased stress.

If you park in a parking garage, why not look for the vacant space that's farthest away from the entrance? You won't have as much competition that way. Plus, you'll get some much-needed exercise — what could make you happier?

Eliminating the number-speak

I happened to be eavesdropping on a conversation (okay, I admit it — I'm nosey!) between two psychologists eating in a nice restaurant one evening, and this is what I overheard: One of the psychologists (a Type A) was telling his friend about all the things he'd accomplished during the past year — how many articles he'd had published, in which prestigious journals, how much grant money he'd been awarded — when the other man (a Type B) politely interrupted and said, "Charlie, I get it — you've had a fantastic year. No question that you're beating the socks off all of us in this academic rat race. But, hey, this is our one night together — let's not spoil it with all those numbers. What I really want to know is how are you — are you healthy, happy, that sort of thing?"

The painful truth is, the rest of the world doesn't care about how *many* successes you've had or how *much* you've accomplished — the only person that stuff is important to is you! Why not just say, "It's been a really productive year," and let it go at that?

From now on, when you're talking to other people, try reducing (or better yet eliminating) all the *number-speak,* including references to your latest golf scores, how much money you've made in the stock market, how much your new car cost, the square footage of your new home, or how big a raise you got last year.

Pretending you're a Dutchman

In the "Type B is very un-American" sidebar in this chapter, I point out that the Netherlands is a Type-B culture. I can attest to that not just because of the statistics, but because I had the good fortune to spend a year there as an invited guest professor many years ago. It was wonderful experience! And, although I didn't learn to speak the language, I did learn the Dutch customs.

My first awareness that Dutchmen don't have the same crazy Type-A work lives that we do in the United States came one day when I returned to the psychology department office a few minutes after noon only to find all the doors locked. After trying in vain to get into the building (I had some work I wanted to get done during lunch), I asked a passerby where everyone had gone. He said, "Sir, they all go home to lunch. They'll be back at 1:30." I couldn't believe it — an entire medical school gone home to lunch. Amazing! Later that day, the chairman of the department explained to me that Dutchmen break their workdays into two parts and refresh themselves in between. I remember thinking to myself, "How *un*-American!"

Shortly thereafter, I had my second lesson in the separation of work and play. The chairman and his wife were hosting a little party for my wife and me, and I was talking about work with several of my new Dutch colleagues. The chairman discreetly pulled me away and told me, "Doyle, you need to stop talking about work. Everyone is being very polite and not saying anything, but that sort of thing is simply not done here. These men and women work all day; after they leave work they want to talk about other things — soccer, family, travel, history, or what life is like for you in the United States. You can talk about work tomorrow at the office." This time I got the message loud and clear — work when you work and play when you play and don't mix the two.

You don't have to leave the country in order to have a more balanced lifestyle. Just adopt some new ways of living and working from some of these Type-B cultures.

Identifying the Three Types of Play

In childhood, work and play are all the same. Play is how a child learns to be a social being — interacting and negotiating with peers — as well as problem-solve. Play is how a child learns to follow rules. Play develops the creative side of the child's emerging personality. And play is how children first learn to experience happiness. As a result, play provides a foundation for similar behavior in adults.

How often have you heard someone at work comment about another employee, "He doesn't play well with others"?

Play is not one particular type of activity — it takes on many forms. The three most common forms are: solitary play, parallel play, and cooperative play. All are important and all should continue throughout a person's life.

In the following sections, I cover each of the main forms of play, and tell you how you can incorporate this kind of play into your adult life.

It's important not only to strike a healthy balance between work and play, but to balance out the various forms of play. Make time for each in your schedule of daily activities.

Solitary play

Solitary play is any fun and joyful activity that you do by yourself. Hobbies are a good example of solitary play. You're occupied with something you enjoy — stamp collecting, woodworking, the *New York Times* crossword puzzles. And, you're doing it *all by yourself,* which makes it the simplest and most accessible type of play. Consider the following examples:

✔ Pete loves to bake, spending hours in the kitchen by himself (his wife knows not to intrude!) preparing rich desserts for family, friends, and neighbors.

- ✔ Toiya enjoys reading — she has ever since she was a child — and can spend an entire weekend alone curled up with her books.

- ✔ Jack collects miniature Chinese figurines — a hobby he picked up while serving in the Air Force overseas. When he finds himself getting stressed out at work, he takes a break and spends a few minutes thumbing through catalogs and thinking about his next purchase.

- ✔ Ramon, an investor, has a collection of pinball machines — some worth quite a bit of money — sitting in his basement. When he's through working or just plain bored, he gets those pinballs moving!

- ✔ Alice loves jigsaw puzzles. Recently, at a flea market, she found a 1,000-piece puzzle — something that should keep her occupied for days.

Do you have a hobby? When's the last time you spent some time with it? If it's been a while, think back to how much pleasure it gave you — maybe it's time to reconnect. If you don't have a hobby, no problem. Start by visiting your local hobby stores and see what sorts of things are available. See if anything catches you attention. You might be surprised at how many fun and interesting activities there are waiting for you.

Parallel play

Do you like to attend college football games on Saturdays in the fall? Are you that guy in the brightly colored vest who spends his weekend beautifying America's highways by picking up other people's roadside trash? Ever had a table at the local flea market, hoping that your junk could become someone else's treasure? Do you enjoy browsing through craft fairs? How about playing bingo? Ever run a marathon? Have you ever taken a pottery class at the local arts center? Do you and your spouse enjoy sitting on the beach, separately reading your favorite books?

These are all examples of *parallel play* — where you're doing something that gives you pleasure alongside others who are doing the same thing. Parallel play is social because of the context in which it occurs. It can also constitute a form of healthy competitive play — for example, you and the fan next to you are cheering for different teams all in the spirit of good-natured rivalry.

If you're an introverted personality — someone who's shy, reserved, and not all that comfortable interacting with other people — parallel play may be easier for you to engage in than cooperative play, which I'll talk about next.

The happiest time

One of the happiest periods in my life was the time when I crewed on the *bateaux* (flat-bottomed boats designed to transport casks of tobacco) down the James River. For a week at a time, hundreds of my fellow Virginians and I dressed in period costume, slept in tents alongside the river, and poled our boats 138 miles all the way to Richmond. We were like kids again — laughing and playing — as we went along.

No one talked about work. No one talked about world events. No one engaged in any meaningful or serious discussions about the economy or politics. No one read a newspaper or watched TV. There was absolutely no way to tell who was the psychologist, the surgeon, or the banker.

What we did instead was nap during the day, drink beer, have water-balloon fights with crews from other boats, and basically act silly. We cooked over open fires, had horseshoe competitions, bathed in the river, and sat up late into the night swapping stories. No one wore a watch — we went by "river time," which translates into something like "We'll get there when we get there and not until." We revisited an earlier time in history when life was less comfortable, but a whole lot more balanced.

This was cooperative play at its best.

Type A's also prefer to engage in parallel play, but for different reasons. Type A's always prefer competition over cooperation and they like to play at things where they have all the control — for instance, one-on-one competition in golf or tennis instead of partnering up with someone else.

Cooperative play

Cooperative play involves interacting with others in some type of pleasurable activity where there's a common goal. Team sports like football, basketball, and soccer are examples of cooperative play. When we lived in Texas, my family and I enjoyed attending barbeque and chili cook-offs, where teams of men and women would work together to create food that tasted out of this world!

Cooperative play is the most advanced, social type of recreation. It *allows* — not forces — people to integrate their skills and energies in a creative way so that the sum is truly greater than the parts. It's a much more intimate type of play.

Cooperative play also fosters a sense of the small "i" that I talk about earlier in this chapter — where each participant is a part of some enjoyable activity rather than the "whole" of it. This type of play is preferred by Type Bs.

What's your favorite type of cooperative play? How long has it been since you engaged with your playmates? Maybe it's time to join in the fun. Here are some possibilities:

- ✔ Card games — like duplicate bridge — that involve partners.

- ✔ Riding a bicycle built for two — better known as riding in tandem.

- ✔ Joining a bowling team — low score buys the beers!

- ✔ A quilting club — my mother belonged to one for years and it kept her feeling youthful despite her advancing age.

- ✔ Book clubs — the reading you do on your own, but the fun is in the group discussions about what you learned and enjoyed about the book.

Chapter 16

Socialization versus Solitude

*K*im headed off west towards the mountains of Tennessee, leaving behind the rolling hills of central Virginia. He was also leaving behind all the problems, responsibilities, and demands of his otherwise hectic, middle-class life. He was leaving behind all those people who defined his day-to-day existence — his son, parents, brother, girlfriend, friends, and clients. Kim was en route to spend an entire weekend with someone who all too often seemed like a perfect stranger — himself. He wasn't running away from the world of socialization; he was only taking a much needed leave of absence. In doing so, he was attempting to rebalance his life with 72 hours of solitude.

In this chapter, I explain why it's important to have enough social connections, help you appreciate the many facets of social support, and show you how having a confidant not only leads to happiness, but can actually save your life. I also explain how you can be alone without being lonely. And I give you some tips on how, when, and where you have the best chance of finding a moment of solitude.

Recognizing That Happiness Doesn't Occur in a Vacuum

Human beings are social creatures. We're also wired for emotions, and we experience those emotions within a social context. We're at our best when we're engaging one another in the course of daily activities — at work and at play. If those activities are productive, constructive, involve mutual coopera-tion, and contribute to our ultimate survival, we tend to feel joyful, happy, and satisfied. If they're unproductive, destructive, or involve conflict, we feel just the opposite — anxious, resentful, and dissatisfied. What's important is the nature of your relationships and the extent to which they're supportive.

Do you have meaningful social ties?

By *meaningful social ties,* I don't mean the usual, "Hey, how are you? What's happening?" kind of superficial connections that make up much, if not most, of your daily routine. I'm talking about relationships — ties — that give your life a sense of purpose and without which you'd be just another lost soul.

One of my clients was dying from Lou Gehrig's disease (ALS). He said, "I'm blessed with good friends — the kind of friends who you could go to in the middle of the night and ask to borrow their new Cadillac to drive from Virginia to California and, without a thought, they'd say yes." Do you have meaningful relationships like that in your life?

What makes a social tie meaningful is that it is unusually close, special, and one that has far greater impact on your life than the more commonplace, casual relationships we all enjoy. I think it is safe to say that not everyone you know would loan you their new car for a cross-country trip "no questions asked." Another way to decide if a relationship is meaningful is to ask yourself, "How would my life change if she wasn't in it anymore?" If the answer is "a whole lot — more than I want to think about," then, no question, you have a meaningful tie with her.

How big is your network?

A *social network* is the *quantity* of relationships that you can draw on for support. *Social support* has to do with the *quality* of that support.

How big is your network? How many people in your life can you really count on?

For Kim, the young man I highlight in the introduction to this chapter, his 8-year-old son remains at the center of his life even though Kim is divorced from his son's mom. Kim's parents sometimes find fault with his modern way of life, but they continue to be proud of him for his many accomplishments. Kim is very close to his sister, even though they live far apart and have distinctly different personalities. And his girlfriend is the newest person in his life who gives his life some sort of meaning.

These five people form the basis of Kim's meaningful social support network. They're his safety net in trying times, his source of motivation and inspiration, the sounding board he relies on when he's faced with difficult decisions and the possibility of major life changes, and his primary source of self-esteem. Kim belongs to these people — and, they belong to him.

Thanks to the marvels of modern technology — e-mail, cellphones, text-messaging — you're probably more connected than ever in terms of the sheer quantity of communications you get per day. But the actual number of *close* connections may be steadily declining. In 1985, one survey suggested that Americans had, on average, three close friends; by the year 2006, this number had dropped to only two. Even more striking was the fact that 25 percent of those surveyed could not point to a single person they were close to. The size of the support network has also decreased, thanks to the shrinking size of American families.

Who's in your network?

As people have become more mobile (moving away from their families of origin), more educated, more affluent, and more independent, the composition of their support networks has changed. Many people under 40, for example, may identify college friends and work associates as their most supportive relationships in place of siblings (due in part to the shrinking size of families) or even parents. Even fewer people would list neighbors as part of their networks. For more and more people, pets have become their significant others. And because more people postpone marriage well beyond their 20s or end up divorced, many of them can't list a spouse as one of the people in their network. Despite these changes, however, people can still have strong social networks and still get good support. As long as your network size is not "zero" and you have a meaningful relationship with those in your network, you're in good shape.

Where's your support?

Some of your closest relationships may be with people who are far away geographically. Most of my best friends, for example, live in another state — the support they afford me is long-distance and not immediately available. My wife, on the other hand, has made many close friends right in our area. That makes a big difference — she doesn't have to go far to enjoy an uplifting lunch (Chapter 13) with one of her girlfriends. Her support is much more accessible than mine is.

Are you receptive to support?

Not everyone takes advantage of the support that's available to them — so it does them no good. If a close friend leaves a voicemail message asking how you are, call her back. If a family member offers to help you move, don't tell him, "No, thanks — I can handle it." If your lawyer gives you some good advice, take it.

Don't be like Chris, a client of mine, who for years suffered from chronic back pain. Chris was a police officer and he lost his job after he was injured. His buddies tried to keep in contact with him — calling him frequently and coming by his house to visit — but Chris made himself unavailable. He wouldn't return their calls and he refused to go to the door when they came knocking. Chris was an angry man. And yet, all the while, he complained, "No one cares about me. No one gives a damn about me now that I can't work." His friends didn't abandon *him* — he abandoned *them*.

What kind of support are you getting?

Support, according to sociologist James House at the University of Michigan, involves "a flow of one or more of four types of support between people." These four types of support are

- **Emotional support:** You need to know that people are in your corner. You need to others to tell you, "I'm here for you no matter what."

- **Informational support:** You need information, guidance, and advice about what to do or how to handle situations. People who can give you this kind of support include lawyers, clergy members, physicians, mental health professionals, and accountants.

- **Tangible support:** This is the chicken-soup type of support. Tangible support includes things like a ride to the doctor's office, a loan of money, help moving to another house, and watching your children so that you and your partner can enjoy a much needed night out on the town.

- **Appraisal support:** You need someone to give you honest, frank, constructive feedback about yourself — for example, that you never seem happy any more. This is not the type of support that typically comes from strangers or from acquaintances.

Giving tangible support when it's needed most

People who've lost a loved one receive lots of emotional support (in the form of hugs and shared tears) and appraisal support ("You're going to be okay. You're a strong person."). But what they get far too little of is tangible support — someone to take care of their kids while they make necessary arrangements or attend the funeral, someone to prepare meals that can be warmed up later and served to guests, someone to take care of pets, and someone to run routine errands.

If you know someone who's recently lost someone she loves, try to provide this type of hands-on support. You'll free up the bereaved person to do what's most important — say goodbye to the person she loves.

Misery loves company — and so does happiness

Emotions are contagious — and in some cases infectious. When you socialize, you may become a happier person or a less happy person. If the emotional tone of the group you're interacting with is positive, you're likely to feel positive yourself. If the reverse is true, you're more likely to find yourself feeling negative — irritable, cynical, pessimistic.

I can best illustrate this point by telling you about two of the most memorable chronic pain rehab groups I conducted over a ten-year period. One I labeled the "Group from Hell"; the other, the "Black Angels":

✔ **The Group from Hell:** This group consisted of four patients, all of whom had been injured at work, had lost their jobs, were in constant pain, and had not benefited from traditional medical or surgical remedies. All four were extremely negative — resentful and bitter about their circumstances, sarcastic, hostile, and highly resistant to my efforts to teach them how to cope with their pain in a way that left them less disabled. Every day, for four seemingly endless hours, they fed off each other's unhappiness, reinforcing their pessimistic, hopeless view of the future. And every opportunity they got, they turned their collective anger toward me — which left me feeling equally dispirited.

✔ **The Black Angels:** This group was made up of three African American ladies who also were struggling with chronic pain, had been injured at work, and had lost their jobs. There was a marked contrast, however, in their attitudes and emotions from the very first day. All three came to the rehab facility with a smile on their faces and a warm, positive greeting. They left the same way four hours later. They laughed, encouraged each other during the fitness training, and generated an atmosphere of enthusiasm. They were eager to learn what we had to teach them and optimistic that rehab would, in the long run, ease their struggle with ongoing pain. And to show their gratitude, on graduation day they presented me with three wooden black angels, which they said would watch over me for the rest of my life. I was touched to the point of tears — and then we all had a group hug and they left, as always, smiling and laughing with each other.

Remember: Pain doesn't make people unhappy — people make themselves unhappy.

Take a minute and think about how connected you are to the world around you and how supportive those connections are. Then organize your thoughts similar to what you see in Table 16-1.

Table 16-1	Social Support		
Who	*Kind of Support*	*Where*	*How Accessible*
Tom	Emotional	Long distance	Somewhat
My accountant	Informational	Close by	Very much
My spouse	Emotional, tangible, appraisal	Close by	Very much
My brother	Emotional	Long distance	Not very

When you're finished with the exercise, ask yourself whether you have an adequate support system. Is too much of your support long distance? Are you making use of the support that's available to you? Would you be happier if you had more support? If you're not receptive to those who want to support you, why not? If you're lacking in support, what can you do to increase it?

The Benefits of Being Connected

Being socially "connected" to the world around you benefits you in two major ways: It keeps you healthy and it makes life more fun.

My friend and former colleague, Dr. Redford Williams at Duke University Medical Center, published a landmark study in the *Journal of the American Medical Association* that looked at the importance of close personal relationships in determining one's odds for surviving heart disease. He and his colleagues noted that heart patients who underwent coronary angiography were three times more likely to die from heart disease within the next five years if they were unmarried or could not identify a *confidant* — someone whom they could share their troubles with. This striking difference in survival rates remained even when the investigators took into consideration the severity of heart disease suffered by each patient. Apparently, keeping unhappiness to yourself can be lethal!

You may find yourself at a point in life where you have no one to confide in — no one to talk to about the important things that are going on in your life, to assist you in overcoming obstacles, or to simply "give you a voice." If this is the case, you need to begin reaching out — go where the people are and let them get to know you. Become a volunteer, find a hobby club to join, or show up the next time they have a young member's event at your local art museum or Fine Arts Center. **Remember:** People don't start out to be confidants — they start out just getting to know one another and things progress from there. If you've already tried that and still feel unconnected, I highly recommend filling that need through some type of counseling relationship — for example, with a mental health practitioner or a member of the clergy. Not only is there no shame in that; it's the wise, smart and right thing to do!

The other major benefit that humans receive from being connected has to do with pleasure. Sigmund Freud once said that a happy, fulfilled life involves a balance of three things — work, sex, and play — all of which are meant to involve other people. Imagine spending your entire life playing by yourself!

Support can save the fetus

In a study examining the relationship between stress and social support in pregnant women, researchers found that women experiencing "high stress" pregnancies were three times more likely (90 percent) to have babies born with complications — including miscarriage — if they also had little or no support from families and friends in the months preceding delivery than if they did have support available (30 percent). Bottom line: Making sure an expectant mother has an adequate amount of support — emotional, tangible, informational, appraisal — goes a long way towards insuring the healthy, normal development of their soon to be born child.

Working with pain clients, I learned that suffering — the emotional component of the *chronic pain syndrome* — is not the result of the pain they experience, but rather the things they give up because of it. We've administered a disability questionnaire to our clients and time after time we find the first thing they give up as a result of pain is recreation — *fun and games*. Ironically, most of these individuals will continue doing routine household chores — mopping, sweeping, and vacuuming, all of which greatly aggravate pain — long after they've stopped socializing with family and friends. Part of the reasoning behind this has to do with the idea that pain and pleasure are incompatible — if you have one, you can't have the other. Not true! The other reason is that in the American culture, people think that if you can't work, then you don't deserve to enjoy yourself. Again, not true!

Looking at the Importance of Solitude

You don't need to talk most people into socializing — after all, humans are social animals. But solitude is another matter. Solitude runs counter to the demands of society, which depends on the efforts of all of us to contribute to the greater good. Taking time for yourself is often viewed as selfish and unproductive.

Solitude is also uncomfortable for many people because they're learned to derive their self-esteem from activities initiated by their "other selves" — that is, their efforts to satisfy themselves by satisfying others. Your "other self" includes such roles as child, student, sibling, grandchild, Girl Scout, athlete, employee, employer, church deacon, neighbor, and citizen. When you serve your "other self" you achieve some measure of happiness — true — but there are also important benefits that come from spending time with your "personal self," that part of you that doesn't need other people to be happy.

The difference between being lonely and being alone

Most people don't understand the difference between being alone and being lonely. Being *alone* just means being by yourself, with no one else around. You can be alone in the shower, alone while driving, alone when you're sleeping, and alone in your office at work. Being *lonely*, on the other hand, means that you're absent from any emotional connection to the world around you — it's as if the whole world in which you live is full of strangers. Some people feel lonely in a crowd, and some people who are completely alone don't feel lonely at all.

One reason that many people avoid opportunities for solitude is that they equate solitude with loneliness. In fact, it's only possible to enjoy solitude — time with yourself — if you're emotionally tied to the social world around you.

✔ **Solitude allows your body to catch up with your mind.** In this crazy aggressive existence that most people live in, we're always tilting forward — our minds are way out in front of our bodies, thinking, analyzing, and planning ahead. Our bodies are just along for the ride. It's only when you stop and get off the merry-go-round of daily life that your mind and body can once again get back into sync.

✔ **Solitude allows your brain to rest.** In a world of overstimulation, our minds are constantly in an overactive mode. Solitude allows your mind to detach from all the endless chatter coming from the environment around you — the radio, the Internet, conversations, street noise, traffic sounds, barking dogs — and rest for a change.

✔ **Solitude jumpstarts the *parasympathetic nervous system* (the branch of the autonomic nervous system that calms you down).** When you're able to get some time to yourself, your muscles relax, your blood pressure decreases, and your heart rate slows. Think of solitude as the anti-adrenaline system that kicks on when there's no longer a need for the fight-or-flight response.

✔ **Solitude prevents burnout.** Burnout is what happens when you're subjected to prolonged, intense, and unresolved stress. You run out of physical and psychological energy, and you act in a disorganized, inefficient, erratic manner.

✔ **Solitude enhances creativity.** Solitude frees the mind up from all the distractions of everyday life and allows it to focus more fully on one thing. It allows your brain to think outside the box and to come up with unique, extraordinary solutions to ordinary problems. That's part of why artists — painters, sculptures, musicians, writers — spend so much time alone.

When you're faced with a difficult problem — where there's no easy solution — allow your brain to *incubate*. Incubation occurs when you step away from the problem, let it go for a while, and come back to it later. More often than not, the solution is readily apparent when you reengage the problem. Why? Simple: While you're off thinking about other things, your brain forgets about all those incorrect ideas you had before you walked away. In essence, incubation gives your brain a fresh start.

✔ **Solitude can be a time of self-discovery.** Solitude is your chance to learn something about yourself. Self-discovery is a process that involves asking and answering four basic questions:

  • Who am I?

  • What makes me unique?

  • Where am I going in life?

  • Am I comfortable with myself?

Self-discovery is something that can — and should — occur at each stage of life. It doesn't matter whether you're an 8-year-old child, a middle-aged woman, or an elderly man; the more you know about yourself the happier you'll be.

✔ **Solitude allows you an opportunity to deal with the big questions in your life.** At various times in your life, you'll be faced with big questions like "Am I enjoying life the way I think I should given my current circumstances — job, finances, relationships?" and "I've been successful at this job for the past 15 years, but is this what I want to do for the rest of my working life?" It takes time and a lot of careful thought to come up with the answers. Such answers are more likely to come to mind in a quiet, introspective moment — solitude — than when you're fully engaged in your usual day-to-day activities.

A friend of mine, for example, was fortunate to be promoted to a top management position early in his academic career. By all accounts, he did a good job — managing to satisfy the demands of his superiors as well as the needs of his subordinates. But as time went on, he began to pay a price for his success. He developed a case of what psychologist Ad Appels, at the University of Maastricht in the Netherlands, calls *vital exhaustion* — excessive fatigue, increased irritability, difficulty sleeping, and feelings of demoralization.

And then something interesting happened: He took a six-month sabbatical and spent his time catching up on his sleep, taking his newborn daughter for long walks, reading, and enjoying solitude. Somewhere during that sabbatical, he began to think about whether he wanted to return to management or simply go back to being an ordinary professor. This question was not an insignificant one — it would determine his salary and his overall status within the university — but it was a question that had never occurred to him before. After careful consideration, his answer was a resounding no. At the end of his sabbatical, he told his superiors what he had decided and they reluctantly agreed to let him step down. They weren't happy — but *he* was!

If you want to know if you're suffering from vital exhaustion, ask yourself the following questions:

- Do you feel fresh and rested when you first wake up in the morning?

- Do you ever feel like a battery that's losing its charge?

If you answered no to the first question and yes to the second question, you're definitely a candidate for vital exhaustion. This alone increases your chances of sudden cardiac death by 42 percent and, if combined with chronic anger, increases your chances by a whopping 69 percent. If this is the case, here are some options you should consider:

- Learn to control your anger better. (*Anger Management For Dummies* is a good place to start.)

- Cut back on smoking and alcohol use as these are highly correlated with vital exhaustion.

- Take a few minutes to meditate each day (see Chapter 23).

- Read Chapter 8 and learn the 5-step method of getting into *flow*.

- Engage in an activity that is uplifting (Chapter 13) both in mind and body.

- Spend less time working and more time playing (Chapter 15).

- Start getting a good night's sleep, exercise more, and eat a healthier diet (Chapter 23).

✔ **Solitude provides an opportunity for perspective.** When you're caught up in the hassles (see Chapter 13) of day-to-day life, all you can see is what's directly in front of you — the problem of the moment. If you want to see and appreciate the big picture of what your life's all about, you have to step back and get a bird's-eye view — and that's exactly what solitude allows you to do.

Solitude = sanctuary

Traditionally, the term *sanctuary* has referred to a place of refuge and safety where a person can escape impending danger and be protected. Think of solitude as your source of spiritual, emotional, and mental sanctuary. It's a safe harbor in an otherwise stormy sea. It's the eye of the hurricane — where it's calm and the winds don't blow. It's a place where you don't have to be on the defensive and where there is absolutely no need for a fight-or-flight response. Solitude affords serenity — one of the many elements of happiness (see Chapter 2).

Chapter 17

Selfishness versus Generosity

In This Chapter

▶ Discovering healthy selfishness

▶ Finding the happy median

▶ Giving without strings

▶ Acting out your intentions

▶ Redirecting your energies

▶ Planning for the unexpected

What does Gordon Gekko, the villainous corporate tycoon played by Michael Douglas in the movie Wall Street, see as the secret to happiness? Greed, of course. Greed — the ultimate act of selfishness — separates winners from losers, as Gekko sees it, and nobody in his right mind wants to be a loser. Greed produces wealth. Greed insures that you'll always have more than you need — whether you're talking about money, food, toys, or square footage. Greed seeks to satisfy self-interest only.

Psychologists Elizabeth Dun (of the University of British Columbia) and Michael Norton (of the Harvard Business School) have a much different take on happiness. Their research suggests just the opposite — namely, that by being generous and giving away money to others, whether they need it or not, people experience happiness. Their findings indicated that an individual's reported level of happiness is not correlated with how much money she spends, but rather on who she spends it on. Giving away as little as $5 a day creates a sense of joy and satisfaction at day's end. Unlike greed, generosity only seeks to satisfy the interests of others.

So, who's right? If your goal is to be happy, should you be selfish or generous? The answer: Both. You need to balance the two.

As I emphasize throughout this part, happiness is found somewhere in the middle of life's extremes — somewhere between work and play (Chapter 15), socialization and solitude (Chapter 16), and so on. In this chapter, I show you how to move away from unhealthy selfishness on the one end and prideful selflessness on the other. I remind you what it really means to be a good scout and why giving for the wrong reasons only leads to unhappiness. And, last, I tie all this to the issue of personal energy and offer some suggestions for how to revitalize your life.

Healthy Selfishness

Most people think the term *healthy selfishness* is an oxymoron. You may have been taught that it's bad to be selfish. And you may have been taught that's it's better to be selfless — to always put others before yourself. *Martyrs* (people who sacrifice their lives for their fellow men) are the extreme example of selflessness and many people believe that martyrdom is the surest route to sainthood.

But consider this: Everything that you do everyday that contributes to your survival is an act of selfishness. The act of eating is selfish — but if you didn't eat, you'd die. The same goes for drinking — severe dehydration leads to death. Sexual activity, even if it's purely for the purpose of procreation is selfish — you're having sex because *you* want children. Working is a selfish act — you want to earn money to spend on necessities and luxuries.

The distinction between *healthy* selfishness and *unhealthy* selfishness lies not in the act itself but in its consequences. Here are some examples of healthy selfishness:

- ✔ Catching up on your sleep when you're exhausted.
- ✔ Participating regularly in religious services to satisfy your spiritual needs.
- ✔ Exercising several hours a week at your favorite gym.
- ✔ Having two drinks of alcohol per day — according to scientists, it relieves stress.
- ✔ Buying yourself a bouquet of flowers to brighten up your office.
- ✔ Lingering in bed for a couple of extra minutes every morning.
- ✔ Being honest because you know how burdensome life can be when it's full of lies (see Chapter 7).

And here are some examples of unhealthy selfishness:

- ✔ Overeating to the point of obesity — it endangers your health and shortens your life.
- ✔ Smoking cigarettes — they're a leading cause of cancer and heart disease.
- ✔ Unloading your anger on a family member just because it feels good.
- ✔ Drinking to excess.
- ✔ Refusing to wear a condom when you have sex.

✔ Blaming a coworker for a mistake you made.

✔ Always beating your kids at games just because you can.

Putting the "I" back in identity

There is such a thing as being too generous — giving too much of yourself, spreading yourself too thin.

Susie was that type of person. She spent every hour of her waking day anticipating and satisfying the needs of her husband, her two children, her elderly parents, her in-laws, her co-workers, and her neighbors. Meanwhile, she totally neglected her own needs. Susie told me once that she waited for the rest of her family to order in a restaurant and then — because she was responsible for the family budget — she always chose the least expensive thing on the menu for herself. "I want them to have whatever they want; I can eat anything," she said. It was only after her divorce from her husband of 30 years that she began to cook things *she* liked instead of always catering to her family's appetites.

Is Susie an exception? No, there are millions of Susies out there, people whose identity, whose sense of self, is inextricably tied to the needs and wants of other people. They're *too* generous with their time, *too* generous with their money, and *too* generous with their energy. They only think of others and never of themselves — and, mistakenly, they think this will make them happy.

There's no "I" in *you*. If someone asks you about yourself, do you say, "I'm Juan's mother," "I'm Dr. Williams's wife," or "I'm Kate Bishop's boss"? If so, then the way you think about yourself has more to do with these other people than it does about you. And the way you think about yourself has a whole lot to do with how happy you are (see Chapter 1). Susie was a good wife and mother — her family would attest to that — but she certainly wasn't a happy woman.

Make today the day you begin putting the "I" back into your own identity. Start by honestly answering the following questions without any reference to your spouse, children, family members, or anyone else.

✔ What do *I* want to do on my day off?

✔ Where do *I* want to go on vacation?

✔ Who do *I* want to have lunch with this weekend?

✔ What book do *I* want to buy for myself today?

✔ What new hairstyle do *I* want?

- Who do *I* want to vote for?
- What kind of car do *I* want?
- Would *I* rather take a nap this afternoon or mow the lawn?

Everyone else around you, whose needs you've spent all your time satisfying, may not like it when you suddenly start putting some "I" back into your identity — and back into your daily schedule of activities. They've obviously had a good thing going and they're not all that eager to have things changed. You'll likely experience some resistance, but you need to persist anyway. They'll get used to the new you — it may just take some time.

Being a good scout

Healthy selfishness is synonymous with being a good scout. The Boy Scout oath not only says that you'll do your best to fulfill your duty to God and country and help other people at all times, it says you'll keep *yourself* physically, mentally, and morally straight. Being a good scout, in short, means finding a balance between serving your own needs and serving the needs of others. Most people think scouting is just about skills — like cooking on an open campfire, learning life-saving techniques, or finding your way out of the forest when you're lost — but it's really more about preparing young people for a lifetime of happiness.

If your parent was an alcoholic

Unfortunately, like millions of other people, I was raised in an alcoholic home. And, like so many children of alcoholics, I learned at a very early age to care for others — my drunken father as well as those who suffered because of his drinking. I was forced to grow up too fast, skipping over much of my childhood and adolescence, and adopting adult roles and behaviors way before I reached my adult years.

Someone asked me once how it was that I was able to assume a high-level management role in a large institution before I was 30 years old. "Simple," I said. "When I was 15 years old — after my father walked out and abandoned us — I had to take care of three small children as if they were my own and run a household while my mother went to work. I already had

15 years of management experience before I took over as head of medical psychology. And, believe me, compared to that, this job is easy!"

All children of alcoholics have psychological "issues," whether they realize it or not. If you're the son or daughter of an alcoholic, even if you've been out of the house for years, do not under-estimate the legacy of alcoholism but do not be discouraged either. Other events and circumstances in life — as well as relationships with healthy folks outside the family — can help you grow and develop into a healthy personality. Support groups like Al-Anon (and Alateen for younger members) can offer a source of real hope, as can more traditional counseling relationships with mental health professionals.

Renewed and redirected energy

Call it exhaustion, call it fatigue, call it burnout — it all amounts to the same thing: Your body is short on energy. As I point out in Chapter 4, it takes energy to generate emotions like anger and joy. And it also takes energy to do those things that are essential to achieving a state of happiness. Without energy, you simply can't be happy.

So, if you feel like a battery that's losing its power, where do you get more energy? You get it from redirecting your energy away from activities that only serve the needs of others and instead toward those pursuits that reenergize and revitalize you.

Instead of spending your entire morning picking up your teenager's clothes from her bedroom floor, why not take a walk around the neighborhood and enjoy the sun on your shoulders? Instead of staying late at the office to catch up on other people's work, why not leave at 5 p.m. and meet an old friend to catch up on what's happening in his life? Instead of running errands and crossing things off your to-do list seven nights a week, why not spend a night or two at home just hanging out with your kids? Instead of going to the office on Sunday morning to get a jump on the coming week, why not go to church and reconnect with your spiritual side?

Some things in life *take* energy and other things *create* energy. Regular exercise creates energy — it leaves you feeling refreshed and renewed. A good night's sleep does the same thing. Laughing creates positive energy. Hugs create an infusion of energy both for the hugger and the person being hugged. These are all activities that fall under the heading of *healthy selfishness*.

Here's an exercise I use with my clients when we're talking about what you have to do to make meaningful changes in your life:

1. **Stand next to a wall in your home or office and put your right hand on the wall.**

2. **Now try to reach the *opposite* wall with your left hand.**

   You'll find that, try as you might, you simply can't do it — unless you let go with your right hand. The message: Sometimes, in order to get where you want to go, you have to let go of something else.

 Take the scout pledge today and honor it every day for the rest of your life. It says, "On my honor, I will do my best to do my duty to God and my country and to obey the Scout Law; to help other people at all times; to keep myself physically strong, mentally awake, and morally straight." What better formula for achieving happiness?

Taking time for yourself

Think about how you spend your time each day. If you're getting 8 hours of sleep every night, that leaves 16 waking hours. Figure out how many of those hours you spend in the service of others (working, running errands, attending meetings, chauffeuring kids around town, cleaning house, paying bills, mowing the lawn) and how many hours you spend purely on yourself (reading the newspaper, taking a nap, soaking in a hot tub, meditating, browsing through your favorite bookstore). If you're like most people, the number of hours you spend on yourself is much smaller than the number you spend on others. In fact, given today's busy world, I'd be surprised if the time you take for yourself amounts to more than two hours per day.

Here's the question I want you to ask yourself: "Am I short-changing myself when it comes to how I allocate my time?" If you spend less than one hour a day addressing your own selfish needs, wants, interests, you are.

If you're employed, how valuable is the time you spend servicing the needs of others? (Figure out your hourly rate at work.) Now, ask yourself: "How valuable is the time I spend with and on myself?" Is it worth the same as what you get paid to work for others? Worth more? Or worth less? Put a real value on it in terms of dollars and cents. Your answer speaks to how much self-worth you have. If you feel like the time you take for yourself is of little value, you won't "waste" your time on yourself. On the other hand, if you see time spent on yourself as valuable, you'll find the time for you. It's as simple as that!

Too Much of a Good Thing: Generosity Gone Awry

Being overly generous can be unhealthy. The trick is to be generous without doing so at your own expense. A parent who takes from his hard-earned retirement savings to bail out his college-age kid who habitually runs up credit card debt and gets in trouble with the law is an example of generosity gone awry. Although this kind of behavior may be well-intentioned, it invariably leads to feelings of resentment, outright anger, and strained relationships with loved ones. Being supportive is one thing — enabling bad behavior through misguided generosity is another.

It's not the thought that counts

When you forget your wedding anniversary and use the excuse that you *meant* to get your spouse something, but your week just got away from you, don't believe her when she utters that all-too-familiar phrase, "That's okay, dear — it's the thought that counts." In the real world, intentions *don't* count — only *actions* do. Even if your wife puts on a happy face (see Chapter 12), you can bet your last dollar that it's not the real deal — she isn't a happy camper!

Everyone is full of good and generous intentions. We think about reaching out to others in need, we fantasize about what we would do and how good we would feel afterward — but unless these thoughts reach the point of action, they never do us or anyone else any good.

The saga of the totem pole

A married woman in her mid-50s whom I had been treating for depression came into my office early one morning in an unusual state of distress. I could tell right away that something had upset her so much that she couldn't control herself. She was tearful, shaking, and had an incredibly unhappy expression on her face. She said, "I had the most awful dream last night. I woke up shaking all over and my heart was pounding — I thought I was going to have a heart attack. And I've been crying ever since."

I asked her to recount the dream and she said, "You know what a totem pole is, right? It's a series of carvings on a pole that Native Americans use to tell a person's life story — the highlights of what that person's life was all about. Well, I found myself standing there looking at my own totem pole. There was a carving of my husband, my daughter, my mother, my mother-in-law, my sister — all the people in my life. And suddenly I realized that one person was missing from my totem pole, and that was me. I wasn't on my own totem pole. Here I am over 50 years old and I'm not a part of my own life."

One day when you look at your totem pole, what will you see? Will you be on there somewhere or will you be like this nice, albeit sad, lady and realize that you've never had a real, loving, generous relationship with the one person who matters the most — you?

If you're not sure whether you're engaging in excessive, unhealthy generosity, ask yourself this basic question: "Can I afford to give this much money, energy, and/or time to this person without being unfair to myself?" If the answer is yes, go ahead. If the honest answer is no, don't. You'll have less regret later on.

When my daughter was very young, I used to read lots of children's books to her. One of our favorites was a story about a little girl who collected dolls from many lands. Page by page, the book depicted dolls from different countries around the world — Italy, France, Holland, China — in native costumes. The child and her mother put each doll she collected in her bed until the bed was full. Then the child suddenly got an unhappy look on her face and said, "But, mommy, there's no room for me!" *Remember:* You need to leave room in your life for yourself.

Giving the Right Way

If you act generously to others, shouldn't you experience the "joy of giving"? It depends. If there is a positive motive behind your generosity — for example, compassion — the answer is "yes". If, on the other hand, your generosity is motivated by a sense of obligation on your part or a need to control others, then the answer is decidedly "no". In other words, there's a right way to give and a wrong way — one way leads to happiness, the other does not.

Giving only because you want to

If you're going to be generous, make sure it's for the right reason. Doing for others because you feel you *have to* rather than because you *want to* will not make you happy.

Too many people go through life acting on the principle of reciprocity — you scratch my back and I'll scratch yours. If someone does you a good deed, you feel obligated to respond in kind. In other words, you're engaging in what I call *reactive generosity.* If you're only giving to people because you feel like you owe them (they had you over for dinner last month, so you feel you should have them over for dinner this month), it'll be obvious to everyone involved. Why? Because you won't enjoy the giving — you'll feel resentful, and that resentment will come out in your behavior.

Stick to giving because you want to, and you'll never go wrong.

Giving without control

How many times have you heard someone say, "After all I've done for you, I can't believe you would act this way"? What that person is saying is, "I'm frustrated because I feel like my generosity hasn't been rewarded."

When you give, you need to give without strings attached — you need to be generous without any expectation of reciprocity or payback. True gifts are one-way transactions. They aren't made out of a sense of obligation, nor do they obligate the recipient.

The generosity hormone

Researchers at Claremont Graduate University in California have found a link between the hormone oxytocin and generosity. In their experiments, subjects injected with oxytocin tended to be more willing to help out a stranger monetarily than those who were not given oxytocin.

Oxytocin is released by the brain in social situations and appears to be the driving force behind our efforts to reach out and help others. The researchers also noted that oxytocin was more likely to be produced in situations where people feel nurtured and safe, and where others act toward you in a loving way — for example, when they give you a hug or a kiss.

Codependency: The ultimate form of control

I define *codependency* as a habitual, compulsive need to control the behavior of others as a means of feeling satisfied with and about yourself. To put it more simply, a codependent person can't be happy unless he's controlling other people. The codependent mother, for example, can't be happy unless her son lives the way *she* wants him to live. The codependent husband can only be happy if his wife acts in ways he approves of. The codependent sister is happy only so long as her siblings do the "right" thing (as defined by her) and she's resentful when they don't.

Eddie and his mom, Joan, had a real problem. Eddie was trying too hard to be the dutiful son and Joan was trying too hard to be the good mother. They were driving each other nuts! To hear Joan tell it, "Every time I turn around, Eddie is dropping by and wanting me to go to lunch or something. Then I have to drop what I'm going to do with my friends and keep him company." She would never tell Eddie this, because it would hurt his feelings, but this is how she feels.

To hear Eddie tell it, "She's just an ungrateful witch. I try to do the right thing by checking in on her now and then, and all I get back is an ugly attitude." He would never tell his mom this because it would hurt her feelings, but this is how he feels.

Neither apparently can be happy unless they go out of their way to satisfy what they perceive to be the needs of the other. So, what's the solution to the problem? Eddie needs to learn that he can be a good son without constantly dropping by his mother's place unannounced. Joan, on the other hand, needs to learn that she's not making herself or Eddie happy by going somewhere she doesn't want to go and then pouting the whole time.

When Eddie gets this compulsive urge to be the good son, he needs to say to himself, "No, not today!" And when Joan feels a similar urge to drop what she'd planned to do today for her baby boy, she needs to say, "Sorry, honey, but I have other plans!" If and when they can both do these things, they can start enjoying one another for a change.

Here are some characteristics of a codependent personality:

- You find yourself saying "yes" when you really mean "no."
- You routinely over-commit yourself.
- You expect yourself to do things perfectly.
- You feel like a victim much of the time.
- You wonder why you never have any energy.
- You rarely say what you feel.
- You find it difficult to have fun and be spontaneous.
- You have trouble standing up for your rights.
- You take things personally.
- You feel unloved even by your loved ones.

Remember: As far as science knows, there is no genetic basis for codependency. It is a learned style of relating to others — in essence, a bad habit — that can be unlearned.

The best gift of all

Someone once said to me "You only truly give when you give of yourself" and I believe that's true. I also believe that it's that type of gift — one that is personal and unique — that makes us the happiest. I'm a writer, so writing this book is my gift to myself. I'm also a counselor and teacher, so every time I have an opportunity to reach out and comfort a friend who is suffering or educate some audience, I do so without hesitation. These are the gifts that create our legacy and the spirit we leave behind.

You may not *think* you're doing for others as a way of controlling their behavior, but you may be doing exactly that. If you give someone a gift of money — not a loan but a gift — do you get upset if she spends it unwisely? Can you hear yourself saying, "If I'd known you were going to spend the money on *that*, I wouldn't have given it to you in the first place." Does it irritate you if you're generous to someone and he doesn't say "thank you"? Do you say things like, "That's the least he could do after I went out of my way to be helpful"?

Part V

Achieving Happiness in Key Relationships

The 5th Wave   By Rich Tennant

...and finally, do you feel well connected to the other members of your department?

In this part . . .

If you're like me, you look for happiness in three types of key relationships: work, family, and with your significant other.

Is your workplace a battleground, where co-workers never say "please" and "thank you," but are quick to act out their hostilities toward each other? Did you know that the emotional climate of the workplace determines whether employees flounder or flourish at their respective jobs? In this part, I show you how to handle anger constructively so that you and others don't leave work everyday feeling resentful and drained.

Would you like to actually enjoy being at home with your family? Simply sharing one meal a day with the entire family can go a long way toward insuring that the rest of your family is happy to see you when you walk through the door at the end of the day. In this part, I provide other strategies for achieving happiness as a family.

And would you like to know which three elements make for a happy relationship and what positive psychology tells us about the benefits of "tending and befriending" those we love? In this part, I fill you in on that and more when it comes to intimate relationships.

Chapter 18

At Work

*E*very Monday morning, it's the same thing: Theresa dreads going to work. For her, work is the place where she is the most unhappy. Her immediate supervisor is a tyrant, screaming about the smallest mistake and treating Theresa and her coworkers with contempt. The days seem long and she's always on guard, never knowing when the next eruption will occur. Theresa came to this job four years ago, a happy person with a laid-back, fun-loving, outgoing personality. Now, she's quiet, introspective, serious, and cynical — she sees no hope for things changing for the better as long as she remains in this job.

Theresa's behavior at work is also changing. She regularly comes to work late and often leaves early if her boss isn't around. She's started snapping at her fellow employees and, from time to time, engaging in malicious office gossip. Theresa knows that her behavior is wrong, but she's so angry about how things are that she acts that way anyway.

Theresa has become a victim of what Dr. Paul Spector at the University of South Florida calls *counterproductive work behavior.* Counterproductive work behavior involves a pattern of negative, aggressive acts — directed at the organization or its employees — that is inevitable when working people get too angry and unhappy.

In this chapter, I help you understand why you may be unhappy at work and what you can do about it. The focus of this chapter is positive — positive ways to cope with anger, positive exchanges you can have with coworkers, and positive strategies for conflict management. I also tell you how to calculate your workplace positivity ratio, which has an awful lot to do with whether you flounder or flourish at your work.

Calculating Your Workplace Positivity Ratio

A leader in the field of positive psychology, Dr. Barbara Fredrickson of the University of Michigan, says that employees tend to flourish (thrive, prosper, achieve success) or languish (finding yourself in a rut, going nowhere, and feeling unhappy) in large part depending on the *positivity ratio* of the setting in which you work. If the positivity ratio — that's your positive emotions divided by your negative emotions — is approximately 3.0 or higher, you're likely to flourish; if it's less than 3.0, odds are that you'll find yourself floundering and unhappy.

Find a quiet time and place, maybe at the end of the day, to review Table 18-1. Circle ten emotions that you observed in yourself and your fellow employees today. Don't focus on which column you're choosing emotions from — just choose ten emotions.

Table 18-1	Emotions Observed at Work
Positive Emotions	*Negative Emotions*
Appreciation	Anger
Contentment	Anxiety
Curiosity	Confusion
Excitement	Disinterest
Happiness	Disrespect
Interest	Dejection
Jealousy	Fear
Joy	Frustration
Satisfaction	Guilt
Validation	Worry

Divide the number of words in the "Positive Emotions" column by the number of words in the "Negative Emotions" column, and that gives you your workplace PR. You want your number to be 3 or above.

You can change your workplace positivity ratio by being more positive at work yourself. In the remainder of this chapter, I give you strategies for doing exactly that.

Making Mom proud: Saying "please" and "thank you"

Almost every morning, Phil eats breakfast at a local restaurant, a small, quiet place mostly frequented by regulars like himself. It's the type of place where the waitresses place your order without even asking you what you want — they know your order because they know *you*! Phil says, "I love this place because it's so friendly and every one here seems to be in a good mood. A great place to start my day!"

During the 20 or so minutes Phil is there, he says "thank you" an average of five to six times. Given the fact that he eats there roughly 350 days a year, that comes to a total of between 1,750 and 2,100 thank-you's per year. Boy, would that make Phil's mom proud! As he explains, "She instilled in me the importance of being courteous, friendly, and civil with other people. She also taught me to say, 'Yes, ma'am' and 'No, sir' to adults."

"Sure, I'm courteous at restaurants," you're thinking. "But what does this have to do with the workplace?" Simple. The word *please* is what you say before making a request as opposed to a demand — and people don't typically respond well to demands. Demands brings out the aggressive sides of our personalities — both overtly aggressive and passive-aggressive — which, in turn, leads to further problems. Similarly, the term *thank you* conveys an appreciation and respect for the other person and what he's doing to make your job easier. If you don't say "thank you," the implication is that you're not appreciative, and everybody likes to feel appreciated.

Start making a habit of saying "please" and "thank you" to everyone you encounter at work — from the janitor to the CEO. Make a special effort to use these terms with the coworkers you have the most difficulty dealing with. Who knows? Maybe this will be the beginning of new and happier relationships with those people. It's worth a shot!

Loving What You Do

Sandra has been a school teacher for 30 years. When she started in the early 1970s, teaching was relatively easy — children respected their teachers and did what they were told. Having kids stay on task — for example, learning multiplication tables or how to diagram a sentence — wasn't all that difficult. The pay wasn't great but, as far as society was concerned, teaching was classified as a "high-value" occupation. That isn't the case anymore! Sandra has to struggle with the kids every school day, from start to finish, all in an effort to educate them. The kids show her little respect; they often don't comply with simple requests; and, there are constant disruptions.

So, how is it that at age 57 Sandra continues to love teaching? According to Sandra, "I suppose a lot of it has to do with the fact that I really believe these are good kids and it's not their fault that they're hard to control — a lot of it has to do with how they're raised. And, you know, I'm actually a pretty good teacher — I should be after 30 years! I guess I just love what I do — simple as that."

Peter, on the other hand, *doesn't* love what he does for a living — or, he wouldn't have been sitting in my office once a week complaining about being unhappy. Peter is a high-priced architect and a senior partner in a major firm. He's so accomplished at what he does that he enjoys the respect of his peers in the community and has amassed a considerable amount of wealth as a result of his labors.

So, why is Peter unhappy? All it took was asking a few key questions to figure that one out: Peter had been succeeding at a career that wasn't of his choosing. All the men in Peter's family going back four generations were architects and, like it or not, that was his destiny. What Peter *really* wanted to be was a big league baseball player — which was not completely fanciful given his natural athletic abilities and his love of baseball throughout his school years. But his family reasoned that there was too much uncertainty associated with a sports career (not all good ball players make it) and, in their opinion, it wasn't a serious, respectable profession. Peter was outnumbered, so he gave in and that was the beginning of a lifetime of unhappiness at work.

Do you love your work? If not, consider the following:

- ✔ **Don't think of your job as an all-or-nothing thing.** Break it down into its various components — meetings, sales, dealing with subordinates — and focus on those activities that you enjoy most. That's where you should be spending most of your time.

- ✔ **Think of your work relative to the other aspects of your lifestyle.** One reason that Sandra enjoyed her work was that it provided escape from major stresses in her home and family life. As she said, "It's a refuge from all that other stuff that I just don't want to deal with right now."

- ✔ **Consider the alternatives — if you weren't doing this, what would you be doing?** Believe it or not, no matter how much you dislike your job, there's always something worse out there!

- ✔ **Try to assign meaning to your work that goes beyond the routine aspects of your job description.** All companies have a mission statement — find out what yours is and be part of that mission.

- ✔ **Get those parts of your job that you don't love behind you early in the day.** From there on out, it's all downhill.

✔ **Make a conscious effort to increase the positivity ratio in your workplace (see "Calculating Your Workplace Positivity Ratio," earlier in this chapter).**

✔ **Act as though you love what you do, even if you don't.** That's right, fake it! In Chapter 12, I tell you how you how you can empower yourself by putting a smile on your face.

✔ **Find a compatriot, a fellow traveler as you journey through the work day, preferably someone who loves her work more than you do.** Who knows? Maybe her optimism and enthusiasm will prove contagious.

✔ **Start looking for a new job if you've tried everything you can think of to be happy at work and nothing works.** Be optimistic (Chapter 5) and tell yourself that there's a job out there somewhere that suits you better.

Establishing Healthy Boundaries

One of the keys to happiness in the workplace is for employees to find the right balance between structure and freedom. Structure involves those formal and informal rules or codes of conduct that govern how you behave at work. More important, structure imposes certain boundaries within which you're expected to freely operate — boundaries that are not to be crossed.

Crossing the line

Back in my academic years, I was once a member of a very powerful tenure and promotions committee, which, in effect, determined whether faculty progressed and prospered in their careers. In one meeting, I made a favorable recommendation about one of the psychologists under my charge, which was subsequently denied by the department chairman — my boss.

Without thinking, I vehemently exclaimed, "I don't think that's fair not to promote this man!" The chairman replied, without raising his voice but clearly unhappy, "What does fairness have to do with anything?" I looked around the room for support, but the other committee members were all looking at their shoes. This wasn't their fight. "Nothing, I guess," I said rather meekly.

After the meeting was over, the chairman asked if I would stay for a minute. He closed the door, sat down across from me, smiled, and said in a quiet, but firm tone, "Doyle, I think maybe you're confused about something. You're a bright young man and I value your input on this committee. But your job is only to make recommendations; my job is to make decisions. If I choose to support your recommendation, I'm sure that makes you happy — it should. But if I choose not to follow your recommendation, I don't expect to hear about it. Do you understand, or are you still confused?"

I had crossed a boundary without realizing it. I did it that once, but never again.

Here's a list of boundaries having to do with power, civility, and intimacy that you probably don't want to cross if you hope to be happy at work:

✔ Don't tell your supervisor that she is incompetent.

✔ Never take it for granted that you'll get a raise.

✔ Don't engage in gossip about fellow employees.

✔ Don't roll your eyes or otherwise act with contempt when someone is giving you constructive feedback about your job performance.

✔ Don't mistake friendly for flirtatious.

✔ Never develop intimate relationships with others with or for whom you work — it's not only risky, it's often against company policy.

✔ Don't goof off just because the boss is away.

✔ Don't treat you coworkers with less respect than you do your family.

✔ Never view those with whom you work as the enemy.

✔ Support is okay, but don't invite co-workers to be therapists.

And, here's a list of healthy boundaries that go a long way toward insuring greater productivity and a sense of well-being in the workplace:

✔ Always say "please" and "thank you" when interacting with superiors and co-workers.

✔ Be personable, but not too personal at work. Your fellow employees don't need to know everything there is to know about your life.

✔ Always remember that even a bad boss is still a boss. Treat him as such.

✔ Where possible, confine work to the workplace — off-site, after-hours socializing is rarely about work.

✔ Treat a one-time kindness as a gift, not a precedent.

✔ If you get paid for eight hours, work eight hours.

✔ Reach out to coworkers in need without intruding in their lives.

Avoiding Toxic Coworkers

Negativity in the workplace is like a virus — sooner or later, it infects everyone. In this section, I cover the main types of toxic workers, and give you tips for dealing with them.

The stress carriers

Ever work with someone who, when she enters the room, seems to instantly create chaos? Before she walked in, people were working away, productive, and in a good mood — but not anymore. Suddenly, tension permeates the air and all the good will between the employees evaporates. What was once a happy work place is no longer. Welcome to the world of the *stress carrier.*

Here are some ways to identify a stress carrier:

- A rapid, loud, or pressured tone of voice
- An aggressive body posture (for example, hand waving or finger pointing)
- A defensive body posture (for example, arms crossed in front of chest)
- A tendency to talk over other people in a conversation
- Fixed, angry opinions
- Use of obscenities
- A tense facial expression (a frown or clenched jaw)
- A jarring laugh
- Head nodding
- Finger tapping
- A tendency to hurry up the speech of others by interjecting comments such as "Uh-huh," "Right," and "I know"

 If you can avoid stress carriers, by all means do so.. Their unhappiness is contagious. If you're around them very much, you'll end up feeling stressed and out of sorts yourself. But, if you can't, inoculate yourself with thoughts like "I'm not going to let her ruin my mood," "I can handle this — it's not like I haven't had to deal with her before," and "This too shall pass!" This'll work the same as getting a flu or smallpox inoculation. ***Remember:*** People can only get to you if you let them. (For more detail about Stress Inoculation Training, check out *Anger Management For Dummies*.)

 Is it possible that you could be a stress carrier yourself? Check out the list in this section and see if you have any of those stress-carrier characteristics. Better yet, ask someone you work with who knows you well to examine the list and tell you what she thinks. Be careful, though: You may not like what she says.

The naysayers

Fred was the chief financial officer (CFO) of a large corporation that was undergoing drastic changes. The chief executive officer (CEO) had abruptly resigned, leaving the institution with significant financial and morale problems. Everywhere you turned, there was an air of uncertainty among those employees who remained. No one was happy.

An acting CEO had been named, whose job it was to carry the institution through this crisis — and she needed the cooperation of Fred and other members of senior management to make this happen. However, Fred was a *naysayer,* the type of person who always has a negative comment, refuses to consider the merits of other people's suggestions, and balks at any attempt to change things.

The acting CEO had strongly admonished Fred on several occasions about always being so negative. But Fred persisted, until one day, right in the middle of a meeting, the CEO had heard enough. She abruptly halted the meeting, telling everyone else except Fred that they were excused. Two hours later, all the senior staff were called to another emergency meeting, at which time the CEO matter-of-factly advised them that Fred had decided to resign immediately and would be leaving by the end of the workday. Everyone was stunned, but not surprised — except maybe Fred.

Would you hang around someone at work who was sick with a cold — coughing, sneezing, wiping his runny nose? I bet you'd stay as far away from him as possible to preserve your health, right? And you wouldn't feel guilty about doing so either. Well, that's exactly what you should do when you run into a naysayer. However, if it's impossible to avoid that person, counter his negatives with some positives of your own — in other words you be a *yeasayer.* For example, you could say "Fred, I understand that you are concerned about what's in our future, I am too. But, I prefer to look at this as a time of opportunity rather than a catastrophe (see Chapter 6 which deals with hardiness)."

No matter how high you are on the organizational chart, no one likes a naysayer. If you're the type of person who can offer *both* criticism *and* positive suggestions, don't worry. But, if you're all negative all the time, your days at your current job may be numbered.

Looking for Win-Win Solutions

Work — all types of work — inevitably involves conflict. Why? Because people who work alongside one an other are either striving to achieve the same goals — recognition and advancement — or they have different views about how things should be done at work. The conflicts themselves, it turns out, are not nearly as important as how you resolve them. And, in doing so, you'll invariably use strategies such as:

- ✔ **Competition:** "I win — you lose. It's that simple."

- ✔ **Compromise:** "It's a give-and-take proposition. Each of us gets a little of what we want even though we don't get all of what we want."

- ✔ **Collaboration:** "Why don't we pool our resources and work together on this problem — be a team?"

- ✔ **Accommodation:** "Whatever — we'll try it your way this time. It's not worth fighting about."

Happy, satisfied employees are the ones who use a mixture of all these approaches to manage conflict, instead of relying on one particular strategy. I cover each of these strategies in the following sections.

Competition

Competition is a win-lose strategy for resolving conflict. Competitive employees attempt to gain power (that's where the term *power struggle* comes from) by winning arguments. Healthy competition involves "winning without intimidating" others. Unhealthy competition is about winning at all costs — it's aggressive and ends up hurting others. Most people don't need to win every battle at work but a win every once in a while keeps them wanting to play the game. Competition can be an advantage (a) when it occurs in an adversarial situation like a court battle or a sporting event and (b) because it signals that the employee is fully committed to some important issue or outcome. In many work settings, competition is viewed as a sign of strength.

Overly competitive employees — those that invariably create a lot of unhappiness for themselves and those with whom they work — exhibit the following behaviors when there's a conflict:

- ✔ They direct personal criticism at the person with whom they're having a conflict.

- ✔ They argue, make demands, and threaten others.

- ✔ They act with contempt — for example, roll their eyes or sigh while you're trying to make your point.

- ✔ They're quick to deny responsibility.

- ✔ They're inflexible — it's their way or the highway.

- ✔ Even their humor is hostile.

Compromise

Compromise is a way of managing conflict in which each party both gains and loses something. You get some of what *you* want and I get some of what *I* want. Think of it as a trade-off, where nobody leaves empty-handed or unhappy.

You know what you want. Now all you have to do is figure out what the other person wants or needs in order to feel satisfied. Ask the other person, "What one thing would it take to make you feel right about resolving this conflict?" If it's in your power to give them that one thing, do so. If it happens that that is the one thing that you absolutely don't want to give in on, ask them if there's maybe something else that would also make them feel right — most of us want more than one thing when we're negotiating with someone else.

Not convinced that compromise is really possible at work? Here are some examples of compromise in the workplace:

- ✔ Edith needs Julie to stay a couple of hours overtime in order to finish a project that has a deadline. She knows Julie had planned to meet her boyfriend after work for a drink. Instead of telling Julie that she *has to* stay late, like it or not, Edith says, "I know you had plans and I hate to ask you to stay until we complete this project. But if you'll agree this once, I'll let you have an afternoon off later this week to compensate you. And I promise I won't make a habit of this." If Julie says yes, she's giving up that after-work time with her boyfriend, but she's gaining an afternoon off later; meanwhile, Edith loses Julie later in the week, but she gets Julie when she really needs her — now.

- ✔ Ted has a full agenda for the staff meeting and, because it's Friday, he knows that the rest of the team wants to get the meeting over as soon as possible. He starts out by telling them, "Look, folks, we have a lot to go over this afternoon, but I'll leave it up to you as to how quickly and efficiently we do that. If you stay focused, you can get out of here early" Ted is giving up control of the meeting (something a lot of executives don't want to do); in return, his staff will have to give up their usual passive (sit quietly and let Ted run the show) approach to staff meetings and become much more assertive and organized. This way, everybody wins.

- ✔ Katie wants a raise, but the budget is tight. Her boss tells her, "I'd love to give you a raise — you deserve it. But honestly, the money just isn't there. What I can do — and what I want to do — is start giving you a lot more responsibility and authority about how things run around here, which will justify a big increase in your salary the next time around. Does that sound like something you can live with?"

Collaboration

When employees collaborate, they *integrate* their ideas and energies so that the whole is greater than the sum of the parts. This happens because:

- **Collaboration generates new ideas.** All parties feel freer to be creative in coming up with ways to solve problems and conflicts. No one idea or opinion dominates.

- **Collaboration signals mutual respect for all parties involved.** People believe their feelings and ideas have value.

- **Collaboration requires a greater degree of commitment than other conflict management strategies like compromise and accommodation.** Each employee feels a sense of true partnership — that is, not only are they part of the problem, they're also part of the solution.

- **Collaboration requires a willingness to move *with* rather than *against* your coworkers.** This means there's less resistance, less tension in the process of finding a new solution to the conflict.

The next time you find yourself in conflict with someone at work, start out with the mindset that you'd like to cooperate with the other person. It increases the likelihood that you'll reach a win-win solution and keep everybody happy.

Accommodation

It's taken me a lifetime to realize just how powerful the word *whatever* is. In conflict situations, where cooperation is the order of the day but there is no possibility of compromise or collaboration, try accommodation. Some people think of accommodation as just another word for giving up or giving in — which, in a highly competitive society, is unthinkable. But it's also a strategy for reducing or eliminating conflict that expresses a desire for harmony.

The word *whatever* can have many meanings, for example:

- Your way is fine; let's go with that.

- I just don't want to fight about this.

- I had my way last time — you can have your way this time.

- This issue is not the hill I want to die on.

- Obviously, this means more to you than it does to me.

- I'm trying to be reasonable here.

- Since you've got the upper hand, what's the sense of fighting about this?

Avoiding anger

In one of my conflict-management classes at the local community college, I asked my students to complete a test measuring different conflict-management styles and also one measuring how often and how strongly they experienced anger in the course of a week. I then took each student's primary conflict-management style and calculated the average amount of anger that went along with it.

Interestingly, those who chose competition as their chief way of resolving conflict with others were far more angry on average than their counterparts who chose compromise, accommodation, or collaboration.

 The next time someone at work says "I know a lot of you think we should go ahead and confront this problem, but I think we should hold off a bit and see what else develops" or "I know you and I don't agree on this, but I feel pretty strongly about my plan of attack," try responding with, "Whatever," and see if the world ends.

Using Anger Constructively

It's not anger that gets you in trouble at work; it's how you *express* your anger. Charlie uses his anger destructively whenever he gets frustrated at his secretary. He hollers at her, berates her, and slams his fist on her desk. Elaine uses a more constructive approach to anger. She asks her secretary to come into her office so that what she has to say to her won't be in public view. She starts out by telling the young woman that, for the most part, she's satisfied with her performance at work, but in this particular instance she finds herself extremely irritated by a mistake that the secretary made. Elaine tempers her anger because she tries to put herself in her secretary's shoes and knows that she wouldn't like it if someone were yelling at her. Unlike Charlie, who just wants to vent his frustration, Elaine's objective is to use her anger strategically to reduce future mistakes.

If you were the secretary, who would you want to work for?

In order to use anger constructively, you first have to decide where you want your anger to take you. If you're Charlie, all you want is to blow off some steam. Elaine, on the other hand, wants to improve her relationship with her secretary — after all, good help is hard to find!

In the following sections, I help you use your anger constructively at work.

Step 1: Think about how you want to feel afterward

Many people believe that expressing anger in some outrageous manner (getting things off your chest) relieves tension and leaves you feeling better afterward. Ironically, nothing could be farther from the truth. Psychologist James Averill at the University of Massachusetts, who has devoted his entire career to understanding anger, asked large numbers of people how they felt after they got angry with someone else. Believe it or not, the vast majority felt like crap: Sixty-nine percent still felt aggravated; 59 percent felt unhappy; and, a third or more felt ashamed, embarrassed, guilty, and anxious. Only one in five reported feeling pleased, good, or confident afterward.

The explanation as to why most of us feel bad after expressing our anger comes from the motives we have for expressing it — in other words, what do we hope to gain? Professor Averill found three motives that pretty much guide all expression of anger — all of which, in my opinion, are destructive:

- The need to assert *my* authority or to improve *my* image — selfish or self-centered anger.
- The need to seek revenge — to get back at a fellow employee in some malicious way. (In the "Counteracting Counterproductive Work Behavior" section, later in this chapter, I show you how this leads to counterproductive work behavior.)
- The need to vent pent-up frustration.

If you choose to use your anger constructively, afterward you will *not* feel:

- Like holding a grudge against a coworker
- Totally justified in continuing to dislike the other person
- Defensive in social situations involving the other employee
- Victimized by that person
- As though you're going to explode any minute
- Pessimistic about being able to work effectively with this person in the future

Step 2: Make anger about the problem, not the person

The focus of Charlie's anger is on his *secretary,* while Elaine's focus in on the *mistake* the secretary made. This is a key distinction between constructive and destructive anger.

Personal attacks make people feel defiant, indifferent, hurt, angry, and rejected — none of which is conducive to improved work performance.

Concentrate on *what* you're angry about, not *who* you're angry at.

Step 3: Look at what's underneath your anger

This step is easier than you think. Why? Because the source of your anger is *you!* Your anger has to do with *your* expectations, *your* values, what *you* demand from your coworkers, *your* level of tolerance, and so forth. Think of anger as a mirror into your heart and soul. Charlie may be angry at his secretary for some flaw or imperfection he can't tolerate in himself. One of the reasons that anger can be constructive is because it tells you something — sometimes a lot — about yourself that you didn't know.

The next time you find yourself angry with someone at work, ask yourself this question: Why am *I* so angry — what does *my* anger say about *me?* You'll learn a lot more than if you ask the other person, "Why do *you* keep annoying me?"

Step 4: Be empathetic

Think about how you express your anger at work and then ask yourself how you would feel and react if you were on the receiving end of that behavior. Gives you a whole different perspective, doesn't it? That perspective is what enables you to use anger constructively.

The ability to put yourself in the other employee's shoes is called empathy and it comes in two forms:

✔ **Mental empathy:** Dr. Avery Weisman, a renowned psychiatrist at Harvard University, summed it up best by describing this type of empathy as "having respect for another person's irrationality."

✔ **Emotional empathy:** Most people are familiar with this kind of empathy. It's when you actually feel the other person's feeling. Their sadness makes you sad. Their nervousness makes you nervous. Their unhappiness makes you unhappy.

Remember: Both types of empathy are important and ideally they both come into play when you're trying to handle your anger more constructively. One is no better than the other — they're just different manifestations of the same thing.

If you'd like to know more about empathy and its relationship to anger, check out two of my books, *Anger Management For Dummies* (Wiley) and *ANGER-FREE: Ten Basic Steps to Managing Your Anger* (Quill).

Step 5: Engage in give-and-take conversation

Constructive anger expression, like all forms of effective communication, involves a two-person dialogue. A *monologue* is when you do all the talking, shouting, or lecturing and the other party sits there passively like a ventriloquist's dummy, speaking only when you let it. In Part IV of *Happiness For Dummies*, I emphasize the importance of balance, and what I'm stressing here is the need for a balanced conversation. First you speak, then she speaks, and so on until you hopefully reach a point of *mutual* understanding.

Step 6: Watch your body language

Most of the reactions people have to other people's anger has to do with nonverbal behavior. Here are some types of body language that clearly do *not* signal constructive anger expression:

✔ Clenched fists

✔ Finger pointing

✔ Hand waving

✔ Grabbing the other person by the arm

✔ Arms crossed at the chest

✔ Narrowing of the eyes

✔ Glaring

- ✔ Frowning
- ✔ Loudly tapping the fingers
- ✔ Speaking rapidly or loudly
- ✔ Excessive head nodding
- ✔ Breathing heavily

Avoid these types of body language if you want to accomplish something useful with your anger.

Psychological research has shown that human beings are much more sensitive to an angry look than they are to any other emotion. We're much more alert to angry faces, for example, than happy faces. It's as though our brain is constantly scanning the environment for the smallest sign of impending anger — so that we can prepare ourselves for the onslaught of negative emotion that may eventually come our way.

Counteracting Counterproductive Work Behavior

Everything you do at work falls into one of two categories — productive or counterproductive. How effective you are as an employee is determined by the balance between the two. If you spend far too much time trying to look busy when you're not, avoiding returning phone calls to someone you should, and arguing with coworkers, your work will suffer. These are all classic examples of *counterproductive work behavior* — which is the type of behavior that employees engage in when they're angry, dissatisfied, and unhappy.

If you want to be happy at work, you *must* find ways to counteract that counterproductive work behavior, which is what I want to discuss in this section.

Giving your employer a full day's effort

In a survey I did with a group of 74 employees at one worksite, I found that five of the most common forms of counterproductive work behavior involved stealing time from the employer. Employees reported often observing their coworkers:

- Coming to work late without permission
- Taking longer breaks than allowed
- Daydreaming rather than doing work
- Leaving work early without permission
- Trying to look busy when you're not

Sound familiar? There is a connection between being an unhappy, disgruntled employee and coming in late or leaving early. You *could* wait until someone or something makes you happier about your job, so that you can start looking forward to working a full day. *Or* you could reverse the connection and decide to see if you're happier when you give your employer a full day's effort; if you do, you'll get more accomplished and feel better about your individual productivity. Of course, I'm all in favor of the proactive approach — reversing that connection.

Treating your coworkers with civility

We live in a reciprocal world — anger begets anger, niceness begets niceness. Problem is, we're all waiting on the other guy to make the first move and then we react accordingly. Most of the things I cover in this chapter — conflict management styles like compromise and collaboration, using anger constructively, and simple things like saying "please" and "thank you" — are considered forms of civility.

The survey I mention in the preceding section suggests a number of uncivil behaviors that you need to avoid:

- Ignoring someone at work
- Being nasty or rude to a client or coworker
- Blaming fellow employees for mistakes that you make
- Insulting others about their job performance
- Refusing to help out at work
- Making fun of people at work
- Being verbally abusive to a supervisor or coworker

You can counteract such behavior by:

- ✔ Always be willing to help a colleague in need
- ✔ Owning up to your own mistakes
- ✔ Treating coworkers with courtesy, not contempt
- ✔ Finding ways to compliment others for their work
- ✔ Laughing *with* others, not *at* them
- ✔ Telling at least five coworkers per day, "Have a good day!"

Being a team player

Teamwork seems to be the mantra of most workplaces today. One industry after another proudly heralds the fact that they've "gone to the team approach." The problem with counterproductive work behavior is that it works *against* the team concept.

Ron, for example, would pick and choose when he wanted to be a team player. As vice president of marketing, Ron was a key player in the day-to-day operations of his company. When Ron was happy with the way things were going (usually because others were doing things *his* way), he was cordial, provided other VPs with vital information they needed, and accessible to everyone. But, when he was not happy, he would act like a *contrarian* — stubborn, oppositional, reclusive — for example, not returning important phone calls and e-mails to his colleagues. On more than one occasion, this cost the company money — large sums of money — not to mention alienating Ron from other members of upper management.

In order for teams to work, the team members must have:

- ✔ **A cooperative attitude:** Unfortunately, Ron is one of those people who cooperates when it suits him and doesn't when it doesn't.

- ✔ **Complimentary skills with others on the team:** Marketing was Ron's area of expertise, which — when he cooperated — complimented his teammates in finance, sales, distribution, product design, and so forth.

- ✔ **Performance goals in common with his team:** One thing I've learned in consulting with both individuals and groups in the workplace is that it's always dangerous to assume everyone has the same goals in mind. Most often, they don't — which means that they often find themselves pulling in different directions at the same time and getting nowhere.

✔ **A common philosophy about how to reach those goals:** Even if everyone on the team agrees on a goal, they may not necessarily agree on
how to best get there. One team member may want to proceed slowly
but surely toward the overall objective, while others may want to move
full speed ahead. In order for the team to work, all the team members
need to agree on how to get there.

✔ **Mutual accountability:** There's no passing the buck when you're a team
player. It's not enough to be accountable to yourself — you have to be
accountable to everyone else on the team. And they have to be accountable to you.

Creating good public relations

One of the most commonly acknowledged examples of counterproductive
work behavior is complaining to people *outside* work about how lousy the
place you work is. A lot of unhappy employees aren't content to complain
inside the workplace; they feel compelled to air the dirty linen with anyone in
the community who will listen.

The thing is, complaining about your job doesn't make you feel any better,
but it makes those to whom you're complaining ask themselves, "If the place
is so bad, why on Earth does she continue working there? Is she not good
enough to get another job?"

The other thing to consider is that an employer's reputation, its credibility,
is an asset — an asset which you as an employee share. When you badmouth
your employer to others, you diminish that asset — and you and they both
lose!

If you can't say anything positive about where you work, it's probably best to
refrain from saying anything at all or, if asked, something fairly innocuous like
"Oh, things could be better but, then again, no job's perfect." If you can't do
that and you have a strong urge to complain about how bad things at work
are, then I would recommend talking to a life coach or therapist — someone
who can be objective and supportive at the same time.

Chapter 19

At Home

lthough happiness may be the ultimate goal of a family, it shouldn't be the primary focus. Instead, focus on the ways in which members of your family treat each other, and the happiness will follow:

- Happy families cooperate; unhappy families compete.

- Happy families share common goals and are accountable to each other; in unhappy families, everybody marches to a different drum and is accountable only to himself.

- Happy families know how to handle anger constructively; unhappy families do not.

- Happy families support each other in good times and bad; in unhappy families, it's every man, woman, and child for himself or herself.

Throughout this book, I offer lots of tips about how to achieve *individual* happiness. In this chapter, I apply many of those same principles to achieving *collective* happiness within a family. For example families need structure — rules, priorities, and goals (Chapter 14); they need to play as well as work together (Chapter 15); family members need to see each other smile (Chapter 12); and, they need to regularly acknowledge how happy they are to be a part of this family (Chapter 11).

Happiness is the glue that binds families together. Without it, families tend to fragment and become distant strangers, even if they love one another. If your family isn't as happy as you know it could be, this chapter is for you.

Setting Priorities

Some families have priorities — things that they feel are most important and crucial to family life and success and that give the family a clearly defined sense of direction and purpose. Other families do not — they're like tumbleweeds, blowing this way and that and getting nowhere in particular.

Take the Johnson family, for example. Their home is full of books and magazines. Every evening, the parents ask their children if they have homework. At the dinner table, they talk about what's happening in the world and even discuss serious topics like abortion, whether kids should have sex in their teens, drug use, and whether it's okay for people to live together before marriage. They watch TV as a family, and on Saturdays they all go to the local library and check out books. When the kids were little, the parents enrolled them in summer reading groups and took them to museums. And the parents are among the few who go to parents' night at their children's school. It doesn't take a PhD to figure out that, in the Johnson family, education is a priority.

For the Elliott family, it's all about game night. All three of their kids are involved in sports — Holly is on the school soccer team, Brad plays junior varsity football, and Mark is in Little League baseball. The parents attend all their games, sometimes dividing themselves up so that they can be at two different games at the same time. The family cheers for their favorite college team on the weekends as they watch the games together in the family den. The father is a member of a sports club and the mother organizes refreshments for Mark's Little League games. This family's number-one priority is sports.

And, then there's the Gutierrez family, whose priority is socialization. They make their home available for all their children's friends. There are big birthday parties for the parents as well as the kids. Last Thanksgiving, there were 25 friends and relatives for dinner, and at Christmas the house is full of people. The parents like to take group vacations with other couples and families rather than just the five of them.

All of these families are happy — they're just happy about different things.

Priorities provide families with:

- ✔ **A sense of immediacy:** What the family needs or wants to do first and foremost
- ✔ **A sense of purpose:** How this family wants to define itself
- ✔ **A sense of importance:** What the family believes is important
- ✔ **A set of shared values:** Values that all the family members share in common
- ✔ **A sense of the future:** Where the family's heading in the days, weeks, months, and years to come

✔ **A sense of stability:** An agenda that doesn't change from one day to the next

Try this exercise to help your family set its own priorities:

1. **Find a time when the whole family can sit down together for at least an hour.**

2. **Pass out sheets of paper and ask each family member to write down three priorities he or she thinks the family has or should have.**

   Give examples like the ones I mention earlier in this section. Also, mention things like honesty, supporting each other, and health. Emphasize that this is not about your individual priorities — it's about what you think the family should be doing as a group.

3. **Then, one by one, have each member do a "show and tell," sharing his list and explaining why he chose the things he did.**

4. **Don't comment right away — wait until everyone has shared their list and then open the door for discussion.**

   Are there any points of agreement — things listed by more than one family member? Are there any glaring omissions? Do family members see any obstacles to achieving these priorities? Is there anyone in the family who seems to not want to get onboard with these priorities? If so, don't criticize them; instead say "It's okay if you don't want to share you priorities with us now, but we really do want to know what you think this family should be doing more of that we aren't or less of than we are." Leave the door open for them go join in later on.

The goal is to end the hour with a firm sense of what you value as a family.

We're a working family

Like most middle-class families, my wife and I made work — having a work ethic, learning how to work, being a responsible employee — a cornerstone of our family values. At the dinner table, we talked about my work — the things I enjoyed and the problems I had — and when the kids were old enough, we encouraged them to find jobs. Both of our children had part-time jobs when they were in high school and they earned extra money working during Christmas holidays and the summer months.

We stressed the importance of being at work on time, of helping out their fellow employees, and showing initiative — which always pays off. And we talked about how education — another family priority — affords a person more options when it comes to employment. So, it should come as no surprise that both our kids have done well in their careers and don't depend on us for financial support. All those dinner conversations must've sunk in!

Since we're definitely Type A parents, what we didn't talk enough about is how important it is to play (Chapter 15 talks about the need to balance work and play). That, our kids have had to learn more on their own.

Deciding What Kind of Parent You Want to Be

People have different hairstyles, wear different styles of clothing, and have distinct parenting styles, too. How your raise you children doesn't just affect how happy they'll be; it affects how they perform in school, whether they take up smoking, how likely it is they'll suffer from depression, and whether they engage in risky sexual behavior.

According to psychologists who study this sort of thing, there are four main styles of parenting: autocratic, authoritative, permissive, and unengaged. The styles differ in terms of how much involvement you have in your child's life and how much control you try to exert over your child's behavior. Table 19-1 illustrates the differences.

Table 19-1	Parenting Styles	
	Parental Involvement	
Parental Control	*High*	*Low*
High	Authoritative	Autocratic
Low	Permissive	Unengaged

I describe the various styles in the following sections. Decide which one fits the relationship you have with your child.

Parenting styles are learned patterns of behavior — which means they can be *unlearned* at any point in life if you choose.

Have each of your kids review the following sections and ask them which one they think fits you. Don't be surprised — and, more important, don't be defensive — if they have a different view of how you parent. Ask them to explain their answer and give specific examples of why they chose that particular style. Maybe the truth lies somewhere in between what you and your kids think.

Autocratic

Autocratic parents tend to be involved in their children's lives only so far as rules and punishment are concerned. They decide what the child does, who the child can be friends with, where the child is supposed to be, and ultimately what the child's life is going to be.

One autocratic mother told me that when her son was just 6 years old, he knew he was going to go to the University of Florida and be an architect. "Ridiculous," I said. "A 6-year-old can't possible conceive of what an architect is or, for that matter, what a university is. The truth is you and your husband decided what you wanted him to be and then made sure he fulfilled your dream."

There is little, if any, back-and-forth dialogue between autocratic parents and their kids — everything is a lecture that embodies the message, "It's my way or the highway!" Children raised by autocratic parents aren't happy, but they *are* angry and afraid — the fear is evident, and their anger is often suppressed. How do they view their parents? As cold, harsh, and rejecting — not a very pretty picture.

If you want to know if you're an autocratic parent, read the following statement and answer true or false:

> As a parent, I *most often* make the decisions about my child's behavior.

If you answered true, you're an autocratic parent.

Authoritative

If you're an authoritative parent, you're highly involved in your children's lives and you're not afraid to exert a reasonable amount of control over their behavior. You're nice, but firm. You have a *presence* in their lives — doing things with them and showing up for things that are important. There is no mistake who is the parent and who is the child, even when they reach their adolescent years. You actually foster independence and self-reliance, which increase with age. You teach your children to be civil and responsible in dealings with others, including family members. You allow your children to find their voice and verbalize their own opinions, needs, wants, fears, and life goals. You punish when it's called for but you aren't heavy-handed — sending your children to a timeout or grounding them is one thing, swearing at and threatening them is quite another. How do the children of authoritarian parents view their parents? As warm, accepting, and loving — despite the fact that parents exert control over their lives.

If you want your child to be a nonsmoker, make good grades, enjoy positive mental health, and not engage in at-risk sex, this is definitely the style you want to choose.

To determine if you're an authoritative parent, answer true or false to the statement:

> I *ask my children their opinion* but I generally end up making the decisions — for example, about curfew or at what age they can begin dating.

If you answered true, you're an authoritative parent.

Permissive

This is the style of parenting that kids love — at least in the short run. Why? Simple: Permissive parents let their kids do as they please, come and go as they like, set their own rules — all in the name of love. Permissive parents are involved in their kids' lives, to be sure, but in a hands-off kind of way. They put few demands on their kids, set few if any limits on their social and emotional behavior (hey, tantrums are okay — they don't mean anything by it!), and allow them maximum independence. The one word that never comes out of the permissive parent's mouth is *no*. It's up to the kids to decide if smoking is bad for them. It's up to the kids to decide what their curfew is, if they have one at all. It's up to the kids whether they do their homework.

How do children view their permissive parents? Kids think their parents are wonderful, cool, and their very best friends. Problem is, these kids also end up being moody, defiant, rebellious, and unable to handle life when they don't get their way. (They also make difficult employees when they enter the workplace and difficult partners in marriage.)

Are you a permissive parent? To find out, answer true or false to this statement:

> My kids may ask my opinion, but I generally *leave it up to them* to make their decisions.

If you answered true, you're definitely a permissive parent.

Unengaged

Unengaged parents are *un*aware of what their kids are up to, *un*available to them emotionally, and *un*willing to assume their responsibilities as a parent beyond that of providing food and shelter, forcing them to attend school, and making sure they have the latest style tennis shoes. Unengaged parents come from all walks of life, from all demographic and socioeconomic groups.

Children of unengaged parents end up alienated from adults as well as peers. They have limited social and problem-solving skills and often use anger as a means of keeping others (whom they view as threatening) at a distance. They're anything but happy. How do these kids see their parents? They don't.

To see if this is your style of parenting, answer the following statement with true or false:

> Do you *know or care* where your child is at all times?

If the answer is true, you're an unengaged parent, and your kids are definitely at risk both to themselves and others. (These children can represent significant danger to society.)

Of course, they're angry

I asked the kids in my middle school and high school anger management classes what kind of parents they had. Only a small number (18 percent) saw their parents as fitting the authoritative style. The rest of them described their parents as autocratic (32 percent), permissive (18 percent), and unengaged (32 percent). No wonder they were angry and totally unable to relate to adults in the school environment — principals, teachers, counselors, even the resource officer assigned to the school. School for these kids was anything but happy.

Balancing Interdependence with Autonomy

When I was a child, I saw a movie that showed how a mother bear loves, protects, and gives her total attention to her cubs for one year . . . and then abruptly chases them up a tree and walks away, leaving them to survive on their own. Thank goodness, humans take a little longer to make sure their offspring can live on their own (called *autonomy*) and with other people *(interdependence)*. Striking the right balance between these two opposite needs is essential to family happiness.

Children begin to strive for autonomy at the end of the first year of life, when they begin to walk. Their development of language makes them even more autonomous because they can tell their parents "No!" Autonomy really comes into its own when children enter their adolescent years. As a parent, you need to foster this emerging sense of independence — but not at the expense of family involvement. In other words, send the message to your child that "I want you to be an individual, but you're still a member of this family."

Interdependence means simply two or more people working together on a common activity or toward a common goal. It's the old idea that two hands — or minds — are better than one. Examples of interdependent behavior among family members include

- ✔ Helping one another prepare family meals
- ✔ Parents helping children with their homework
- ✔ Everyone helping out with the yard work
- ✔ Attending to one another during illness
- ✔ Doing household chores together — washing dishes, doing laundry
- ✔ Taking care of family pets

✔ Playing cards and other types of games

✔ Outdoor recreational pursuits like cycling, fishing, camping

✔ Working on school projects together

In the following sections, I show you how to foster independence without getting into power struggles with your kids and I talk about why it's important that each member of the family have a clear job description.

Sharing power

The concept of power is fundamental to family life. People talk about ways in which parents can *empower* their children, about *power struggles* between parents and children, and the *power differential* that exists between siblings of different ages. How families handle the "power relationships" that emerge — and change — over time in large part determines how happy they end up being.

Where there is a significant imbalance of power — for example, an autocratic father sets all the rules for his teenage daughter and threatens to punish her if she doesn't comply — problems exist. At the very least, in this example, the daughter feels *powerless,* which can be a breeding ground for feelings of depression, defiance, or hostility. At the worst, the father and daughter will become estranged from one another.

For parents, the trick is to find age-appropriate ways of beginning to share power with their kids starting at an early age and continuing until they reach adulthood. Believe me, I know this task isn't an easy one. Parents are often reluctant to relinquish power — "This is my house. I pay the bills here. And, I know what's best for you." And children generally want more power than they can handle at each stage of their development — "I'll be okay with my friends at the beach. I don't know why you worry so much. You just need to chill out." This conflict is precisely what makes family life sometimes seem more like a wrestling match than anything else.

Have a family discussion — with the *whole* family — about power. Don't allow these issues to play themselves out in an unconscious, unspoken, uncivil, and ultimately unhappy way. Other ways of sharing family power at different ages include: telling your 7-year-old that she can have a friend over to play and letting her decide which friend to invite; sending your 11-year-old to the grocery store to pick up some items for dinner; letting your son pick out which kind of pizza the family will eat; letting the kids decide what the family watches on TV sometimes (my guess it won't be CNN or Fox News); and, letting adolescents of driving age chauffeur the younger children to dance class and other after-school activities.

Making sure everybody has a job

Imagine being hired for a job and not having a job description. They give you an office, a desk, and some filing cabinets, but no one ever tells you what you're there for. Or, imagine that you're on a baseball team, and you're all suited up for the game, but the coach has never told you what position he wants you to play. You just sit on the bench, waiting, but there's nothing for you to do that can make you feel a part of this team.

In happy families, everyone has an assignment, a job, a purpose, something he or she can contribute to family life. There are no spectators, and no one is allowed to sit idly on the sidelines. (This builds a foundation of commitment which is vital to developing a hardy personality — more about this in Chapter 6).

Children — even very young ones — need to know what is expected of them. For example, you may tell your 4-year old, "Your job is to pick up your toys after you're through playing with them. That's not mommy's job." Adolescents need to know that their job is to spend a certain amount of time helping out at home — even though a million exciting and enticing opportunities exist elsewhere. The same goes for parents, whose jobs go way beyond simply putting bread on the table and chauffeuring kids around town (see Chapter 21).

Change the family dialogue to include the phrases *It's my job to . . .* and *It's your job to. . . .* Assuming everybody does his or her job consistently and well, how can the family help but be happy? If someone in the family isn't happy because she doesn't like her particular job (for example, cleaning up the kitchen after dinner) tell her it's fine with you if she swaps with another family member (maybe her brother hates having to walk the family dog) just as long as everyone ends up with a job.

Fighting Fair

All families fight. The question is: "Do they fight fair?" Children fight for increased autonomy; parents fight for more respect. Families fight over ideas, values, how to spend money, curfews, who can drive the car, and the list goes on. There are winners and losers and sometimes there's even compromise.

Happy families fight, too — they just do it fairly. In happy families:

> ✔ **Parents and children fight "for" rather than "against" things.** It's one thing if a child fights for what he considers a more reasonable curfew — it's quite another if he simply defies his parents at every turn, even when they're trying to be reasonable.

✔ **Parents use nonphysical means of discipline.** This includes things such as grounding, time-outs, restriction of privileges like driving the family car, and extra chores.

✔ **Conflicts are more often managed in noncompetitive ways.** This includes: *compromise* (each person giving up something), *accommodation* (going along with what the other person wants to avoid further conflict), and *collaboration* (both parties working together to reach a mutually agreed upon resolution to the conflict). Happy families don't often compete with one another, nor do they go out of their way to avoid conflicts, both of which end up leaving family members angry. (In the preceding Chapter 18, I show you how these ways of managing conflict also come into play in the adult work-a-day world.)

✔ **Family members don't treat each other with contempt.** They don't belittle, cuss, or demean each other — all of which are meant to inflict maximum damage on the other person, a person they supposedly love. (In the following Chapter 20, I talk about how this type of behavior, often learned in families, can ultimately ruin intimate partner relationships such as marriage.)

✔ **Family members show emotional and behavioral restraint.** In short, there are self-imposed limits to how emotions — like anger — are expressed. A mother may think about wringing her daughter's neck, but she doesn't. Family members allow themselves to be irritated or angry, but they stop short of rage or what I call *toxic anger*. (To appreciate the difference between anger and rage, check out *Anger Management For Dummies* [Wiley].)

✔ **Fighting is just *one* thing family members do — it's not the *only* thing they do.** There are far more positive interactions than negative ones.

The mantra of a happy family

A happy family is one characterized by mutual support, interdependence, shared power, and at least one time a day when everyone gets together for a meal. All these ingredients are captured in what I believe should be the family's *mantra* (a sacred word, phrase, or formula that has magical power):

We are all in this together.

I encourage family members to silently recite this mantra throughout the day — in good times and bad. And, on occasion, actually repeat the phrase out loud. For example, when your children are upset with you because you won't let them have something they want, look them straight in the eye and say, "Hey, remember: We're all in this together." I guarantee this will go a long way to defusing family conflicts and supporting the importance of family unity — together.

The Family Table: Sharing the All-Important One Meal a Day

The modern-day family finds itself in a major time crunch. Too much to do and not nearly enough time to get it all done. Parents are pulled one way (work, work, work!) and kids another (school, sports, dance classes, studying for SATs). You're lucky if you have one meal a day together — but, actually psychologists say that may be enough.

The all-important one meal a day isn't about the food as much as it is about the chance to maintain those meaningful social ties (see Chapter 16) essential to a happy family life. Mealtime is when family members can

- ✔ Catch each other up on what's going on in their lives

- ✔ Negotiate changes in family rules

- ✔ Ventilate (allow to breathe, as it were, in contrast to venting which describes a volcanic eruption of raw emotion) their feelings without being judged

- ✔ Ask for advice

- ✔ Reinforce each other's individual achievements

- ✔ Plan future events

- ✔ Make sure everyone is doing their family "jobs"

- ✔ Have intelligent discussions about current events

- ✔ Talk about spiritual issues

- ✔ Revisit their biological roots

It's a time when family members can support one another be reminded that they belong to something greater than themselves.

In today's super-busy world, getting together routinely for a particular meal — for example, dinner at home — may be difficult. That's fine — then have breakfast together if that fits your family schedule better or meet for dinner at a restaurant. What is important when it comes to happiness is not the time or location, but rather the fact that the family spends some meaningful time together each and every day.

Don't be a slave to family rituals

A slave, by definition, has no choice about what he does in life from one minute to the next.

Sallie is a good example of someone who is a slave to family rituals. Her teenage daughter comes home from school and announces, "There's a big basketball game tonight. Everybody's going to be there. So, let's get to the gym early, okay?"

Sallie, who just got home from work, replies, "I haven't started dinner yet and that's going to take a while." *Ritual # 1:* Our family must always sit down for a complete, full-scale evening meal no matter what's going on.

Sallie fixes dinner, the family eats, and when they're finished the daughter says, "Okay, let's get going or we'll be late." Her brother and dad are ready to go, but Sallie isn't — "You all go ahead. I've got to clean up the kitchen." The family protests, "Come on — you can clean up later after we get home." But Sallie is adamant about *Ritual # 2:* You can't leave dirty dishes on the counter no matter what.

Looking rather unhappy, the family — without Sallie — heads off for the game. As if Sallie didn't feel bad enough realizing she was missing out on a good time with her family while they were gone, she felt even worse when the get back home and her daughter ran in and shouted, "What a great game! You should have seen it. It came down to the wire — but we pulled it out. It was fantastic! The gym was packed. Everybody asked where you were."

Remember: Rituals are just patterns of habitual behavior that make life a little more predictable and stable. But they shouldn't be set in stone and you shouldn't be a slave to them. Never pass up a good time just to get the dishes done!

Chapter 20

In Intimate Relationships

*B*eing in love is one thing. Being happy with your life partner is quite another.

Mel and Katherine found that out the hard way. What seemed like a happy marriage ended abruptly after 30 years, not long after their last child left home. Mel asked his wife to sit down one evening — an evening like any other — and they had the following conversation:

> **Mel:** I don't want you to get upset, but I'll be moving my stuff out in the morning.
>
> **Katherine:** What do you *mean* you're moving out? Moving to where?!
>
> **Mel:** The apartment I signed a lease on yesterday.
>
> **Katherine:** I don't understand. Why are you moving into an apartment?
>
> **Mel:** Because I'm getting a divorce. I've already seen a lawyer and he's putting together the paperwork.
>
> **Katherine:** Divorce. Why? What's wrong?!
>
> **Mel:** I'm just not happy — I haven't been for years — and I thought it was time to do something about it.

Despite Katherine's pleas that they go to marital counseling, Mel had made up his mind and there was no turning back. What made this especially difficult for Katherine was the fact that she didn't see it coming. "I thought we were a happy couple," she said. "We never had a cross word, worked together to raise three healthy children, took care of our parents, worked in the yard together, paid our bills on time." But apparently, something was missing — something important.

In this chapter, I examine why intimate relationships aren't always as happy as they seem and tell you what you can do to avoid ending up like Katherine and Mel.

Understanding What Being a Partner Really Means

When you're in a long-term relationship — whether it's within a marriage or not — you have a partner. Your partner is your most intimate companion. And it's companionship — not love, not sexual gratification, and especially not just having someone with whom you can split the monthly mortgage payment — that leads to happiness in intimate relationships.

Answer the following questions to see how good of a companion you are to your partner:

1. **How willing or eager are you to accompany your partner through life's journey?**

   - Not very: 1

   - Somewhat: 2

   - Very much: 3

   - Absolutely 4

2. **How willing are you to treat your partner as an equal in all things?**

   - Not very: 1

   - Somewhat: 2

   - Very much: 3

   - Absolutely: 4

3. **Do you enjoy a sense of togetherness with your partner?**

   - Not really: 1

   - Somewhat: 2

   - Very much: 3

   - Absolutely: 4

4. **Can your partner confide in you?**

   - Not really: 1

   - Somewhat: 2

   - Very much: 3

   - Absolutely: 4

5. **Do you do your fair share of day-to-day tasks and responsibilities?**

   - Not usually: 1

   - Somewhat: 2

   - Pretty much: 3

   - Absolutely: 4

6. **Are you and your partner united in meeting the challenges of every-day life?**

   - Not really: 1

   - Somewhat: 2

   - Pretty much: 3

   - Absolutely: 4

7. **Do you and your partner match up well in terms of interests and personality?**

   - Not really: 1

   - Somewhat: 2

   - Pretty much: 3

   - Absolutely: 4

8. **Do you and your partner cooperate more than you compete when it comes to resolving conflicts?**

   - Not really: 1

   - Somewhat: 2

   - Pretty much: 3

   - Absolutely: 4

9. **Do you not only allow for, but appreciate, any differences that exist between you and your partner?**

   - Not really: 1

   - Somewhat: 2

   - Pretty much: 3

   - Absolutely: 4

10. **Do you value your partner as much as you value yourself?**

    - Not really: 1

    - Somewhat: 2

    - Pretty much: 3

    - Absolutely: 4

Having a confidant is good for your heart

Dr. Redford Williams, a former colleague of mine at Duke University Medical Center, found that patients undergoing coronary angiography (X-ray exam of blood vessels after injection of a radiopague material) were three times less likely to die from heart disease within five years if they were married and/or could identify a confidant with whom they could share their troubles. Interestingly, these remarkable differences in survival rates remained even when Dr. Williams took into account the severity of disease suffered by each patient.

Add up the point values of your answers. A score of 25 or above indicates a strong relationship, at least from your end. If you want to know how good a companion your partner is, have your partner take the test. The combined scores should tell you the state of your relationship.

Balancing the Me with the We

A happy couple is one where the two partners retain their own separate, individual identities while working together to meet life's many challenges and accomplish mutual goals.

A friend of mine who's a minister refused to continue the traditional marriage ritual where the bride and groom light a joint candle — symbolizing their union — and extinguish their respective individual candles. He argued that it was a mistake to ask the couple to forsake their individual identities in order to enter into the sanctity of marriage — and he was right!

On the other hand, it's equally naïve to imagine that you can be in a committed relationship (one with no "back door") — and be happy together — without adjusting your interests, needs, and lifestyle to those of your partner.

The hard part is deciding just how much of an adjustment to make — and that's where the idea of balance becomes important. For example, in my earlier example of Katherine and Mel, the problem that led Mel to seek a divorce was that he made too many adjustments to suit his wife and essentially ended up with a marriage that was all about the two of them and not enough about him. He complained, "I'm tired of always doing what she wants to do or what the kids want to do. It's my turn now. I'm going to do what I want from now on. I'm going to play golf with my friends, go where I want to go, eat the things I like, spend my money on things that I want." For 30 years, it had all been about Katherine, his children, his parents, and his in-laws — and now it was all about Mel.

Think about how you spend your time on the weekends — who you're with, the kind of activities you engage in, where you go, and so on. Now decide which of these are *we* activities and which are *me* pursuits. Examples of *we* activities include things such as:

- Meeting another couple for dinner
- Going to a movie together
- Attending church together
- Working in the yard together

Me activities include

- Spending some time by yourself browsing through a local bookstore
- Checking out the local flea market on your own
- Playing basketball with your buddies
- Going to the spa with your girlfriends
- Reading
- Having lunch alone with a close friend

Your disease is not my disease

For years, I worked with people who suffered from multiple sclerosis (MS) and the families of people with MS. The effects of MS are crippling not only for the person who has the disease, but also for the quality of the person's relationships — especially intimate relationships.

I once was asked to address a large group of spouses of MS patients at a regional conference. The experience was incredible — and sad. I started out by asking the audience how their spouses' illness had changed their lives. One by one, they stood up and told heart-wrenching stories about how they could no longer enjoy life.

One young man in particular caught my attention when he described — in tears — how he had given up everything he loved since his wife contracted MS. He no longer joined his friends on weekend cycling tours in the Virginia mountains, no longer played pickup basketball with his friends from high school, and so on.

When I asked him why he had ended all those activities, he answered rather angrily, "Because she can't do those things anymore because of her damned MS, and I have to stay home with her all the time." I told him, as nicely as I could, that I thought he was making a mistake. I could tell he was already beginning to resent his wife and her disease, because of the disabling effect it had on their marriage. I assured him that the world wouldn't end if he joined his friends on a biking expedition while his wife stayed at home with a friend.

I told him, "If you give up all the things you enjoy doing just because your wife has MS, you might as well have MS, too!"

How balanced are these activities? If the numbers are too unbalanced (more than 80 percent for one type of activity and less than 20 percent for the other), it's time for a change.

The key to happiness lies in balance.

Thinking of Happiness in a Relationship as a Three-Legged Stool

Psychologists who study what makes for a successful and loving relationship have narrowed it down to three components:

- ✔ **Passion:** "I'm crazy about her."
- ✔ **Shared interests:** "We enjoy the same things — travel, golf."
- ✔ **Intimacy:** "I feel really close to him."

Think of your relationship as a three-legged stool. If all three legs are in place, you have a secure feeling. If not, the relationship gets a bit wobbly!

A relationship that's based on a combination of passion and intimacy but lacks shared interests is said to be a *romantic relationship*. A relationship that combines intimacy and shared interests but lacks physical passion is seen as a *companionate relationship*. And a relationship that combines passion and shared interests, but lacks intimacy, is referred to as a *shallow orfatuous* (means silly) *relationship*. What kind of stool are you sitting on?

Passion

In the three-legged stool analogy, *passion* is physical passion — the feeling of arousal you get when your partner walks into the room and catches your eye. Your heart begins to pump faster, your blood pressure goes up, and everything about you gets turned on from head to toe. I'm also talking about the sexual interaction that comes from such feelings — holding hands, hugging, touching, and having sex. Passion is all about biology and adrenaline. Passion is about excitement!

Rate how you feel about your partner on a scale of 1 to 10 (with 1 being no passion at all, and 10 being passion through the roof). Now, using this same scale, rate how you think your partner feels about you — better yet ask your partner! How do your ratings match up? Are they within a point or two of each other, or has one of you said 3 and the other said 9? Do you both feel that there's enough passion in your relationship?

Passion doesn't have to be sex. You can be passionate with your partner in a myriad of ways.

If one or both of you feels that there isn't enough passion in your relationship, I recommend reading *Sex For Dummies,* by Dr. Ruth Westheimer (Wiley). There you can find ways to bring more passion into your relationship, so that you're both satisfied.

Shared interests

The best thing about having a partner who shares your interests is that you have a built-in playmate, someone to enjoy life with. My brother Gene and his wife, Syl, are a great example of this. They've been married for 50 years and they've enjoyed the same activities, activities that give their lives meaning and pleasure. Early on, they both bowled in a league; they were both in the Masonic Order (she was in the Eastern Star, he was a Shriner); and they spent many hours beautifying their yard. They grew exotic orchids. They were both heavily involved in Little League baseball when their son was growing up —as a coach and announcer at the games. They spent a lot of time bass fishing (my brother is still sore that his wife caught the biggest fish!). They go on gambling junkets. And they love to travel. They both compete in shuffle-board leagues. And, above all else, they're both collectors — he has his coins and marbles, she has her figurines. No wonder they're a happy couple!

On a scale from 1 to 10 (where 1 means you and your partner have no shared interests, and 10 means you do everything together), rate the degree to which you and your partner's interests overlap. Ask your partner how he or she would rate this facet of your relationship.

If you're on the low end (1 to 4) as far as shared interests go, try cultivating an interest in one thing that your partner enjoys. Ask him what he likes about that activity and if that's something he thinks you could learn to like. Learn all you can about the activity — the more you know, the more it may appeal to you. If he's an avid golfer and you're not, maybe you could both work as volunteers at a PGA golf tournament in your area — my wife and I have done it several times and it's fun. Or, find a new activity that neither you nor your partner have been involved in before but which interests you both. The important thing here is not the activity itself, but the fact that it's an opportunity for the two of you to do something enjoyable together.

Intimacy

When most people see the word *intimacy,* they immediately think of sex. But the kind of intimacy that leads to happiness in a relationship involves much more than sex. It means

- ✔ Having a closeness not found in other relationships
- ✔ Knowing the other person's secrets — secret wishes, desires, fear, and vulnerabilities
- ✔ Being cozy, warm, friendly, and comfortable
- ✔ Sharing confidences about things that matter most in life
- ✔ Communicating in an informal way
- ✔ Allowing each other to penetrate your innermost selves
- ✔ Sharing yourselves emotionally
- ✔ Knowing everything there is to know about each other
- ✔ Letting your guard down — and trusting that your partner won't take advantage of you
- ✔ Thinking of the two of you as "one"

On a scale of 1 to 10 (where 1 is no intimacy at all, and 10 is absolutely intimate), how would your rate your relationship? Ask your partner to rate your relationship, too.

If your relationship is short on intimacy, make a point of having some time alone with each other (That's right — no kids!) every day. For example, take a short walk together after dinner — 30 minutes tops. Once a month, just the two of you go away somewhere "special" to catch up on what's going on in each other's lives. Spend 10 minutes of time cozying up to one another after you wake up in the morning and before you begin another busy day — or, take the last 10 minutes of the day right before you go to sleep to do the same thing.

Intimacy doesn't require a lot of talk — just holding each other quietly for a few minutes can speak volumes about how you feel about each other.

Avoiding the Dreaded "C" Word: Contempt

John Gottman, psychologist and author of *10 Lessons to Transform Your Marriage* (Crown Publishers), believes that one aspect of communication between married couples inevitably leads to irreconcilable unhappiness and the ultimate downfall of the relationship: contempt. If you treat your partner with contempt (saying things like, "You're a fool!", "You make me sick to my stomach," "I don't know what I ever thought I saw in you in the first place," or "I must have been out of my mind to want to marry you."), all you can expect in return is unhappiness. Why? Because people who are on the receiving end of contempt feel humiliated, embarrassed, rejected, and demeaned — hardly a recipe for happiness.

Contempt involves criticism that is both hostile and conveys a feeling of disgust (translated: You do not please me!). It also communicates an utter lack of respect for your partner — which is why, for example, you roll your eyes when she is talking to you about herself. Contempt is frequently seen in one-sided relationships where one party feels superior to the other. And, it has a number of negative effects on how you treat your partner, such as the following:

- Contempt will keep you from acting in a caring manner towards your partner.
- Contempt will cause you to treat your partner uncivilly.
- Contempt will prevent you from comforting your partner or her from comforting you.
- Contempt will stop you from acting with compassion towards your loved one.
- Contempt will rule out any hope of your complimenting your partner for something she has done in your behalf.
- Contempt makes your partner think you are unconcerned about his welfare.
- Contempt is the opposite of cordial — welcoming, good-natured, polite.
- Contempt flies in the face of courteous behavior.

According to Gottman, the antidote to contemptuous behavior lies in observing your partner more closely and looking for something she's doing right. Find something you can admire in her — maybe she's an unusually truthful person, someone who's kind to strangers, or she makes a mean cherry pie. And, once you find it, let her know that you appreciate that part of her. By doing so, you elevate her status *in your eyes* which slowly-but-surely lessens that feeling of superiority that I mentioned earlier. The more you see her as an equal, the more you will admire her and she you.

Making Empathy the Norm

Empathy — the ability to walk in another person's shoes — is the key to a happy relationship. An empathetic relationship is one in which each partner makes every effort to know what's going on in the mind and heart of the other. Empathy makes all these other things — acceptance, appreciation, forbearance, forgiveness, tolerance, and understanding — possible. Empathy sometimes means giving your partner a second chance. Empathy can open the door for alternative explanations as to why people in relationships behave the way they do — for example, "She's not really mad — she's probably just tired. After all, she works hard all day, just like I do."

Nearly all people in intimate relationships have moments of empathy here and there, but for many people empathy is more the exception than the norm. With happy couples, empathy *is* the norm. It's consistent, predictable, and expected.

In the following sections, I fill you in on the two main types of empathy and how you can ensure they're a part of your relationship.

Emotional empathy

Former president Bill Clinton scored some major political points when he spoke the now famous words: "I feel your pain." Human beings love that type of emotional empathy — having someone able to relate to how they feel. It's a form of emotional validation. When I work with chronic-pain patients, who show evidence of tremendous suffering — anger, bitterness, despair — I always say to them, "Of course, you feel upset and misunderstood. Of course, you're frustrated and aggravated. Of course, you feel like none of your doctors believe you. I would, too, if I were in your shoes." I mean those words — and they know that I mean it. Communicating my emotional empathy to my clients gives me a lot of credibility that I wouldn't have otherwise.

If you want to score some major marital points, listen to what your partner is saying. If your partner says, "I'm tired," hear your partner's voice. Instead of defending yourself against your partner's feelings, by saying something like, "It's not *my* fault you're tired" or, "What am I supposed to do about it?" say something like, "Of course, you're tired. Of course, you're upset. Of course, you're anxious." And mean what you say.

Rational empathy

Avery D. Weisman, professor emeritus of psychiatry at Harvard Medical School, in his wonderful and insightful book *The Coping Capacity* (Human Sciences Press), refers to another type of empathy, one that requires "a respect for another person's irrationality." He's talking about *rational empathy,* which he suggests is a real, authentic desire to view the world through the other person's eyes. Rational empathy doesn't mean that you necessarily adopt your partner's way of seeing things — it just means that you try to understand and consider it. Rational empathy, in effect, keeps married couples from ending up strangers speaking a foreign language.

Empathetic surgeons

Researchers at St. Louis University School of Medicine looked at the relationship between empathy and explanations for surgical outcome among 40 orthopedic surgeons. They found that those surgeons who were more empathetic — those who tended to adopt the patient's point of view — were less likely to attribute failed back surgeries to psychological problems in the patient. In other words, they were less likely to think it was all in their patients' heads. That's the kind of surgeon I'd rather have.

To master the art of rational empathy, you must:

- ✔ Be open-minded
- ✔ Be considerate when sharing your beliefs and ideas with your partner
- ✔ Be an active listener
- ✔ Place no demands on your partner
- ✔ Be willing to take turns in a discussion, no matter how heated it gets
- ✔ Let your partner finish his or her thoughts and sentences, without interrupting
- ✔ Be courteous and civil at all times
- ✔ Be accepting of the fact that there is more than one way to see things
- ✔ Be respectful of the other person
- ✔ Know that showing contempt is dangerous

Intimacy and empathy go hand in hand. The more you and your partner share with one another, and the more you know about one another — beyond just the superficial things in life — the easier and more natural it is to "walk in their shoes."

Tending and Befriending: Reaching Out to Those You Love

Greg and Cindy have been arguing for hours about his having too much to drink at a friend's wedding. Both are angry and some harsh words have been exchanged. "Nag, nag, nag — that's all you I get from you. I can't even enjoy myself without you having something to say about it," says Greg. To which, Cindy responds, "Enjoy yourself? Hell, you were just plain drunk!" They're nearing the point where Greg will predictably withdraw from the conversation and enter a world of silent brooding, while Cindy prepares to seek him out, apologize for losing her temper, and assure him that, of course, she wants him to enjoy himself.

According to Dr. Shelly E. Taylor, Director of the UCLA Social Neuroscience Laboratory, this scenario is all too common in men and women in dealing with stress and conflict. Stress triggers the fight-or-flight response in men and the tend-and-befriend response in women. Both are driven by sex-linked hormones — testosterone for males and oxytocin for females — and both are built-in response patterns that have evolved over the history of mankind.

Tending and befriending — reaching out to those you love — comes easy for most women. It's their nature. And it goes a long way toward easing marital tensions and making for a secure and happy relationship. In other words, the fact that I've been happily married for over 40 years has more to do with my wife than it does with me. Like most men, my natural tendency has always been to attack or cut and run when things get too heated.

But men can learn to tend and befriend. And so can women for whom tending and befriending doesn't come naturally.

Not exactly what she wanted to hear

I had a client who found a lump in her breast, had it biopsied, and went to her doctor to find out if whether was malignant. Her husband volunteered to go along for support. However, when they were told that the test was positive for cancer and she would have to have a mastectomy, her husband reacted angrily and caused a scene in the doctor's office. To make matters worse, when they went home to digest the news, her husband got drunk and spent the rest of the day blaming her for her cancer. He actually said, "We really don't need this right now — the expense and all — and besides you should've taken better care of yourself!" This was not at all what this poor woman wanted to hear as she faced the choice between death and disfigurement.

You and your partner may not have faced anything as serious as cancer, or you may have faced situations just as serious. Either way, you have the power, in every situation, to be either the kind of person your partner can depend on as a source of strength, or the kind of person who adds to your partner's pain. You can get ready for moments as difficult as this one by being there for your partner in the more ordinary, day-to-day struggles. That way, when a crisis arises, you'll have gotten in all kinds of practice, and you'll be supportive without even having to think about it.

Asking the crucial question: Are you enjoying the journey?

Most of us have it backwards when it comes to intimate relationships. They see the relationship as the destination — when they're single, they think, "If I just had a partner, everything would be okay." So they do everything they can to find a partner as quickly as they can. After they're in a relationship, they can relax — from that point on, they figure, things will take care of themselves, right? Wrong! A relationship isn't a destination — it's a journey. For some, it's a reasonably smooth journey that lasts a lifetime; for others, it's an all-too-brief and rather rocky journey that ends in a breakup or divorce.

The question that couples should ask themselves over and over throughout their relationship is: "Are we enjoying the journey?" If the answer is yes, then you're happy. If the answer is, "Um, I'm not sure," "Well, sort of," or "No," then you're not.

Tending and befriending others involves five main elements of social behavior:

- ✔ **Be sympathetic or empathetic toward your partner.** For example, you can say, "I know you're scared — so am I. But we'll get through this."

- ✔ **Don't be afraid to reach out and make physical contact.** Giving your partner a hug, patting her on the back, holding her hand — all these things signal to your partner that you're in her corner and she's not alone.

- ✔ **Ask your partner, "Are you okay?"** That one question helps your partner begin to feel better. And it opens the door for him to share what's in his heart.

- ✔ **Be optimistic.** People need support most when they feel helpless and hopeless. They need someone to tell them that better times are ahead. You can be that someone for your partner.

- ✔ **Focus on your partner's needs, not your own.** Make whatever you say and do about your partner. For example, don't start out by saying, "Your getting upset only upsets *me*. It only makes *me* feel guilty, like I haven't done something I should have." Trust me, that's really not what your partner wants to hear.

Identifying the Three Most Important Words in a Relationship

I bet you thought I was going to say the three most important words in a relationship are "I love you." Even *more* important are the words, "I am sorry." These three words can do more for a relationship than any others. Whether it's "I'm sorry I was so selfish," "I'm sorry I hurt your feelings," "I'm sorry I forgot about our anniversary," or "I'm sorry I had too much to drink at the wedding," saying you're sorry communicates to your partner that you accept responsibility for your part of the relationship and that you take ownership for any transgressions you bring to it.

And that's really the basis of all mature relationships — accepting responsibility for your own actions. Even the most childish and irresponsible people in the world can say, "I love you" and mean it. But it takes a real adult to say, "I'm sorry." Which are you?

Love isn't enough

My parents tried unsuccessfully for 23 years to find happiness in their marriage. It was difficult, to be sure, given the fact that my father was an alcoholic with a short temper and my mother could give as good as she got when they were fighting, which was most of the time. What I think was wrong in this up-and-down relationship was the fact that both of them were too proud and too stubborn to say to the other, "I'm sorry." I never heard either one of them utter those all-important words — and I think that's why their marriage ended in divorce.

It isn't enough to love your partner. You need to accept responsibility for your faults, your mistakes, the negatives you bring to the relationship. When you do *that,* your relationship has a good chance of surviving.

Part VI
The Part of Tens

The 5th Wave   By Rich Tennant

"Okay, you were depressed because you didn't win, but couldn't you have been happy enough about finishing second to pick up the $100,000 check?"

In this part . . .

I offer ten quick strategies for raising a happy child (no small task!) and ten personal habits that adolescents and adults can employ in their efforts to become happier people. Achieving happiness is not only about knowing what to do, but also about avoiding possible certain roadblocks and pitfalls that lead to *un*happiness. In this part, I point out those roadblocks so you can dodge them.

Chapter 21

Ten Ways to Raise a Happy Child

*B*eing a parent is an incredibly challenging job, especially when it comes to your child's emotional development. When they're born, most children appear to be happy: They smile and coo — evidence of how satisfied they are with the nourishment and comfort provided by their parents. But this soon begins to change as their lives become more complex and their needs grow. The childish anger that typically emerges by the third month of life is the child's way of communicating that, from his perspective, the parent is failing to meet his needs.

Although most infants are happy, maintaining that happiness throughout childhood and adolescence and into adulthood isn't a given. For the most part, if children aren't happy, it's *not* because they're bad or have some major psychological problem — it's because they haven't been *taught* how to be happy. And if they're not happy when they're children, you can bet they won't be happy as adults. As a parent, one of the greatest gifts you can give your child is the gift of knowing how to be happy. Helping your child learn what it takes to achieve happiness is a parental gift that keeps on giving.

In this chapter, I show you ten ways to teach your child how to be happy on his own — without relying exclusively on *you* for his happiness. Teaching your child how to be happy is no different from teaching him to use the bathroom, tie his shoes, or ride a bike — all skills that are best learned early in life.

Make Sure Your Message Gets Through

If you want to teach your child something, you need to put yourself in her world — and recognize that her world is different from yours. Your kid is not a "little adult" who, though smaller in stature, is fully capable of understanding grown-up ideas and language and following grown-up commands.

Listen to your child and adapt your language to hers. If you're trying to teach her that being satiated is a good thing — and one of the key ingredients to happiness (see Chapter 2) — tell her, "Being satiated means the same thing as *being full,* honey, like when you're full of ice cream. It means you don't need any more."

If your child can't understand you, he can't learn from you. I once had a neighbor — an engineer — who shared with me that he had explained to his 2-year-old son the difference between AC and DC electricity so that he wouldn't stick his finger in the wall socket anymore. A 2-year-old doesn't understand — or need to understand — the finer points of electrical wiring. He just needs to know not to stick his finger in the wall socket. Focus on the message you're trying to convey to your child, and then figure out the *best* way — not the most complicated way or the most technical way — to convey that message.

Be Your Child's Emotional Coach

Nowadays, kids have all sorts of coaches — football coaches, gymnastics coaches, soccer coaches, people who coach them to get higher SAT scores, and coaches for the high school debate team. Regardless of the sport or subject, a coach is there to help kids become successful and competitive. What many kids seem to lack, however, is someone to coach them on their feelings — anger, fear, sadness, and happiness — and what to do with them.

That's where parents come in. As the first and potentially most influential adult in your child's life, you have a unique opportunity to be his emotional coach. Here are some tips to keep in mind:

- ✔ **Make raising a happy child your primary goal.** Put happiness ahead of other important goals — such as education, athleticism, popularity — all of which contribute to your kid's success but do not, by themselves, make for a happy child. Not sure about that? Take a look at all the unhappy, troubled, young celebrities and professional athletes — not to mention all the grade-anxious adolescents heading off to prestigious universities in hopes of making their parents proud — and you'll see the truth in what I'm saying.

- ✔ **Be active and hands-on when you're interacting with your child.** Rearing a child is no time to be passive! Take your kid places where

Happy days

Believe it or not, from my entire childhood, I have memories of just two happy days with my parents — one day I spent with my mom, the other I spent with my dad.

With my mother, it was on my tenth birthday. She managed to get rid of all the other children for a whole day, which she spent talking with me, letting me help her around the house, and letting me help make my own seven-layer birthday cake. It was a masterpiece in the making — we carefully stacked each layer, one on top of the other, as they came out of the oven, cementing them together with mint-green icing, until it was complete. The cake was beautiful, but what was even more beautiful was the fact that I had my mother all to myself for one day in my life and she seemed happier than I had ever seen her.

The day I spent with my father was just as memorable. He was a fisherman, but he rarely let us kids go along with him. Mostly, fishing was his time to relax, forget all the stresses of his life (including a family he couldn't afford!), and drink a lot of beer. For some inexplicable reason, one day he up and announced that I could come along with him. Talk about surprised! The day was more than I expected. My father sat on the bank and fished. He didn't really interact with me all that much, but he let me run around freely playing and entertaining myself. He gave me money to buy food and drinks (a rare thing, indeed). He was in an uncharacteristically good mood — no yelling or criticizing. And, for once, he didn't seem to be in a hurry to move on to something else. He seemed happy, content — which allowed me to feel the same.

I'm grateful for those two days. They may not seem like much to you, but they meant — and continue to mean — the world to me.

you're happy and explain to him what it is about this place that creates positive feelings for you. For example, if you're happy at the beach, take your child there and say something like, "I'm so happy when I'm at the beach, because I can swim and read and be with my family, and those are my favorite things to do." Ask him where he thinks he would be happy — at the movies? the zoo? — and take him there.

✔ Do the same with activities. For example, if you enjoy reading, take your child to a local bookstore or the library and let him share in your pleasure as you browse about the store. If you love the smell of a new book (come on, who doesn't?), find a book you like, open it up, put your nose inside and take a big whiff. Then ask your child if he'd like to smell it, too. Show him book covers you like and see if he can find book covers that he likes, too. It doesn't matter if your child can read and understand all the words in the book — you can still find ways to share the experience.

✔ Find games your child wants to play and play *with* him — don't just tell him to find a friend or sibling to play with. Kids *love* it when their parents get down on the floor with them and play. Talk with your child about the happiest, best times in your life (see Chapter 8), so he can begin wanting to experience such times himself.

✔ **Be proactive.** Don't wait until you see that you child is unhappy before you do something about it. Be ahead of the curve. Get your child up early on Saturday morning and say, with all kinds of enthusiasm, "Let's go have a really happy day — just you and me!" Be like Brando in *The Godfather,* and make the kid an offer he can't refuse! I guarantee you, he'll remember that day for the rest of his life.

Distinguish between Needs and Wants

Human needs are few: air, water, food, shelter — things that directly contribute to survival. The rest of life is made up of wants. Your kid may *want* to get along with her peers, *want* to do well in school, or *want* to spend endless hours playing video games. Believe it or not, every kid *wants* to find some way to elicit the love and approval of her parents. *All* children want that — even when they say they don't or act as if that's the farthest thing from their minds.

Your job as a parent is to help your child find acceptable and effective ways to satisfy her wants so she can have some hope of being happy. You need to show her *which* wants — to be the "boss" in children's games, getting a new toy every time she goes to the mall, having the last word in family discussions — will not bring joy to her life. (Chapters 2 and 3 give you the background you need to have this kind of conversation.)

Show Your Child That Generosity Begins at Home

The smallest of children can learn the joy of giving. At the holidays, when you see people ringing the bell for the Salvation Army, give your little one a little money to put in the kettle, and let *him* be the one to drop it in. (Put some money in yourself, too, so he sees that giving is something *you* value, too.) If your family attends church or temple, give your child some coins to place in the offering plate — and make sure he sees you putting money in the plate as well.

By the way, giving isn't just a religious thing. If you don't attend religious services, you can use the same principle to donate to charities. For example, every time you give your child his allowance, you can talk to him about charities that he may want to donate some of his allowance to. You can even use this as an opportunity to talk to your child about the things that matter to him. If he's an animal lover, maybe he'd like to give a portion of his allowance to the local Humane Society or the ASPCA. If he's a pint-size environmentalist, maybe he'd like to donate to Greenpeace or the Sierra Club.

Generosity involves not only giving material things, but also giving your time and attention. Be generous toward your child by allotting him at least as much time as you spend preparing meals, washing clothes, or talking with family and friends on the phone. If you're eating with your child in a restaurant, turn off the cellphone and make him the center of your universe. (Over the years, I've noticed that, without fail, the kids who misbehave the most in restaurants are those who are ignored by their parents.)

Engage in generous activities as a family. You can volunteer to work at a soup kitchen one afternoon a month, or you can help out at the local animal shelter. If you have an older person in your neighborhood, suggest to your child that he offer to rake the neighbor's leaves or shovel her driveway.

And when your child does something generous — whether that's offering to help you empty the dishwasher or giving some of his allowance to a charity — be sure to let him know how proud you are of him. You may be surprised by how happy your child is to get your approval. This is how you teach generosity — and generosity leads to happiness.

Who's the rich one?

As a parent, it's hard to know for certain whether you've done a good job in raising your kids. You hope so, but you're always looking for a sign that you've done your job well. My son, Chris — a wonderful young man — told me a story that was truly an affirmation of everything his mother and I had done over the years to build a happy, functional family.

Chris and a college friend were Christmas shopping, and Chris was apparently buying some unique, thoughtful, **and fairly** costly gifts (at least for his budget!). His friend — who came from a wealthy family — asked him, "Why are you buying such nice gifts for your family? Why are you going to so much trouble?" Chris laughed and said, "Because they're my family and I love them."

The other boy had no response — he looked confused. That was one of those watershed moments when my son began to appreciate why he was so much happier than his friend, despite the differences in their respective pocketbooks.

Teach Your Child Mastery

The most unhappy children I've seen in my life are the middle school and high school kids I interact with in my anger-management classes. It doesn't take a rocket scientist to understand why they're so angry toward everyone they encounter: They're lost children; misfits in a world where all the other kids are good at something — academics, sports, making friends — and they're not. The saddest thing, though, is that these kids *know* they're misfits! They have no discernable adaptive skills, they're not aware of their own talents, they've never been taught how to problem-solve — so, all that's left is their anger. They are, in effect, the *masters* of anger.

It's as simple as this: Your job as a parent is to teach your child to be good at something. Here are just some of the things you can help your child be a master of:

- ✔ **Reading:** Reading is a lifelong source of joy for many people. Read to your child — even after she's learned to read herself. ***Remember:*** Don't just buy your child books; ask her about the books she's reading.

  My editor remembers falling in love with the *Anne of Green Gables* series when she was a child, telling her grandma how much she loved the books, and being delighted when her grandma read the books, too, just so she could share the experience.

- ✔ **Writing:** This can include everything from having good penmanship to learning proper grammar to telling good stories. At its most basic level, writing is important as a form of communication. But when kids get into writing poems or short stories, it can be a great source of happiness.

- ✔ **Playing well with others:** Kids need to learn to get along with others. They need to learn to follow rules, learn what "fair play" means, and learn to take turns — all of which can be learned from playing games. Children who end up succeeding in life have mastered the art of cooperation — being a team player. Kids who cheat and are always crying "foul" when they don't get their way will be doing the exact same thing as adults later on in life.

- ✔ **Being interested in what other children want or like:** All children start out as the center of their own universe. They expect others — parents and kids alike — to be interested in what *they* want, which is reasonable up to a point. But your child also needs to appreciate that the world is full of lots of different people whose interests also need to be considered. That's the real value of having brothers and sisters or playmates from next door — the child learns to *share* the world. Explain to your little one that "as bright as the sun is, it is only one planet in the entire universe," and so it is with human beings.

REMEMBER

✔ **Coloring within the lines:** When kids learn to color within the lines, they're setting the stage for good organizational skills later on in life.

Coloring outside the lines is okay, too. If your child has an interest in art — whether drawing or painting or clay or papier-mâché — encourage that! If you don't have a creative bone in your body, check in with the art teacher at your child's school and get some ideas for things you can do to help your child have more fun with art at home. Or sign her up for art classes at your local art center or community center.

✔ **Studying:** Keep the focus here on having good study skills — for example, getting homework done before watching TV or playing video games, knowing how to prepare for a test, and taking notes in class or on reading assignments. If your child has good study skills, and she works hard at school, that's all that matters.

I've always seen schools as an arena where children first learn to achieve success, but I can't stand those bumper stickers that say, My Child Is an Honor Roll Student at Such-and-Such School. I want to yell out the window, "Sure, teach your child to want to achieve great things in school. But for goodness' sake, be proud of her even when she *doesn't* make it to the top of the academic ladder, as long as she puts forth her best effort." (The problem is, I've never found a red light that was long enough for me to say all that!)

✔ **Being respectful of others:** A disrespectful child will grow up to be a disrespectful husband, neighbor, and employee. Respect is just another way of saying "I *value* you and what you do." Start by always saying "please" when you want your child to do something and "thank you" when she does it. Respect her opinion when it differs from you own — just because she disagrees doesn't mean she's an idiot. Respect is also about *boundaries*. Teach your child that it's never okay to open another person's mail, get in his mother's purse, rummage through his sister's dresser drawers, or take things that don't belong to him. All of us have a *right* to both privacy and ownership.

✔ **Playing sports:** It doesn't have to be anything super-competitive — Ping-Pong will do.

✔ **Leading:** Leaders aren't born — they're made. That's not to say that some kids don't initiate activities more than others; they do. But leadership skills and attitudes can be developed in *all* children. The best thing parents can do is give kids opportunities to lead — it can be as simple as telling a child, "You're in charge of the family today — you choose how we're going to spend our day."

✔ **Playing a musical instrument:** If you don't play an instrument yourself, you can still talk to your child about which instruments she likes and get her started with lessons or let her play in the school band or orchestra.

✔ **Competing:** You want your child to have a healthy perspective on competition. It's great for her to want to win and to work hard to excel, but you need to teach her that competition can be unhealthy, too. Winning isn't everything, and competing with honor is key. (See the next section, "Help Your Child Be a Happy Loser," for more on this.)

Nobody can be a master of everything. Look for your child's natural interests and strengths and work to help her develop those. Of course, you still want to introduce her to new activities and help her get better at the things she's not as good at, but don't expect her to be the next Beethoven if she hates the piano and has no musical aptitude. Also, it's only natural for you to want to share your interests with your child. If you were a jock in high school, maybe you're dying to get your child into sports. The key is to pay attention to *her* interests and be happy *yourself* when she finds something *she's* happy doing.

Help Your Child Be a Happy Loser

Don't let your child grow up thinking that happiness is tied to winning — it's not. But if your child *thinks* it is, he'll drive himself nuts by constantly trying to win — at anything and everything — and he'll hate himself and be unhappy when he loses. So how do most kids get the crazy idea that winning is everything? *From their parents.* If you charge out onto the ball field and scream at your child when he loses a game (or yell at the umpire when he makes a call you disagree with), you're teaching him that winning matters more than anything — more than being kind, more than being respectful, more than *anything.* If you don't teach your child to be a happy loser when he's young, trust me, he'll be a *sore* loser when he grows up.

Major-league jerk

When my son was a kid, he played minor-league baseball, for 8- to 12-year-olds. At that age, it's all about pitching. If a kid can get the ball over the plate, you win. Otherwise, the pitcher walks every batter and your team loses big time.

One day, my son's team was definitely losing big time. The boy who was pitching couldn't get the ball anywhere near home plate, and the other team was far ahead. Finally, the coach came out and pulled the pitcher. The boy's feel-

ings were understandably hurt and you could see he was crying as he headed to the bench. When the game ended, all the parents for both teams ran out onto the field to either congratulate or console their children. The losing pitcher's father went up to his son, said, "*I'll* give you something to cry about!", and slapped the boy across the face. What a horrible lesson that boy learned that day: *Winning is everything, and if you want to make me happy, you'd better win.*

Some parents believe that it's wrong — in fact, psychologically damaging — to beat their kids at a game. If I had a dollar for every time I heard some parent say, "You need to let them win regardless — it's how you build self-esteem," I'd be a much richer man today. Of course, you want your child to learn to win, but it's just as important to show him that losing isn't the end of the world.

Encourage All Forms of Play

Play is a major source of happiness for children as well as adults. Not only does it make children happy, but it serves as the foundation of a human being's social development. The lessons people learn from childhood play highly influence their adult social lives.

But play doesn't come in just one form. Here are the main forms of happiness:

- ✓ **Solitary play:** Sitting quietly and entertaining herself with some object or age-appropriate activity (like coloring). Kids between 2 and 5 years old frequently engage in this nonsocial type of play. Children who are comfortable with solitary play end up as adults who are comfortable with solitude and don't feel lonely when they're alone.

- ✓ **Parallel play:** Playing alongside another child. During this same time period, kids may start to play together but still engage in separate activities. For example, two children may play in a sandbox, each doing her own thing.

- ✓ **Associative play:** Playing with another child. As children grow older and enter their preschool years, they may interact with one another when they play (for example, playing house or school).

Children also need to be exposed to competitive play (including sports, such as baseball or soccer) as well as cooperative play (where they work together, such as putting together puzzles). They need to play at games with rules (like board games) and without rules (drawing a picture). As a parent, you should encourage *all* forms of child play.

Allow for Imperfections

At any age, striving for perfection can be burdensome, to put it mildly. Perfection is an ideal, not a reality. If you insist on having a perfect child, you'll only end up disappointed and unhappy — and your child will see that disappointment in your eyes.

All human beings (including you!) have flaws, warts, frailties, and imperfections that, along with certain unique talents, define our personalities. So many young people in today's world are literally *killing* themselves (suicide among adolescents is on the rise) trying to live up to their parents' unrealistic and unattainable goals. Kids need to know that there is no such thing as perfection. They need to know that a C isn't the end of the world. And they need to know that if they're not the most popular kid in school, that doesn't make them a loser.

Bottom line: Your child needs you to give her a break now and then. She needs to hear you frequently say, "I love you. No one is perfect."

Teach Your Child Commitment and Perseverance

Two of the most invaluable lessons a parent can teach a child are commitment and perseverance. In Chapter 6, I tell you how being a player, not a spectator, is one of the three elements of a hardy personality — someone who is resilient and self-reliant; fully committed to life. Encourage your child to explore possibilities — try out for the track team; try out for the cheerleading squad; try out for the debate team. Never discourage her by saying things like "I don't think you'd be good at that" or "That's silly — why would you want to do that?" If she keeps trying to find the right fit — which takes commitment — she eventually will.

Perseverance means not being a quitter. You need to give your child a chance to finish something important, to feel the sense of pride and accomplishment that only comes at the end, and to be happy with himself as a result. A lot of adolescents who head off to college want to come home (and stay) sometime during their first semester because "It's too hard and I'm not making the grades I made in high school." (If you think that's uncommon, just ask any college administrator.) Parents should be encouraging, not accommodating — tell them they need to stay and work things out. In most cases, that's just what they'll do and they'll thank you later on (and so will the college — it needs your tuition dollars!).

Let Your Child See You Happy

Emotions are contagious. If your child sees you looking sad and unhappy all the time, she'll most likely end up feeling the same way. The good news is that the same is true for happiness: If your kid sees that *you're* happy, she'll likely be happier herself. Children need to see you smile (see Chapter 12), they need to hear you laugh, and they need to hear you say, "Today's a happy day!" once in a while.

Scientists call the contagiousness of emotions *emotional mimicry.*

Al was almost 40 years old when he came in for counseling. I asked him what problems he was having and he said, "I'm not sure. I just don't seem to be as happy as most of my friends, even though I have a better job and more creature comforts than some of them. We go out and do things socially and they laugh and seem to enjoy themselves, while I sit there and watch. I feel somehow disconnected from what they're all about." When I asked Al, "Would you say your parents were happy people, angry people, or anxious people?", he said,

> Truthfully, I don't know. They rarely showed any emotion around me. I remember lots of times when we ate dinner and my mother would talk to me and then my father would talk to me, but they wouldn't look at or talk to one another. Sometimes they would go weeks without talking and just leave notes for each another. Our house was always pretty quiet and I spent a lot of time in my room.

Al had no recollection whatsoever of either of his parents ever looking happy. It's not surprising that *he* was having trouble being happy, too.

Kids are like sponges: They soak up everything around them. The single greatest things you can do to help your kids be happy throughout their lives are to be happy yourself, and to share your happiness with them.

Chapter 22

Ten Roadblocks to Happiness

A chieving happiness is a journey, and as with any journey, there are many potholes and roadblocks along the way. Think of this chapter as a big orange cone, giving you enough warning to swerve out of the way.

An Unrealistic Sense of Self

You can easily tell that Jenna and Jamie are sisters — they're both brunettes, they have the same laugh, and they both love pizza. But when it comes to personality, they couldn't be more different. Jenna sees herself as "super-woman," able to succeed at anything she sets her mind to, and she expects perfection in herself and others. She's brimming with self-confidence and what I describe in Chapter 5 as exuberant optimism. Jamie, on the other hand, has a much more negative view of herself — she downplays her abilities and constantly looks at life as a glass half-empty. Neither, unfortunately, has an accurate sense of self. Jenna *over*estimates what she's capable of, while Jamie *under*estimates her abilities. And this is why neither one is happy.

No matter what — or how much — she accomplishes, it's never enough for Jenna. She always expects more of herself: "I should've studied more for that test and then I would've gotten an A+ instead of an A–." Her bar for success is ever-increasing and always seems to be just beyond her reach, leaving her frustrated more often than not. Jamie has the opposite problem — she feels inadequate because she hasn't enjoyed enough success in life. Why? Because she's constantly selling herself short: "I shouldn't have tried out for that job — I knew I wouldn't get it." By doing so, Jamie is denying herself opportunities to appreciate her many strengths.

Start listening to yourself. How often do you think or say the word *should?* According to cognitive psychologists, *should* is one of the most toxic words in everyday language. It conveys people's expectations of themselves and others: "She shouldn't do that," "He should keep his mouth shut," or "I'm such an idiot — I should've known better." It also guides people's behavior, making them want to do more (or less) than they're capable of and less than what would make them happy.

Entitlement

A sense of entitlement — a feeling that you have a right to something — is the root cause of most people's unhappiness. Parents are unhappy when they don't get the love and respect from their kids that they think they're entitled to. Husbands are unhappy when they don't get all the sex they think they're entitled to from their wives, and wives feel just as unhappy when there's too little intimacy in the marriage. Employees feel unhappy when they fail to get the raise they feel entitled to, the promotion, or the freedom to take a day off from work whenever it suits them. Employers are unhappy if their workers don't put forth effort they believe they're entitled to.

Here are some things you are *not* entitled to:

- ✔ A spouse who always thinks as you do
- ✔ Children who always love you
- ✔ Employment — now or in the future
- ✔ Good health and a long life
- ✔ A computer that never crashes
- ✔ Cheap gasoline
- ✔ The respect and admiration of your peers
- ✔ A stable economy
- ✔ A car that starts on a cold morning

If you think you're entitled to those things — and more — you may as well forget being happy. Instead, get used to feeling miserable.

Think of life as a never-ending series of negotiations. Work to *earn* the respect you want, instead of demanding it. Work for that promotion — don't just wait to receive your entitlement. Negotiate ways to be happy in your marriage — make it more about give and take and try to appreciate your spouse's needs as well as your own.

Toxic Anger

Being happy when you're angry all the time is impossible. And that's what *toxic anger* is — experiencing intense anger on a daily basis. Anger is not inherently bad, but it can lead to health problems, unemployment, legal difficulties, financial woes, and dysfunctional relationships when you have too much of it. When it comes to anger, you need to think in moderation — it's fine to get irritated or just plain mad, but rage is *always* a problem.

Here are some things you can do to manage your anger better and prevent it from being a roadblock to happiness:

- **Ventilate more and vent less.** Venting is about blowing up and losing your cool. Ventilation is what you do when you let your anger breathe, when you talk about your feelings in a reasonable and civil manner.

- **Manage your stress better.** Not everything in life is a catastrophe. Most of what you encounter on a daily basis has to do with manageable problems — so if it's broke, fix it!

- **Let go of the angry past.** I have a rule that if I haven't worn a piece of clothing for three years, it's time to give it away. The same should be true of old anger. If you're still angry about something that happened long ago, find a way to forgive and forget. Unburden yourself from the past and free yourself up to deal with the emotions of today.

- **Confess you anger.** Spend 15 minutes a day writing down all your negative feelings — anger, hurt, sadness — read what you wrote, and then literally throw away the piece of paper. This simple act can help you prevent your anger from one day to the next.

- **Assert yourself.** Don't be a doormat, letting other people walk all over you. On the other hand, don't aggressively attack everybody who does something you don't like. Find the middle ground where you stand up for yourself without answering anger with anger.

If you think you may be having trouble with anger, check out my book *Anger Management For Dummies* (Wiley).

Resentment

Resentment is the residual of unexpressed, unresolved anger. It's like the stain that you see in a cup when you never finish drinking the coffee, the carbon that builds up in an automobile engine, or the creosote that lines your chimney when you burn too much wood too slowly. Resentful people look at life through darkened glasses, expecting the worst and being on the ready to defend themselves from harm. In effect, yesterday's anger gets in the way of today's happiness.

When I hear people say, "He's been angry at me for years," I correct them by telling them that anger is an emotion and, thus, an experience that is time-limited. Anger comes and goes much like waves on a beach. Staying angry very long is physically impossible. What *is* possible, however, is feeling resentment for years, even a lifetime. Emotions come and go, but resentment can — if you let it — last forever.

Getting angry isn't always a choice, but letting go of anger is. Based on my own research, I've concluded that 70 percent of people resolve their anger in less than half an hour. If your anger lingers beyond that point, it most likely will turn into resentment. Don't be afraid to tell yourself, "Time's up," as you approach that 30-minute mark.

Greed

The message of the popular 1987 movie *Wall Street* couldn't be clearer than when Gordon Gekko (Michael Douglas) shouts to stockholders, "Greed is good!" Gekko believes that greed creates competition, separates the winners from the losers, and is what ultimately translates into wealth. He makes a compelling case.

But greed also gets in the way of happiness — and for these very same reasons. If greed makes you the winner, then everyone else around you — family, friends, colleagues — end up feeling like losers. Greed may, in some cases, lead to wealth, but as I show you in Chapter 3, wealth does not ensure happiness — if it did, I wouldn't have had so many wealthy people as clients over the years. Lastly, greed is all about competition, but happiness comes more from *cooperation* — an effort to act in harmony with the world around you.

Greed is not just about ambition (that is, about doing well in some aspect of everyday life). Instead, it's about *exuberant* ambition — unlimited and insatiable ambition — that comes from wanting a bigger slice of the pie than anyone else has. Greed is another name for narcissistic ambition, where your own self-interests predominate over all others and where you feel entitled to be greedy, to take more than your fair share.

Why do an increasing number of highly paid corporate executives end up in prison these days? Are they just another example of stupid crooks? No. What they are is greedy — they aren't satisfied by making millions of dollars a year. They want *more* — and they feel they have the right to take as much as they want, no matter how much it hurts other people or destroys the very institutions that made them rich in the first place.

Greed isn't just about making money. People who are greedy about food end up struggling with their weight. People who are greedy about alcohol often end up alcoholics. People who are greedy about time tend to overschedule their days, having too many appointments in too little time. Those who are greedy about communication, tend to do all the talking without letting anyone else get a word in.

What are you greedy about? Is it keeping you from finding happiness?

Aggression

Aggression literally means "moving against the world." Two types of aggressive behavior occur between human beings — achievement-driven aggression and combative aggression. Achievement-driven aggression can lead to happiness, but combative aggression definitely does not.

People who have achievement-driven aggression are

- Competitive
- Forceful in pursuing their goals
- Persistent
- Determined
- Direct in their communication

People who have combative aggression are

- Confrontational
- Impatient
- Demanding
- Intense
- Domineering

Achievement-driven aggressiveness often leads to happiness, which is the result of a sense of accomplishment that comes from having done a job well. It gives you something to be satisfied about and a reason to feel grateful — both active ingredients in genuine happiness (see Chapter 2).

Combative aggressiveness, on the other hand, means you're engaged in combat with everything and everyone that comes your way. Combativeness is about overpowering people, often as a means toward whatever it is that you believe you're entitled to in life.

Achievement-driven aggression involves competing or fighting *for* something you value, whereas combative aggression always entails competing *against* the world.

Take a soul-searching moment and think about the characteristics of these two types of aggression. Ask yourself — and be honest — which of these attributes best describe you. Are you a mixture of the two or predominantly one or the other type of individual? Ask someone who knows you well to rate you, too. Maybe you'll discover something about yourself that you didn't know before — and begin to understand why happiness has eluded you.

Depression

Tens of millions of people worldwide are unable to experience happiness for one simple reason: They suffer from depression. Depression is so prevalent that it is referred to as the "common cold of mental illness." When you're suffering from depression, you're not just having a bad day. You're experiencing a range of symptoms, including:

- Low energy, lethargy, and malaise
- Loss of appetite
- Sleep disturbance
- Spontaneous crying
- Irritability
- Negative self-image
- Guilt
- Suicidal thoughts
- Diminished sexual interest
- Social withdrawal
- Loss of pleasure

The persistence and severity of these symptoms are what define just how depressed you are.

The psychiatric term for this loss of ability to experience pleasure — which prevents you from enjoying everything from food to sex — is *anhedonia,* a condition that may well reflect a breakdown in your brain's reward system. Depression depletes the brain of dopamine, which is vital to the sensation of pleasure and, ultimately, happiness.

The good news is that depression is a treatable disorder. If you read the list of symptoms and realized that you've experienced three or more of them during the past month, talk to your personal physician or a mental health expert. The best time to treat a mood disorder is before it becomes disabling. (For a comprehensive and complete discussion of depression and its treatment, turn to *Depression For Dummies,* by Laura L. Smith, PhD, and Charles H. Elliott, PhD [Wiley].)

Loneliness

You can be alone and still be happy, especially if you've managed to get into flow (see Chapter 8). But loneliness is another matter. *Loneliness* is an absence of an emotional connection with the world around you. You can be lonely in the midst of a large gathering of people, and not feel lonely when you're by yourself. Happiness is more about *belonging* — having meaningful social ties to family, friends, and community — than about having money, power, and success.

Here are some ways you can become a more connected person and ward off loneliness:

- ✔ **Be a community volunteer.** Try to find activities where you're actively engaging with other volunteers, such as Habitat for Humanity (www. habitat.org), where you work on building a house. (And you don't even have to know how to pound a nail!)

- ✔ **Become a regular at a local eatery or coffee shop.** You can eat or drink coffee anywhere, but if you make one place part of your daily routine, you'll start to feel like you belong there — and you'll get to know the other regulars.

- ✔ **Sign up for a course at your local community college or adult education center.** Taking a class is a great way to make friends and learn at the same time.

- **Get involved in historical reenactments.** They're still fighting the Civil War just about every week somewhere in the South, and the Renaissance is alive and well at Renaissance fairs throughout the country.

- **Sign up for a yoga class.** You'll be able to be in the company of other people without having to be "on" the whole time.

- **Join a local theater group.** If acting isn't your thing, paint scenery, sell tickets, or work as an usher.

- **Join a civic group, such as the Junior League, the Lion's Club, or the Optimists Club.**

- **Become a member of a hobby club, like a knitting group or a camera club.** You can learn, play, and socialize all at once.

- **Attend religious services and enjoy the fellowship.**

Vindictiveness

Are you one of those people who believes in an "eye for an eye"? When you get angry, do you say things like, "You'll get yours — I'll see to it," "Remember, what goes around comes around," or "Your time will come — you just wait"? If so, like it or not, you have a vindictive streak.

Simply put, vindictiveness is about getting even, settling scores, answering one hurt or insult with another. On the surface it's about anger — and, expressing anger in some vengeful manner. But vindictiveness is *really* about hurt and pain. Vindictive people think that by hurting the person who caused them pain — whether physical or emotional — they'll somehow feel better. The problem is, they won't!

As far as I know, forgiveness is the only antidote to vindictiveness. At some point, you have to say to yourself, "I forgive that person for hurting me. What she did was wrong, but I forgive her. I won't forget what she did, but I forgive her." Repetition counts, so say that to yourself as many times as it takes to let go of the hurt.

Keep in mind that forgiveness isn't easy. It's a choice you make — no one can make you forgive another human being. It takes time. And it requires support and demands sacrifice — for example, you have to give up being the victim, you have to quit insisting that life has to be fair, and you have to surrender your right to revenge. (If you're having trouble forgiving, check out *Anger Management For Dummies* [Wiley], where I go into more depth on the subject.)

Drug Abuse

Patients in an ever-growing number of drug and alcohol treatment facilities throughout the world are learning one immutable truth: Chemicals are no substitute for real happiness. The euphoric high that accompanies drug use is only momentary and is more an illusion that a reality. Drugs don't make you feel safe. They don't generate a sense of satisfaction, gratitude, or serenity — each an essential ingredient to happiness. And, of course, there are the predictable negative consequences — just ask an alcoholic the morning after a drinking binge.

Drugs are, for many people, a form of self-medication, used in an attempt to escape feelings of chronic unhappiness associated with mood disorders such as depression, pathological anxiety, and even boredom. I know because for several years I worked in an inpatient drug-rehab program and I saw what happens when people begin to detox — it isn't a pretty sight.

If you're consuming more than two alcoholic drinks per day (one if you're female) and/or you typically have more than four drinks at one sitting (three if you're female), you do not qualify as a responsible drinker. You need to cut back on your consumption — and if you can't do it on your own, you need to get some professional help.

Chicken or egg?

Drug addicts experience *anhedonia* (the lack of the ability to experience pleasure) following withdrawal from their drugs of choice. One possible explanation is that addicts take drugs in the first place to artificially create a sense of pleasure because their brains are incapable of doing so on their own. Another possibility is that the misuse of mind-altering drugs produces changes in the chemical workings of the brain, which result in a loss of pleasure. Either way, addicts are not happy people.

Chapter 23

Ten Things You Can Do Today to Foster Happiness in Your Life

The main theme of this book is that happiness is no accident. You have to work to achieve happiness — the greater and more consistent the effort, the greater the eventual reward. In this chapter, I offer you ten simple, effective strategies that, if you make them part of your daily routine, will help you reach your goal of a life full of positive emotion. Think of them as prescriptions, think of them as the ten secrets to a happy life, think of them as the Ten Commandments of Happiness, think of them anyway you like — just make sure you turn thinking into action!

Establish and Stick to a Morning Ritual

If you want your day to be positive, you need to get off on the right foot. One way to do that is to have a little ritual that you can start the day with — something predictable, something that you do come rain or shine, something that doesn't take too much time or energy but sets the stage and emotional tone for everything that comes after it. Rituals are examples of *automatic* behaviors that you do without thinking — and, that's what you want early in the morning when you're getting ready for the day ahead. Think of it this way: What starts off positive stays positive.

I begin each day going to a little coffee shop for breakfast, reading my paper, and spending 20 minutes with myself. I think of it as my little sanctuary — a time of peace and tranquility before I'm swept away by all the demands of the external world. My morning ritual strengthens and fortifies me for the day ahead.

My wife, on the other hand, gets up before I do, lets out our dogs, and spends 20 minutes reading the newspaper and petting Max and Dixie. That's her time for herself — and the dogs — and, I'm careful not to disturb it. (It's one of my many excuses for lingering in bed until the last possible minute!)

Your morning ritual could involve exercising, meditating, praying, remembering all the things you have to be thankful for, or writing compassionate notes to family and friends in need. (I cover each of these topics later in this chapter.)

Eat a Healthy Diet

A healthy diet is a source of energy and nutrients, both of which contribute to physical and emotional well-being.

Take, for example, the banana. Did you know that bananas not only provide a boost in energy (just ask athletes!), but they also help improve a person's mood? Bananas contain a protein, tryptophan, which converts into serotonin, a brain chemical that sets the tone (positive or negative) of emotions. In that sense, bananas work on the same principle as antidepressants, which also elevate levels of serotonin.

To make sure you're eating healthy, you need to:

- **Eat a nutritionally balanced diet that includes daily food choices from all five of the basic food groups:**
  - The bread, cereal, rice, and pasta group: 6 to 11 servings
  - The fruit group: 2 to 4 servings
  - The vegetable group: 3 to 5 servings
  - The milk, yogurt, and cheese group: 2 to 3 servings
  - The meat, poultry, fish, dry beans, eggs, and nuts group: 2 to 3 servings
- **Eat three meals every day.** Make sure you start with a good breakfast — it sets the stage for a healthy day.

- **Watch your portion sizes.** If you're eating crackers or chips, put them in a bowl or on a plate instead of eating straight out of the box or bag. Decide ahead of time how much you're going to eat and stick to it — that way you won't keep reaching into that box or bag after you're full.

- **Eat when you're hungry and make healthy choices when snacking.**

- **Use sugar sparingly.**

- **Limit your caffeine intake to 250 mg per day.** That's equivalent to three cups of coffee. (Read the label on your favorite soda to see how much caffeine it has.)

- **Eat a *minimum* of 1,200 calories per day.** If you're not trying to lose weight, you'll probably need closer to 1,800 to 2,000 calories per day.

- **Opt for lean meats and low-fat foods.**

- **Drink eight 8-ounce glasses of water per day.** Often, when people think they're hungry, they're really thirsty.

For much more information on diet and nutrition, check out *Dieting For Dummies,* 2nd Edition, by Jane Kirby, RD, and the American Dietetic Association (Wiley), and *Nutrition For Dummies,* 4th Edition, by Carol Ann Rinzler (Wiley).

Exercise

That old saying "Move it or lose it" is true. If you don't get enough physical exercise, you have less energy and stamina to work at achieving happiness. The simple tasks of everyday life become chores, and no one looks forward to doing chores! To reconnect with the joy of living, you have to get your body moving again in a way that goes beyond your normal daily routine.

Many people confuse exercise with activity — routine physical activities such as housework or going up and down the stairs at home and work. Exercise is rigorous in nature — it gives your heart and body a workout, which means working up a sweat! You can exercise in a gym (on machines such as a treadmill or elliptical trainer) or on your own (by walking or jogging, for example).

What's the best form of exercise? According to a friend of mine who owns and operates his own health facility, the best exercise for you is the one you'll agree to do. In other words, as far as your body is concerned, what matters isn't *how* you exercise but how *often* you exercise. And you'll exercise more often if you're doing an exercise you like. It's common sense, really: If you can't stand swimming, what are the odds you'll make swimming a part of your daily routine? Not good. The goal is to find an exercise you really enjoy, because if you enjoy it, you'll do it more often.

How much should you exercise? I recommend exercising daily for 25 to 30 minutes or exercising four times a week for 45 minutes. For much more information on the different types of exercise, how to know you're fit enough to exercise, and how to measure your progress, check out *Fitness For Dummies,* 3rd Edition, by Suzanne Schlosberg and Liz Neporent, MA (Wiley).

Get Enough Sleep

Sleep is essential to health and happiness. Yet, millions of people suffer from acute and chronic sleep deprivation. As a result, they:

- Show signs of increased irritability
- Have difficulty concentrating and remembering things
- Are ineffective at work
- Have a low tolerance for stress
- Are prone to emotional outbursts
- Lack stamina or endurance
- Are accident-prone
- Struggle to get out of bed in the morning
- Come across to others as pessimistic and sad
- Doze off during boring meetings or while watching TV

Does this sound familiar? If it does, you're definitely not getting enough sleep. How much is enough? Children need around ten hours per night. An adolescent needs eight to nine hours. Adults require seven to eight hours. And seniors can get by on roughly six hours unless they're unusually active — for example, doing a lot of physical labor or continuing to work full-time into their retirement years. (Seniors often nap at least once during the day, which means they can get by with a little less sleep at night.)

Here are some tips on what constitutes *good sleep hygiene* — things that make getting a good night's sleep more likely:

- **Avoid daytime naps lasting more than 30 minutes.**
- **Go to sleep at approximately the same time every night, even on weekends.**

- ✔ **Don't exercise or engage in any stimulating activity (including work) just before you go to bed.** Have a buffer period of about an hour between when you put down the activities of your day and when you close your eyes.

- ✔ **Don't use alcohol, tobacco, or caffeine within four hours of bedtime.** You may think, "But alcohol makes me sleepy — won't it help me sleep?" It may make it easier for you to fall asleep, but it'll also make your sleep restless and cause you to wake up throughout the night.

- ✔ **Don't use the bedroom for things other than sleep and sex.** That means no TV or reading while in bed.

- ✔ **Don't go to bed angry.**

- ✔ **Unclutter your mind.** You can't do anything to change what happened during the day, so what's the point in rehashing all that stuff? And you can't totally prepare for what tomorrow will bring.

- ✔ **Make sure you're sleeping on a good mattress.** The money you spend on a new mattress is money well spent. The typical mattress lasts only about 10 to 12 years.

Sleeping pills — both over-the-counter and prescription — are never a good option for getting enough sleep. If you use them too often, they can produce negative side effects including daytime drowsiness, anxiety, and rebound insomnia when you stop taking them. Never take sleeping pills without consulting your doctor.

If you follow all the tips in this section and you're still having trouble getting enough sleep, you may have a sleep disorder. For more information, check out *Sleep Disorders For Dummies,* by Max Hirshkowitz, PhD, ABSM, and Patricia B. Smith (Wiley).

Meditate

Meditation is the oldest technique known to man for producing a state of inner calm and relaxation. All religions include meditation, in one form or another, as a primary way of achieving a spiritual connection. It has a variety of medicinal benefits — lower blood pressure, decreased muscular pain, improved sleep — in addition to leading to improved self-esteem and a general sense of well-being.

Meditation feels good because it increases the brain's level of dopamine, a neurotransmitter that is key to the experience of pleasure.

TECHNICAL STUFF

Are you suited for meditation?

Strange as it may seem, *extraverts* (outgoing, sociable, adventure-seeking, risk takers) are much more likely to practice meditation regularly than are *introverts* (quiet, thoughtful, reserved people). Maybe it's because introverts already spend a considerable amount of time in quietude, whereas, for extraverts, meditation is something unusual and, thus, refreshing. Who knows?

The key is that meditation works whether you're as chatty as Rachael Ray or as reclusive as Greta Garbo.

To meditate, all you have to do is:

1. **Sit quietly in a comfortable position.**

2. **Close your eyes.**

3. **Breathe through your nose and focus on each breath you take.**

4. **Each time you exhale, repeat a soothing word (such as *one*) or a phrase (such as *I'm relaxed*) to yourself.**

   Continue this process for 10 to 15 minutes. Breathe easily and naturally. Keep a passive attitude throughout. The goal here is to *let* something positive happen, not *make* it happen.

TIP

These are just the bare bones of meditation. For much more information on meditation, including specific meditation exercises and guided meditations on a CD, check out *Meditation For Dummies,* 2nd Edition, by Stephan Bodian (Wiley).

Make a Spiritual Connection

Do you believe in a *higher power,* a being or entity that transcends human existence that you can turn to at various times for various reasons (reassurance, guidance, peace of mind, hope)? If you do, you may be more likely to be happy — if only because you don't feel so alone as you struggle with the ups and downs of everyday life and can "hand off" your problems when they become burdensome.

It doesn't matter which religion you practice, or whether you actually consider yourself religious at all (plenty of people think of themselves as spiritual, but don't follow any particular religious faith). What matters is how *often* you make that spiritual connection. Research has shown that just showing up at a religious service of some sort once a week cuts your odds of developing heart disease literally in half. Now there's something to be happy about!

In Chapter 6, I draw a link between hardiness and happiness. Interestingly, hardy people — those who have an internal sense of control, are actively committed to life, and are able to turn catastrophes into challenges — seem to have a greater spiritual connection than do non-hardy folks.

Be Thankful

Gratitude is one of the identifiable key ingredients to achieving happiness. First your needs are satisfied and then you're grateful — that's how it's *supposed* to work. But for many unhappy people, that's not the case. They find themselves neither satisfied nor thankful for what life has provided in the way of material things or opportunities.

If you don't want to be one of those folks, begin or end your day with five minutes of quiet reflection on the things you have to be thankful for as you either look ahead to the day before you or recount how your day went. This is not a time for self-criticism (could've, should've, would've) or focusing on that half-empty glass. It's your time to dwell on the positive — the blessings of everyday life — and appreciate the fact that much of what ends up making you happy comes from sources outside yourself.

Here are some examples of things you may be thankful for:

✔ Be thankful for your partner, who is there to comfort and support you in good times and in bad.

✔ Be thankful for your health.

✔ Be thankful that you are healthy enough to help others in need.

✔ Be thankful to the higher power (if you believe in one) that offers hope to the hopeless and help to the helpless.

✔ Be thankful for being sober (if you have a history of alcoholism).

✔ Be thankful for being in a positive mood (if you're prone to depression).

✔ Be thankful to your children for giving your life meaning and purpose.

Prayers of supplication versus prayers of gratitude

Sometime in my middle-age years — I'm not sure exactly when — I transitioned from nightly prayers of *supplication* (humble entreaties to God for things I thought I needed to make me happy) to prayers of *gratitude* for all that I had already received. I realized I was way ahead of the curve on the so-called good life — in other words, I already had more than my fair share of positive experiences in marriage, family, friends, economic opportunity, and career. To keep asking for more would, in my opinion, have been arrogant and ungrateful.

Today, if I ask God for anything, it's on behalf of others — for example, my children who are young and have a lot of life left to live, friends who struggling with the inevitable events and circumstances unique to old age, and my beloved dogs. And, here's the kicker: *The less I ask for, the more I continue to receive.*

✔ Be thankful for the sunshine.

✔ Be thankful that you have enough money to take care of the basic necessities of life.

✔ Be thankful if others see you as intelligent, witty, or creative.

✔ Be thankful that you have the good sense to be thankful.

Think and Feel with Compassion

All world religions and all truly great figures in the history of mankind have one thing in common: They teach, preach, and exemplify compassion. Mother Teresa, Gandhi, Jesus, and Martin Luther King, Jr., all were champions of compassion.

I was raised in the segregated South during the days before and after the civil rights movement, and I believe Martin Luther King had compassion for white Southerners whom he saw as being prisoners of long-standing cultural racism. Thus, by seeking to free his own people, he freed whites as well, making the "new South" a much safer, more just, and attractive environment in which to live.

If you're not sure if you're the kind of person who regularly acts with compassion, ask yourself the following questions:

✔ Do I believe that people who are less fortunate deserve my love?

✔ Am I nonjudgmental when I consider other people's misfortunes?

✔ Do I believe that one of the primary reasons I was put on this Earth is to help others in need?

✔ Do I have an "I'm for them!" attitude toward my fellow human beings?

✔ Do I believe that "What goes around, comes around" — in other words, that compassion breeds compassion?

If you answered "yes" to most or all of these questions, you're well on the road to happiness. If your answers suggest you're a little "light" when it comes to compassion, you might start by *acting* with compassion (that is, lend a hand where it's most needed — see the next section) and see if that doesn't change how you think and feel about others.

Lend a Helping Hand

My Aunt Judy was right when she told me, "Doyle, God put us on this Earth for one reason and one reason only — not to make money, not to win every race we choose to run, but to help our fellow man." I'm not talking about compassion — acting in sympathy toward the less fortunate among us (I cover that in the preceding section); I'm talking about lending a helping hand just because you can and because you'll end up feeling happier if you do.

The best type of support is the kind that's unsolicited — like my neighbor who started mowing my 2-acre yard one day without asking. I went outside, stopped her, and said, "You don't have to do this — I know you've got plenty of other things to do today." Her reply said it all: "I know, but I *want* to do it — I'm doing it as much for me as I am for you."

What have you done lately to help someone else? You don't have to be a knight in shining armor. The simplest things count, too. For example, in your everyday life you can do the following:

✔ When you see a young mother trying to get out to the car with a cart full of groceries and a few crying kids, you can offer to push the cart for her and put the groceries in her trunk.

✔ When you notice that your neighbor's sidewalk is covered with snow, you can shovel it for him.

✔ When you see your kid struggling with his homework, you can sit down and offer to help him figure it out.

✔ When you see that the dishwasher needs to be emptied, you can empty it (and save your spouse or parent from having to do it).

✔ When you learn that your best friend lost her mother, send her some flowers along with a note expressing your love.

✔ When someone you know (even if you don't know them all that well) is going through a difficult time, add him to your prayer list.

✔ When you see a turtle crossing a busy street, stop your car, pick it up, and take it safely to the side of the road.

✔ When you see a notice in the newspaper soliciting volunteers for some worthy cause, pick up the phone and offer your services.

✔ When your local bookstore invites customers to purchase books that they will distribute to underprivileged kids, buy a couple and help open up a child's mind.

Have a Sense of Humor

Lighten up! Try not to take life so seriously. Put a smile on your face (see Chapter 12). Don't just read the sports page in the newspaper — read the comics! End the day by listening to your favorite late-night comedian. Spend some time with an irreverent friend, someone who has a healthy respect for the absurdities of life. According to the Bible (or The Byrds), "There's a time to laugh and a time to cry." Make sure you have the right balance between the two.

Chapter 24

Ten Thoughts That Lead to Happiness

*H*appiness is a case of mind over matter. What you have in your mind — your thoughts — matter. Angry thoughts lead to anger, sad thoughts lead to sadness, and happy thoughts lead to happiness. In this chapter, I offer you ten positive thoughts that will help you find happiness.

Life Is Ahead of You — And That's Where Your Focus Should Be

Focusing on the past is easier — after all, you know what that was. The future — what's ahead of you — is far less certain. But think about it: Isn't that uncertainty part of what makes life exciting and interesting? Something really wonderful — a new career opportunity, a new relationship — may be about to happen in your life. Your future is full of possibility; your past is already settled.

I'm always happy on New Year's Day. Why? Because that's the day I officially forget about the previous year and begin to look forward to the year ahead. I spend a few minutes reflecting on the unique challenges and opportunities that came my way during the past 12 months, and then I let that go so I can eagerly anticipate what lies ahead. It's like being reborn once a year — I get a fresh new start, feel renewed energy, and give thanks for all the good things that haven't happened yet but I'm guessing will.

People who are weighed down by the past are rarely happy. They spend far too much time looking backward instead of forward and, as a result, often overlook the positive things in their day-to-day lives. Are you one of those folks who's walking through life with your head on backwards?

Begin each day with a few minutes of quiet time where you can reflect on all the positive possibilities that lie ahead in the next 24 hours. Open yourself up to the unknown, unforeseen circumstances of the day and trust that you'll be able to deal with and benefit from whatever is in front of you.

It's Never Too Late to Say You're Sorry

We all screw up sometimes — we say things we regret later, we hurt other people's feelings, we're arrogant and selfish. (Hey, I speak from personal experience!) Although you can't go back and undo your mistakes, you can say "I'm sorry" and mean it.

Is there a time limit — a statute of limitations — on apologies? No. It's never too late to let someone know that you feel bad about behaving badly. She'll appreciate your apology, whether it comes five minutes later or two years after the fact.

Apologizing for some transgression in your past is like removing a pebble from your shoe. It makes journeying through life a whole lot easier and less painful.

Thinking that you're sorry for having hurt someone, by itself, is not enough. The apologetic thought needs to be acted upon. The person you hurt needs to hear you say, "I'm sorry for what I said or did," and so do you. Silent apologies may *feel* good, but they don't *do* a lot of good.

We're Here to Help Each Other

My Aunt Judy put this thought in my head when I was a young boy and it's been there ever since. She explained that we're not on this Earth simply to get educated, earn money, buy things, mow the grass, or take out the trash. Those things have to do with survival. The ultimate purpose of life is to support, love, encourage, and assist one another in every way we possibly can. If you're doing that, you're happy. If not, you're not.

All you have to do is ask

The ever-popular golfer Chi Chi Rodriquez loves to tell this story: As a youngster, his father confronted a man in the middle of the night who was stealing bananas from their backyard. The man was their next-door neighbor, who had lost his job and was having trouble feeding his family. Expecting his dad to be angry — because they had little to eat as well — Chi Chi was surprised when his father cut a big bunch of bananas from the tree and gave them to his neighbor, saying, "If you need something to eat, just ask and I'll give you part of what I have — you don't need to steal." That life lesson was not lost on Chi Chi, who has been an incredibly generous man throughout his long and prosperous career, helping those much less fortunate than himself.

Take a minute and ask yourself the following questions:

- ✔ Who have I helped today?
- ✔ Who needs my help today?
- ✔ What can I do that would be helpful to someone I care about?
- ✔ What's keeping me from being helpful?
- ✔ How do I feel after I've been helpful to someone in need?
- ✔ If those I care about can't rely on me for help, who can they rely on?

Get going and do something good for someone! You'll be happy you did.

I've Had My Fair Share

Whether or not life is finite, I choose to think it is. When someone asks me why I don't drink alcohol anymore, I answer by telling him, "Because I've had my fair share already." My answer may not satisfy him, but it satisfies me. By thinking that I've had my fair share — that hypothetical quantity allotted to me in a lifetime — it was easier to get sober without thinking that I was being deprived of something that was rightfully mine for the taking. One reason most alcoholics have trouble stopping drinking, I'm convinced, is that they *don't* feel they've had their fair share of booze yet. Until they believe they've had their fair share, no intervention in the world will likely prove effective. Along with the thought that you've had your fair share of something comes the feeling that you are satiated, satisfied and content — all key ingredients to achieving happiness (see Chapter 2).

If you want to quit smoking once and for all, repeat over and over to yourself, "I've had my fair share of nicotine." If you want to lose weight, tell yourself at some point during every meal, "I've had my fair share of food for right now — it's time to stop eating." If you're tired of always dominating social conversations and want to hear what others think for a change, tell yourself, "I've had my fair share of air time — I want to let someone else take center stage." If you're tired of always being angry about one thing or another, say to yourself, "I've had my fair share of anger for one lifetime," when you feel your buttons being pushed. (You can find many more solutions to excessive anger in *Anger Management For Dummies*.)

You Don't Have to Get over the Bad Things in Life — You Just Have to Get beyond Them

As a therapist, I'm frequently asked by my clients, "How long will it be before I get over this?" My answer is always the same: "You won't ever get over it — the best I can do is help you get beyond it." Initially, this response is anything but comforting to the person who hears it because she thinks, quite naturally, that until she does get over this bad thing, she can never hope to be happy again.

The simple truth is that our brains hang on to bad memories, just like the good ones, forever. Getting beyond a bad event doesn't mean that you forget that it happened — it just means that you have to detach emotionally and move on with your life.

When Juan's brother died tragically of cancer at age 40, Juan was grief stricken. He couldn't bring himself to talk about his brother — how much he missed him, all the good times they'd had together — without becoming tearful and feeling overwhelmed by sadness. When these feelings persisted after four months, Juan realized that he needed help and he went into counseling. It took a while, but eventually Juan got to the point where he could enjoy the good memories of all the years his brother was a meaningful part of his life. Juan has moved beyond his brother's untimely death, even though he'll never get over it.

In the appendix, I list a reference for Viktor Frankl's *Man's Search for Meaning* (Washington Square Press). I highly recommend this book if you're struggling to get beyond some unfortunate circumstance in life.

Life Isn't Fair — And the Sooner You Accept That Reality, the Better

Admit it: You want life to be fair, and you have your own idea of what fairness is all about. If your kids are healthy, if people appreciate all the hard work you do, and if you get the promotion you think you deserve at work, you think that's fair. If your child gets sick, if no one appreciates your hard work, and if you get passed up for a promotion at work, you see those things as unfair. If so, you're not alone. Most people associate "fairness" with good outcomes and "unfairness" with circumstances that don't work out the way they want them to.

In Chapter 1, I tell the story of Cecil, a 60-year-old gentleman who began life with a childhood illness resulting in a physical handicap. Cecil's secret to being a happy man was that he and his entire family accepted just how "unfair" his situation was, but then they moved on with their lives, treating Cecil as though he was normal, in every sense of the word.

Let philosophers and theologians spend their lives pondering what's fair and unfair. Put your energies into experiencing and dealing with life in more practical terms — for example, what works and what doesn't when it comes to achieving happiness.

When in Doubt, Pole Left

For over a decade now, every summer dozens of *bateaux* (boats) along with hundreds of crew members journey 138 miles down the James River in Virginia. Crew members push the boats forward with long, sturdy poles, just as their predecessors did in the 1800s. Each day on the river is different — some days are uneventful, while others are filled with hazards, some serious enough to disable the boat and injure the crew.

The bateaux men have a saying that captures their thinking when they're faced with some oncoming obstacle: "When in doubt, pole left." The idea behind this saying is that, at a time of actual or potential crisis, indecisiveness is dangerous. Even if you're not sure how things will turn out when you suddenly change course, doing *something* is always better then doing *nothing*. If you do nothing, you know where you'll end up — on the rocks!

People who navigate the changing waters of life without a plan for how to react to adversity — to be decisive, take risks, change course — typically encounter more unhappiness than they would otherwise.

Water Flows Downhill

There's a simple truth in that statement. Invariably, water does flow downhill. And that's why this thought is so important. Too often, people try to make life seem more complicated than it is. We're too analytical, we look for hidden agendas, and we second-guess everything and everyone. Even Freud once said, "Sometimes a cigar is just a cigar."

Many of my disabled chronic-pain clients have difficulty accepting help from others, including close friends and family. Why? Because they view these offers of help in a negative light — "They feel sorry for me. They think I'm not man enough to get the job done now that I'm in pain." The simple truth is these good folks just want to help, that's all.

The simple truth is . . .

I often use children's books with adults in my anger-management classes. Each book usually contains one important lesson about how to better manage emotions. One of my favorites is *I Was So Mad* by Mercer Mayer (Western Publishing). Most of the book is about a young boy who continues to be mad because he's told "no" by his family every time he wants to do something — filling up the bathtub with frogs.

He gets so angry he finally decides to run away from home. But before he can leave, his friends come by and invite him to play ball. His mother says "yes" and suddenly he's not mad anymore. The simple truth: People — children and adults — get frustrated and angry when they can't do what they want, but that soon ends when they find something they *can* do that gives them joy. Happiness and anger can't coexist. So the next time you find yourself frustrated by the way things are, look for something positive you *can* be happy about.

I Have What I Need

Humans have few actual needs — the things that are vital to our physical survival. We need air, water, food, shelter, and a certain amount of sleep, and that's it. Everything else — jewelry, cars, fine clothes, a vacation home, a big-screen TV, $200 tennis shoes — are things we *want* out of life. Understanding the difference between needs and wants goes a long way toward finding happiness.

In Chapter 1, I talk about the fact that, although young people are happy, people typically report becoming even happier as they grow older. One reason for this, I think, is that for somewhere in midlife most people's wants begin to decelerate, even though their needs remain the same. You still *need* to eat, drink, and stay warm, but you may not *want* a new car every three years.

I Deserve to Be Happy

In my lifetime, I'm amazed at how many people I've met who don't feel like they deserve to be happy. And I'm not just talking about clients who have come to me for counseling — I'm also talking about my family and friends. They talk about surviving, "just trying to make do," settling for whatever comes their way, or doing what it takes to hang in there.

Repeat to yourself out loud ten times each morning: *I deserve to be happy. I deserve to be happy. I deserve to be happy.* Because you do.

Deserving something — like happiness — and feeling *entitled* to it are two different things. An entitlement means you have a legal *right* to that thing, which in this case you don't. What you deserve is a chance, an opportunity to pursue and ultimately discover a sense of happiness. This book can provide a road map for achieving happiness, but it can't give you permission to take the journey. That you have to provide yourself!

Appendix

Resources

· ·

I include in this book everything you need to know to achieve happiness, but you may want to delve further into a particular topic of interest. Luckily, information about positive psychology is currently available from a variety of books and Web sites that will add immeasurably to the good stuff that's contained in Happiness For Dummies. The resources listed here are only a limited sample of what's out there for you to consider — but they represent a good starting point.

Self-Help Books

Here's a list of self-help books I recommend:

- *The Beethoven Factor: The New Positive Psychology of Hardiness, Happiness, Healing and Hope,* **by Paul Pearsall (Hampton Roads):** In this book, Dr. Pearsall tells you how to be a "thriver" — someone who faces adversity head on and grows in the process — and not just a survivor in today's stressful world. He uses stories of hardy personalities, including the composer Ludwig von Beethoven, to inspire the reader.

- *Codependent No More: How to Stop Controlling Others and Start Caring for Yourself,* **by Melody Beattie (Harper/Hazelden):** For two decades now, this book has helped millions of people achieve happiness by focusing more of their energies on self-care instead of taking care of others. The message here is simple: Don't leave your happiness up to others — you make it happen!

- *Connect: 12 Vital Ties That Open Your Heart, Lengthen Your Life, and Deepen Your Soul,* **by Edward M. Hallowell, MD (Pantheon):** This thought-provoking book will help you learn how connected — emotionally, physically, and socially — you are to the world around you. You'll love the tips at the end of the book on how to create a more connected life — it's easier than you might imagine!

- *Don't Sweat the Small Stuff and It's All Small Stuff,* **by Richard Carlson, PhD (Hyperion):** This book offers readers a refreshingly new perspective on day-to-day life stress. It contains 100 simple behavioral prescriptions for how to remain calm in the face of a stress-filled life. If you're the type of person who tends to panic when things don't go your way, this is the book for you.

- *Feeling Good: The New Mood Therapy,* **by David D. Burns, MD (Harper Collins):** A bestseller for over two decades, this book teaches people to deal effectively with depression. It's full of scientifically based therapeutic strategies for developing a more positive outlook on life.

- *Forgive for Good,* **by Dr. Fred Luskin (Harper):** This book, written by a leading scientist, offers a nine-step method of forgiving yourself and others and moving beyond the role of victim following mistreatment, tragedy, and hurt.

- *Finding Flow: The Psychology of Engagement with Everyday Life,* **by Mihaly Csikszentmihalyi (Basic Books):** This highly readable book shows not only shows how the psychological experience of "flow" contributes to happiness, but, more important, offers practical strategies for becoming more fully engaged in life.

- *Learned Optimism: How to Change Your Mind and Your Life,* **by Martin E. P. Seligman, PhD (Pocket Books):** If you're a person who too often views life as a glass half-empty, this book will teach you how to live a more optimistic life. Dr. Seligman shows how optimism comes into play in all areas of life — work, parenting, education, sports, politics, and health.

- *Living a Life That Matters,* **by Harold S. Kushner (Anchor Books):** Written by the author of the bestselling book *When Bad Things Happen to Good People,* this book helps the reader appreciate the importance of doing things that matter in the world — which is how we know that we matter. Full of timeless spiritual wisdom and advice that paves the way for a sense of personal integrity.

- *Man's Search for Meaning,* **by Viktor E. Frankl (Washington Square Press):** A riveting account of Dr. Frankl's experience as a psychiatrist and survivor of the Holocaust. According to Frankl, the primary thing that motivates human behavior is the search for meaning in everyday life, which is also one of the keys to achieving happiness.

- *One Small Step Can Change Your Life: The Kaisen Way,* **by Robert Maurer, PhD (Workman):** Whatever change you're trying to make in your life — stop smoking, lose weight, become a happier person — this book is a must! It shows you how to overcome your brain's built-in resistance to change by thinking and acting small when it comes to building new behavior. Its success lies in the fact that its message is counterintuitive.

✔ *Opening Up: The Healing Power of Expressing Emotions,* **by James W. Pennebaker, PhD (Guilford):** Emotions — positive or negative — need to be expressed. If you're happy, you need to share it. Otherwise, it doesn't do you or anyone else any good. Although this book focuses a lot on negative feelings, the advice and perspective it offers holds true for positive feelings, too.

✔ *The Power of Flow: Practical Ways to Transform Your Life with Meaningful Coincidence,* **by Charlene Belitz and Meg Lindstrom (Three Rivers Press):** This book contains an expanded definition of "flow" that results in a natural, effortless unfolding of a person's life in a way that moves you toward harmony and happiness. It includes 14 strategies for achieving synchronicity, including creating silence, following your intuition, and taking risks.

✔ *Punished by Rewards: The Trouble with Gold Stars, Incentive Plan $, A's, Praise, and Other Bribes,* **by Alfie Kohn (Houghton Mifflin):** This book explains why traditional rewards don't make for happy students. What works are the 3 C's: collaboration, choice, and content. A revolutionary approach to modern-day learning.

✔ *The Relaxation Response,* **by Herbert Benson, MD, and Miriam Z. Klipper (HarperTorch):** This book, which remains a bestseller 30 years after it was originally published, shows how inextricably the mind and body are connected and how exercising the built-in relaxation response can foster health and well-being in all of us.

✔ *The Resilience Factor: 7 Keys to Finding Your Inner Strength and Overcoming Life's Hurdles,* **by Karen Feivich and Andrew Shatte (Broadway):** This is a skill-oriented book that offers an ABC method of promoting resilience in dealing with life's unexpected challenges, surprises, and setbacks. Readers describe this book as insightful, practical, amazing, and encouraging.

✔ *Social Intelligence: The New Science of Human Relationships,* **by Daniel Goleman (Bantam):** This nationally-recognized author explains how we are hardwired for social connections and how this leads to happiness. Goleman tells how negative emotions poison us and how positive emotions nourish us.

✔ *Tuesdays with Morrie,* **by Mitch Albom (Doubleday):** An inspiring real-life story of a dying man who continues to experience the joy of living, all the way to the end. This book is full of the kind of wisdom and philosophy that leads to a happy life.

✔ *What You Can Change and What You Can't: The Complete Guide to Successful Self-Improvement,* **by Martin E. Seligman (Vintage):** A pioneer in the field of positive psychology, Dr. Seligman shows how disciplined effort can lead to effective lifestyle changes that contribute to happiness. If you're someone who spends far too much time trying to change those things you really can't, this is the book for you.

✔ ***Wherever You Go, There You Are: Mindfulness Meditation in Everyday Life,* by Jon Kabat-Zinn, PhD (Hyperion):** Its appeal is that it makes learning to meditate simple and easy. Readers are instructed in techniques such as "non-doing" that are based in the 2,000-year-old history of Buddhist meditation, which focuses on living fully in the present, observing ourselves, and experiencing life without judging it.

Other Relevant Books

Here is a select list of other inspirational and motivational books that relate to the concept of happiness. I admit it: These are some of my personal favorites!

✔ ***Anyway: The Paradoxical Commandments: Finding Personal Meaning in a Crazy World,* by Kent M. Keith (Putnam):** This wonderful little book explains how living a paradoxical life — one that runs contrary to common sense and popular opinion — can lead to happiness. Something for your bedside table!

✔ ***Ben Franklin's Wit & Wisdom* (Peter Pauper Press):** Selections from Franklin's *Poor Richard's Almanack,* which continue to serve as a guide for how to live a happy and healthy life in today's world.

✔ ***The Diary of Anne Frank* (Pan):** A timeless, true story of personal courage and happiness in a young woman living under the tyranny of Nazi Germany. It's a story of faith, nobility, and survival of the spirit.

✔ ***Jonathan Livingston Seagull: A Story,* by Richard Bach (Avon):** A poignant story of how difficult it can be to achieve ultimate freedom and realize your true spiritual potential.

✔ ***The Mulligan: Everyone Needs a Second Chance in Golf and in Life,* by Wally Armstrong and Ken Blanchard (Thomas Nelson):** An internationally acclaimed writer and a professional golfer team up to use golf as a metaphor for how giving ourselves a second chance in life leads to happiness. Entertaining and full of wisdom.

✔ ***The Road Less Traveled,* by M. Scott Peck, MD (Touchstone):** The well-known psychiatrist and author talks about how to achieve spiritual growth and health. A forerunner to positive psychology, Peck emphasizes the importance of loving relationships, serenity, discovery of one's authentic self, and serendipity — all topics covered in *Happiness For Dummies.*

✔ *Cirque du Soleil The Spark: Igniting the Creative Fire That Lives Within Us All,* **by John U. Bacon and Lyn Heward (Doubleday Canada):** This fictional narrative adopts the underlying philosophy of Cirque du Soleil as a means of living a meaningful life. If you've ever been to a circus, you'll love this book!

✔ *When All You've Ever Wanted Isn't Enough* **by Harold Kushner (Pocket Books):** Many people find that material rewards aren't enough to achieve happiness. Something vital is missing — a sense of purpose. This book helps you focus on that.

Biographies of Self-Actualized People

There are many biographies and autobiographies of celebrated people cited as examples of self-actualized personalities by psychologist Abraham Maslow. In addition to those I list here, Maslow included people such as Pablo Casals, Albert Einstein, Aldous Huxley, Thomas Jefferson, Abraham Lincoln, Pierre Renoir, Albert Schweitzer, and Walt Whitman. Reading about the life of someone who has achieved happiness can serve as an inspiration in your own life.

✔ *Benjamin Franklin: An American Life,* by Walter Isaacson (Simon & Schuster)

✔ *Churchill: A Biography,* by Roy Jenkins (Plume)

✔ *General Patton: A Soldier's Story,* by Stanley P. Hirshson (Harper)

✔ *Hemingway,* by Kenneth S. Lynn (Harvard)

✔ *His Excellency: George Washington,* by Joseph J. Ellis (Knopf)

✔ *Mandela: The Authorized Biography,* by Anthony Sampson (Vintage)

✔ *Mark Twain: A Life* by Ron Powers (Free Press)

✔ *Autobiography: The Story of My Experiments with Truth,* by Mohandas K. Gandhi (Dover)

✔ *The Autobiography of Eleanor Roosevelt,* by Eleanor Roosevelt (Da Capo)

Web Sites

If you who find yourself experiencing persistent unhappiness, consider seeking out the services of a qualified mental-health professional — a clinical psychologist, psychiatrist, or counselor — or a trained coach to assist you. You can begin by checking out the appropriate listings in your telephone book for services in your local community.

Check out the following Web sites for information and guidance in selecting a qualified provider:

- **The American Psychiatric Association** (www.psych.org/public_info) provides information about mental health disorders and options for treatment.

- **The American Psychological Association** (www.apa.org/pubinfo) provides information about depression and other emotional disorders that lead to unhappiness.

- **Mental Health Organization by State** (www.cdc.gov/mentalhealth/state_orgs.htm) provides links to mental-health agencies and private organizations in each state that serve the mentally ill.

- The **National Alliance for the Mentally Ill** (www.nami.org) is an organization that serves as an advocate for people and families experiencing mental illness. Information is available about both the causes and treatment of illnesses that affect children and adults.

- The **National Institute of Mental Health** (www.nimh.nih.gov) reports research about a variety of mental health disorders.

- The **National Mental Health Association** (www.nmha.org) is a nonprofit organization that provides information and help regarding mental-health issues.

- **WebMD** (www.webmd.com) provides an array of information about physical and mental-health issues, including information about psychological treatments, drug therapy, and prevention.

If you're looking for one Web site that explains what positive psychology is and how it contributes to health and happiness, go to the University of Pennsylvania Positive Psychology Center site (www.ppc.sas.upenn.edu). This single site contains information regarding the definition of positive psychology; readings and videos; questionnaires; a list of resources for teachers and researchers; and conferences and other educational programs.

Index

Notes

Notes

Notes

Notes

Notes

Notes

Notes

Notes

BUSINESS, CAREERS & PERSONAL FINANCE

Accounting For Dummies, 4th Edition*
978-0-470-24600-9

Bookkeeping Workbook For Dummies†
978-0-470-16983-4

Commodities For Dummies
978-0-470-04928-0

Doing Business in China For Dummies
978-0-470-04929-7

E-Mail Marketing For Dummies
978-0-470-19087-6

Job Interviews For Dummies, 3rd Edition*†
978-0-470-17748-8

Personal Finance Workbook For Dummies*†
978-0-470-09933-9

Real Estate License Exams For Dummies
978-0-7645-7623-2

Six Sigma For Dummies
978-0-7645-6798-8

Small Business Kit For Dummies, 2nd Edition*†
978-0-7645-5984-6

Telephone Sales For Dummies
978-0-470-16836-3

BUSINESS PRODUCTIVITY & MICROSOFT OFFICE

Access 2007 For Dummies
978-0-470-03649-5

Excel 2007 For Dummies
978-0-470-03737-9

Office 2007 For Dummies
978-0-470-00923-9

Outlook 2007 For Dummies
978-0-470-03830-7

PowerPoint 2007 For Dummies
978-0-470-04059-1

Project 2007 For Dummies
978-0-470-03651-8

QuickBooks 2008 For Dummies
978-0-470-18470-7

Quicken 2008 For Dummies
978-0-470-17473-9

Salesforce.com For Dummies, 2nd Edition
978-0-470-04893-1

Word 2007 For Dummies
978-0-470-03658-7

EDUCATION, HISTORY, REFERENCE & TEST PREPARATION

African American History For Dummies
978-0-7645-5469-8

Algebra For Dummies
978-0-7645-5325-7

Algebra Workbook For Dummies
978-0-7645-8467-1

Art History For Dummies
978-0-470-09910-0

ASVAB For Dummies, 2nd Edition
978-0-470-10671-6

British Military History For Dummies
978-0-470-03213-8

Calculus For Dummies
978-0-7645-2498-1

Canadian History For Dummies, 2nd Edition
978-0-470-83656-9

Geometry Workbook For Dummies
978-0-471-79940-5

The SAT I For Dummies, 6th Edition
978-0-7645-7193-0

Series 7 Exam For Dummies
978-0-470-09932-2

World History For Dummies
978-0-7645-5242-7

FOOD, HOME, GARDEN, HOBBIES & HOME

Bridge For Dummies, 2nd Edition
978-0-471-92426-5

Coin Collecting For Dummies, 2nd Edition
978-0-470-22275-1

Cooking Basics For Dummies, 3rd Edition
978-0-7645-7206-7

Drawing For Dummies
978-0-7645-5476-6

Etiquette For Dummies, 2nd Edition
978-0-470-10672-3

Gardening Basics For Dummies*†
978-0-470-03749-2

Knitting Patterns For Dummies
978-0-470-04556-5

Living Gluten-Free For Dummies†
978-0-471-77383-2

Painting Do-It-Yourself For Dummies
978-0-470-17533-0

HEALTH, SELF HELP, PARENTING & PETS

Anger Management For Dummies
978-0-470-03715-7

Anxiety & Depression Workbook For Dummies
978-0-7645-9793-0

Dieting For Dummies, 2nd Edition
978-0-7645-4149-0

Dog Training For Dummies, 2nd Edition
978-0-7645-8418-3

Horseback Riding For Dummies
978-0-470-09719-9

Infertility For Dummies†
978-0-470-11518-3

Meditation For Dummies with CD-ROM, 2nd Edition
978-0-471-77774-8

Post-Traumatic Stress Disorder For Dummies
978-0-470-04922-8

Puppies For Dummies, 2nd Edition
978-0-470-03717-1

Thyroid For Dummies, 2nd Edition†
978-0-471-78755-6

Type 1 Diabetes For Dummies*†
978-0-470-17811-9

*Separate Canadian edition also available
†Separate U.K. edition also available

Available wherever books are sold. For more information or to order direct: U.S. customers visit www.dummies.com or call 1-877-762-2974.
U.K. customers visit www.wileyeurope.com or call (0) 1243 843291. Canadian customers visit www.wiley.ca or call 1-800-567-4797.

INTERNET & DIGITAL MEDIA

AdWords For Dummies
978-0-470-15252-2

Blogging For Dummies, 2nd Edition
978-0-470-23017-6

Digital Photography All-in-One Desk Reference For Dummies, 3rd Edition
978-0-470-03743-0

Digital Photography For Dummies, 5th Edition
978-0-7645-9802-9

Digital SLR Cameras & Photography For Dummies, 2nd Edition
978-0-470-14927-0

eBay Business All-in-One Desk Reference For Dummies
978-0-7645-8438-1

eBay For Dummies, 5th Edition*
978-0-470-04529-9

eBay Listings That Sell For Dummies
978-0-471-78912-3

Facebook For Dummies
978-0-470-26273-3

The Internet For Dummies, 11th Edition
978-0-470-12174-0

Investing Online For Dummies, 5th Edition
978-0-7645-8456-5

iPod & iTunes For Dummies, 5th Edition
978-0-470-17474-6

MySpace For Dummies
978-0-470-09529-4

Podcasting For Dummies
978-0-471-74898-4

Search Engine Optimization For Dummies, 2nd Edition
978-0-471-97998-2

Second Life For Dummies
978-0-470-18025-9

Starting an eBay Business For Dummies, 3rd Edition†
978-0-470-14924-9

GRAPHICS, DESIGN & WEB DEVELOPMENT

Adobe Creative Suite 3 Design Premium All-in-One Desk Reference For Dummies
978-0-470-11724-8

Adobe Web Suite CS3 All-in-One Desk Reference For Dummies
978-0-470-12099-6

AutoCAD 2008 For Dummies
978-0-470-11650-0

Building a Web Site For Dummies, 3rd Edition
978-0-470-14928-7

Creating Web Pages All-in-One Desk Reference For Dummies, 3rd Edition
978-0-470-09629-1

Creating Web Pages For Dummies, 8th Edition
978-0-470-08030-6

Dreamweaver CS3 For Dummies
978-0-470-11490-2

Flash CS3 For Dummies
978-0-470-12100-9

Google SketchUp For Dummies
978-0-470-13744-4

InDesign CS3 For Dummies
978-0-470-11865-8

Photoshop CS3 All-in-One Desk Reference For Dummies
978-0-470-11195-6

Photoshop CS3 For Dummies
978-0-470-11193-2

Photoshop Elements 5 For Dummies
978-0-470-09810-3

SolidWorks For Dummies
978-0-7645-9555-4

Visio 2007 For Dummies
978-0-470-08983-5

Web Design For Dummies, 2nd Edition
978-0-471-78117-2

Web Sites Do-It-Yourself For Dummies
978-0-470-16903-2

Web Stores Do-It-Yourself For Dummies
978-0-470-17443-2

LANGUAGES, RELIGION & SPIRITUALITY

Arabic For Dummies
978-0-471-77270-5

Chinese For Dummies, Audio Set
978-0-470-12766-7

French For Dummies
978-0-7645-5193-2

German For Dummies
978-0-7645-5195-6

Hebrew For Dummies
978-0-7645-5489-6

Ingles Para Dummies
978-0-7645-5427-8

Italian For Dummies, Audio Set
978-0-470-09586-7

Italian Verbs For Dummies
978-0-471-77389-4

Japanese For Dummies
978-0-7645-5429-2

Latin For Dummies
978-0-7645-5431-5

Portuguese For Dummies
978-0-471-78738-9

Russian For Dummies
978-0-471-78001-4

Spanish Phrases For Dummies
978-0-7645-7204-3

Spanish For Dummies
978-0-7645-5194-9

Spanish For Dummies, Audio Set
978-0-470-09585-0

The Bible For Dummies
978-0-7645-5296-0

Catholicism For Dummies
978-0-7645-5391-2

The Historical Jesus For Dummies
978-0-470-16785-4

Islam For Dummies
978-0-7645-5503-9

Spirituality For Dummies, 2nd Edition
978-0-470-19142-2

NETWORKING AND PROGRAMMING

ASP.NET 3.5 For Dummies
978-0-470-19592-5

C# 2008 For Dummies
978-0-470-19109-5

Hacking For Dummies, 2nd Edition
978-0-470-05235-8

Home Networking For Dummies, 4th Edition
978-0-470-11806-1

Java For Dummies, 4th Edition
978-0-470-08716-9

Microsoft® SQL Server™ 2008 All-in-One Desk Reference For Dummies
978-0-470-17954-3

Networking All-in-One Desk Reference For Dummies, 2nd Edition
978-0-7645-9939-2

Networking For Dummies, 8th Edition
978-0-470-05620-2

SharePoint 2007 For Dummies
978-0-470-09941-4

Wireless Home Networking For Dummies, 2nd Edition
978-0-471-74940-0